IMAGES
of America

BREWERIES OF THE GOLD COUNTRY

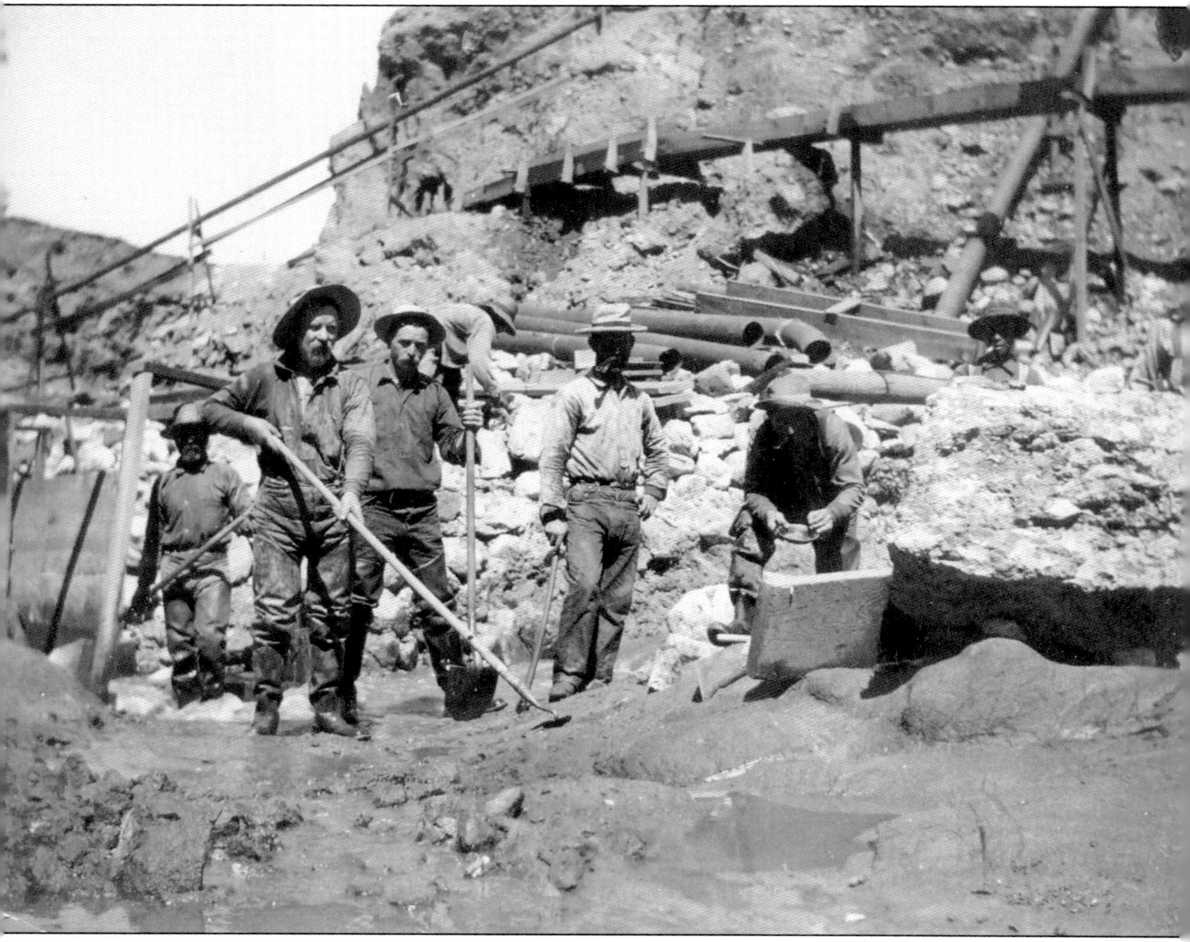

It is known who the customers were—the thousands of miners who poured into California's gold fields—but the history of the breweries of the Motherlode remains relatively intangible. Work on a placer mining claim or in a hardrock mine was hot, dirty, and paid much less than the flyers and adventure stories promised. Often these men turned from mining back to their traditional occupations, finding life much easier and more profitable. A handful of those were brewers. They provided locally and regionally crafted lagers, ales, and steam beers for the "thirsty thousands." (Courtesy Amador County Archives.)

On the Cover: The Sutter Creek Brewery was established as early as 1861 by Wilhelm Cremer and George Seiser, both from Germany. The brewery quickly changed hands to Leopold Rabolt, a naturalized German immigrant, who made delicious steam beer into the 1880s. At the time of this 1891 photograph, John Raddatz and Albert Ludwig had just renovated the "old Rabolt property;" the brewery continued producing into the teens. By 1930, the brewery was no longer operating, an industrial victim of Prohibition. The original wood-framed brewery building seen on the cover was razed in the early 20th century. Still standing is the stone granary that held the locally grown grains used in the brewery's fermentation process. (Courtesy Amador County Archives.)

IMAGES
of America

Breweries of the Gold Country

R. Scott Baxter and Kimberly J. Wooten

ARCADIA
PUBLISHING

ISBN 978-0-7385-7621-3

Published by Arcadia Publishing
Charleston, South Carolina

Printed in the United States of America

Library of Congress Control Number: 2011929297

For all general information, please contact Arcadia Publishing:
Telephone 843-853-2070
Fax 843-853-0044
E-mail sales@arcadiapublishing.com
For customer service and orders:
Toll-Free 1-888-313-2665

Visit us on the Internet at www.arcadiapublishing.com

We would like to dedicate this book to our parents, Bob and Judy Baxter, and Gary and Paula Wooten, who instilled in us the importance of our history. We would also like to thank Brad Paisley for reminding us of all the helpful and hurtful things alcohol can do.

Contents

Acknowledgments

This volume would not have been possible without the assistance of many regional archives, museums, historical societies, archivists, and historians. Among those whose help was critical are Lisa Hopkins, Gretchen Kingsbury, and all the volunteers at the Amador County Archives; Shannon Van Sant and the Calaveras County Archives; Calaveras County Historical Society and Museum; John McCabe and the El Dorado County Historical Museum; Debbie Poulsen and Placer County Museums; Searls Historical Library; and the Tuolumne County Historical Society. In addition, we would like to thank Judith Marvin and Foothill Resources; Janette Molin; Mary Lou D'Agostini; Ruth Gottstein of Volcano Press; Michael Backovich; Larry Cenotto; Pat Crosby, president of the Golden Chain Council; Elaine Zorbas; Syd Whittle and HMdb.org; Leroy Radanovich; Carolyn Feroben and the Mariposa Museum and History Center; and Cherry Simi. Our thanks also go to our editors John Poultney and Amy Perryman. Finally, special thanks go to our children (for all the peanut butter and jelly sandwiches), Gary and Paula Wooten, Rebecca Allen, and Jenny Upchurch. Trying to keep track of all those who helped us over this large geographic region is difficult; we apologize for anyone we have overlooked.

INTRODUCTION
BREWING ON THE MOTHERLODE

"Beer is proof that God loves us and wants us to be happy."

—Benjamin Franklin

In contrast to common knowledge, gold and silver were known to exist in what is now California long before it became part of the United States. For a variety of reasons, these resources were not exploited while the region was solely occupied by its native inhabitants, nor when it was governed by Spain and then Mexico. However, in the initial years of governance by the United States, the territory's mineral wealth was exposed by the discovery of gold at Sutter's Mill (now Coloma State Park). The result was the great California Gold Rush of 1849. Thousands of would-be miners and entrepreneurs, from around the globe, flooded into California. Most headed directly for the Motherlode, also known as the Gold Country.

The Motherlode is a geological formation of gold-bearing deposits from one to four miles wide and 120 miles long. Trending north-south, it is situated along the western foothills of the Central Sierra Nevada Mountains. This formation runs from Madera County in the south to Sierra County in the north. Initially, miners focused on the loose placer gold found in the gravel deposits along the region's many creeks and rivers. They eventually followed this loose gold to the source, the hardrock matrix, into which they tunneled for many miles.

The life of the miner during this time was difficult and uncomfortable, with long days spent placer mining in ice cold water and later toiling away in sweltering hardrock mines hundreds—even thousands—of feet underground. With few creature comforts, many miners turned to one that would help pass the time. This one simple comfort was alcohol. Some preferred spirits, others wine, and still others beer. At that time, only small quantities of these beverages were being produced at the few small settlements in the territory. For the most part, reasonably palatable alcoholic beverages were expensive, as they were imported by ship from Europe and the eastern United States.

However, it did not take long for some enterprising individuals to see a niche market for locally produced alcoholic beverages, chief among them beer. The reasons for the local production of beer over wine or spirits are many; among them were the portability of the ingredients for making beer and California's climate, which lent itself well to the rapid production of these same ingredients. Breweries were soon established almost as quickly as the ramshackle towns they serviced. Within a few short years, communities with unique names like Hangtown, Angels Camp, Mokelumne Hill, and El Dorado boasted one or more breweries. Many initially started out in tents, log cabins, or other temporary structures. As communities became better established, additional time, money, and energy were invested in the breweries. With ever-increasing investment, some breweries eventually became architectural and engineering masterpieces. Many breweries also housed their own saloons to dispense their products, becoming social hubs for the local community.

The following is a brief and simplified description of the brewing process during the latter half of the 19th century and the first two decades of the 20th century. There were many variations to the process, and the intent here is to provide a basic overview to the uninitiated.

In the strictest sense, beer is a simple brew of water, grain, yeast, and frequently hops. Added together in the correct proportion and under the correct conditions, the result is a pleasantly intoxicating beverage that has been enjoyed for thousands of years. Such concoctions were noted more than 5,000 years ago in Egypt. The recipe for the manufacture of beer has changed over time and varies by region, but the essentials remains the same.

Grain—traditionally barley—is soaked in water, prompting it to sprout or germinate. During this stage of development, much of the starch in the kernel of grain is converted to sugar to provide the newly forming plant with needed nutrients to grow. It is the sugar the brewer wants, not the plant. To keep the plant from utilizing the sugar for its own needs, the growth process must be stopped. To do this, the grain is dried out, essentially killing the sprout and preserving the sugar. This is usually done by spreading out the grain on a level floor and allowing it to dry. This process is often sped up with the aid of heat. This step in the beer-making process is known as malting, with the end product known as malt, or malted grain. In some instances, the malt is roasted, which generally leads to a darker and more flavorful beer. Some breweries produced their own malt, while others purchased it from another source, including specialized facilities called "malt houses." While not as common in California as elsewhere, there were malt houses that only produced malt for sale to other parties.

The malt is then added to a vat of heated water, which leaches the sugar from the malted grain. In more modern times, malt-extract syrup is used in place of malted grains. Generally added to this heated malt concoction are hops. A relative of cannabis, hops are a vine-like, flowering plant that can reach many feet in height and are frequently grown on specialized farms. Hops are added as a preservative and flavoring agent. Hops are grown in many varieties, some specific to particular geographical locations. Hops are generally a bittering and aromatic agent which, when used in various quantities and combinations, add a great deal to the odor, flavor, and shelf life of a beer. At this point, the concoction is known as wort.

Once cooked for the desired time and at the desired temperature, the wort is transferred to a mash tub. After the wort has cooled to a predetermined temperature, yeast is added. The yeast acts in a manner similar to that used in making bread. The yeast, a bacteria, essentially eats the sugars from the malt, and their waste product is alcohol. This is known as fermentation. Another byproduct of fermentation is carbon dioxide, the gas that commonly gives both beer and other carbonated beverages their bubbly fizz. It is this same carbon dioxide that makes bread rise. After a few days or weeks, the fermentation process is complete, the yeast having digested all or most of the sugar in the wort. From there, the beer can be placed in kegs or bottled. Small amounts of malt or sugar were generally added at this time to provide carbonation to the beer. With slight variations of ingredients, temperature, and methods of production, a wide variety of beers can be produced. These are often tailored to the tastes of particular regions, to climatic conditions, and technological restrictions.

Currently, many consumers seek beer that is low in calories and carbohydrates, but historically, beer made up much of a person's caloric intake for the day. Men, women, and even children drank beer for breakfast, lunch, dinner, and for refreshment in between. Such notables as Ben Franklin and Thomas Jefferson were known to drink beer with their breakfast. Beer was even considered a staple ration in many militaries around the world. Sailors and soldiers were known to mutiny and riot when rations of beer were restricted. Such an incident nearly brought the famous Pilgrims of Plymouth Rock to an inglorious end. These traditions continued for many centuries in the United States. With that in mind, the reader may have a better understanding of what an important commodity beer was during this time. Beer was considered a necessity, but substandard beer was avoided if at all possible.

Unfortunately, traditionally made beer does not have an incredibly long shelf life; it spoils rather quickly, especially in warm climates. To counter this, some brewers added extra hops, which worked as a natural preservative. Legend has it this led to the development of India Pale Ale (IPA). This highly hopped beer was reportedly developed for the long transit to, and to survive the hot climate of, the British province of India. For the most part, however, shipping beer over long distances was not practical. Aside from the spoilage, it is also heavy, making transit expensive. In contrast, dried grain and hops are relatively light and not prone to spoilage if kept dry. Yeast, a bacteria, reproduces itself once activated, meaning very small quantities, or cultures, can be used and reproduce indefinitely. The natural result of these factors was that it was usually more practical to manufacture the beer near where it was to be consumed, provided there was a ready source of water—hence the many breweries that sprang up in the earliest days of California's statehood.

By a chance of history, the California Gold Rush occurred during the same time that Germany was experiencing an extended period of widespread social upheaval. During the mid-19th century, millions of Germans emigrated from their homeland in search of a better life and simple safety of life and limb. Many of these emigrants followed the stories of easy wealth to California—so much so, that it was not long before persons of German descent made up more than 20 percent of the population in many California communities. Staying true to the modern stereotype, these newly arrived immigrants knew their beer. It is to these pioneering German immigrants that credit likely goes to the development of "steam beer." Often referred to as the United States's only indigenous brew, steam beer was developed in California as a way of producing a palatable beer within the region's climatic limitations.

With names like Krahner, Fausel, Wieland, Krauss, Strohm, and Gross, California's German population formed the backbone of the fledgling state's brewing industry. It is the rare occasion in researching breweries of this period that at least one of those involved does not have a Germanic surname. As a disclaimer, the authors must apologize in advance for the likely misspelling of many of these names. Their pronunciation and spelling was foreign to many record keepers, and some immigrants "Anglicized" their names to make them easier to understand for their new countrymen. As a result, many of the family names incorporated in this text have had multiple spellings, and in such instances the authors have chosen to employ the most commonly utilized spelling.

Over a period of 70 years, California's Gold Country was home to hundreds of local breweries. It all came to an abrupt end in 1919 with the implementation of the Volstead Act, which outlawed the sale of alcohol. Generally referred to as "Prohibition," it forced the closure of all commercial breweries. Although repealed in 1933, the Volstead Act effectively killed all local breweries; only the largest brewers were able to hold together during the decade-plus hiatus. It has only been in recent decades that ventures into regional brewing have returned to the Motherlode, with some local breweries gaining national recognition. The final section of this volume provides contact information for these new pioneers brewing in California's Gold Country.

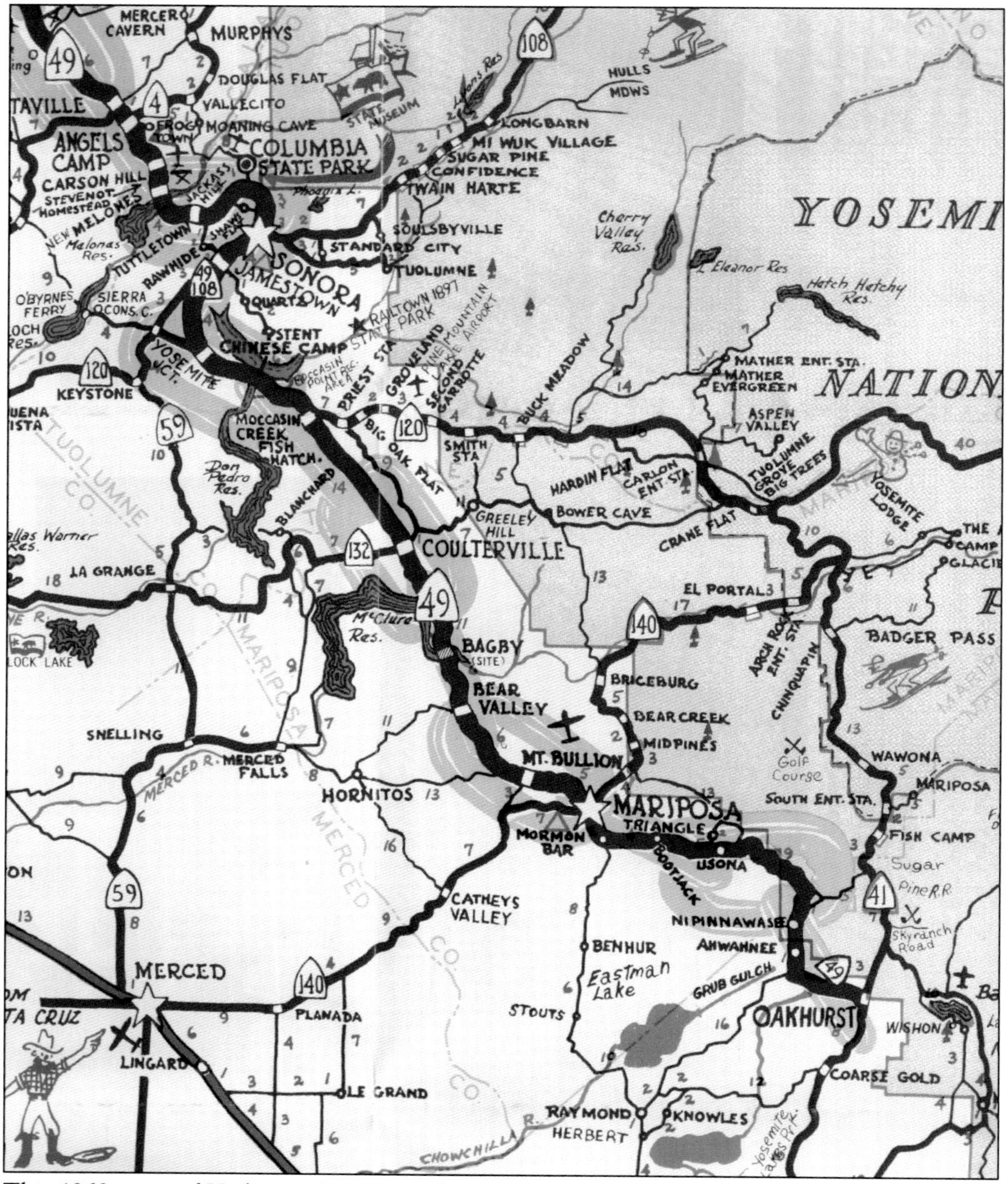

This 1960s map of Highway 49 runs north from Oakhurst, Madera County, through Mariposa and Tuolumne Counties. The Mother Lode State Highway Association was established in 1919 to link the mines and communities of the 11 counties of the Motherlode together with a modern roadway. While it may be hard for those driving Highway 49—with its tight curves, steep grades, and almost non-existent shoulders—to think of it as modern, it was when constructed. The idea for the road commission, later called the Golden Chain Council, was put forth by Archie Stevenot, a mining supervisor in Calaveras County. He had the foresight to realize that the gold mines would eventually play out, and that the rich history of the Motherlode region would draw the newly emerging automobile tourism industry. (Courtesy Golden Chain Council.)

One

Madera, Mariposa, Tuolumne Counties

The Southern Mines

"In heaven there is no beer (no beer!)
That's why we drink it here
And when we are gone from here
Our friends will be drinking all the beer"

—Soggy Bottom Boys

Oakhurst, in northern Madera County, is at the very beginning of the "Golden Chain" Highway, or Highway 49. Aptly named for the forty-niners who came to the Motherlode seeking their fortunes, the highway winds northwards over 300 miles from its junction with Route 41. Originally known as Fresno Flats, Oakhurst had a large population of miners in its early days; no documentation of a brewery in the community was uncovered.

The route to the more northerly gold fields quickly moved into Mariposa County. Founded in 1850, this county would appear to be nearly dry if one were to look only at its historic brewers; but if one looked at the liquor distributors and saloon keepers in the county's early voter registers, it becomes obvious alcohol was readily available and consumed by the local populace. Mariposa's breweries appear to have concentrated around the town of Mariposa, the county seat, with breweries in Mariposa, Agua Fria, and Hornitos. Some of these breweries lasted only a few years and little documentation exists. Others became fixtures in their communities. Today, Mariposa County is more famous for Yosemite National Park than it is for its historic breweries.

The Golden Chain Highway leaves Mariposa County, passing into western Tuolumne County. The southern portion of the route is relatively sparse in population, both historically and today, and winds through Moccasin, Chinese Camp, and Montezuma. The highway then loops northward, encompassing the early mining communities of Jamestown, Sonora, Columbia, and Tuttletown. Not surprisingly, where the miners were, so were the breweries. Within this region, there were several breweries; others may have existed in smaller, nearby communities.

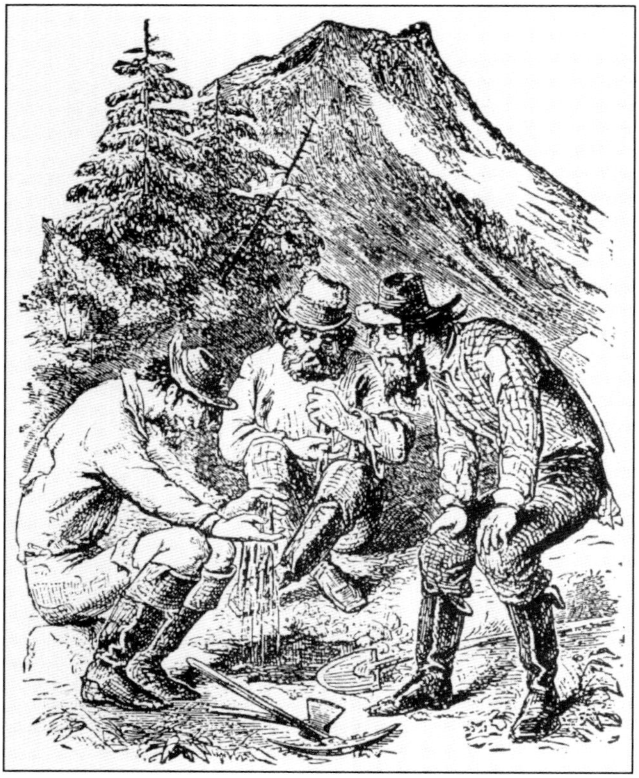

The story of brewing in the Motherlode is three-fold: mining, beer, and transportation. The tale starts with the advent of mining, beginning with the discovery of gold in 1848. This 1885 etching from Elliott & Co.'s *Calaveras County* depicts a traditional image of independent claim miners, a reality that quickly changed with the advent of hardrock mining, when many became wage laborers. With their wages, miners bought beer. As the population of miners grew, the scarcity and price of imported commodities, including beer, rose.

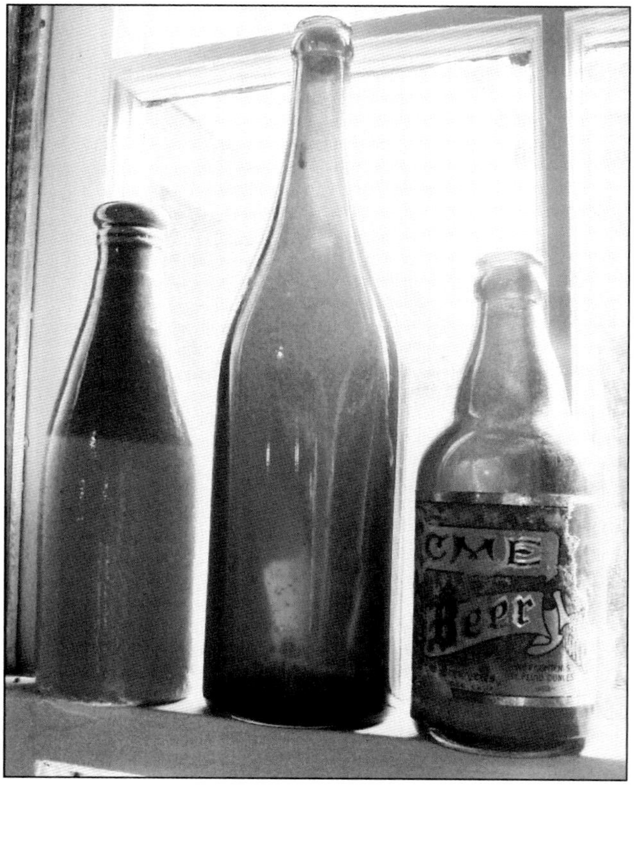

Beer was first imported to California's larger cities, such as San Francisco and Sacramento, in heavy, stoneware bottles, like the bottle on the left. While the establishment of commercial breweries took time, beer could be brewed on a small scale—as seen with many modern microbreweries—including in a tent or barn. As brewing became an established industry in California, stoneware bottles were recycled or replaced with glass bottles, a technology that has also changed with time. (Courtesy authors' collection.)

At the same time breweries were being developed, so were the roadways that would lead between the mines, allowing for the freighting of both grains for brewing and the final product. The earliest roads between the mines were unreliable at best. Mud and snow in the winter and dust in the hot, dry summers made passage of people and goods impossible at times. According to forty-niner David Leeper, "The roads were so wretched that supplies could only be got to the mines by pack-animals." As seen in this 1920 Division of Highways publication, freighting with horse and wagons was still common practice on these "modern" roads (and often horses were more reliable).

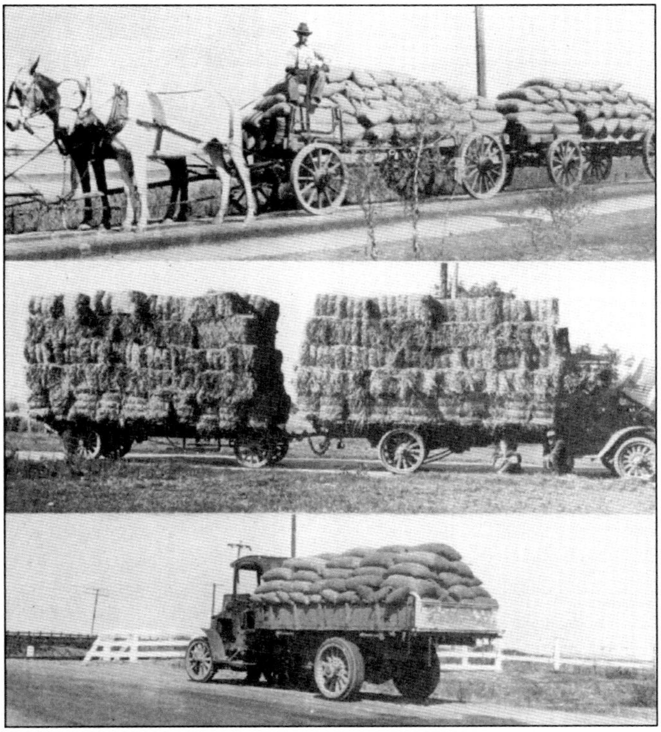

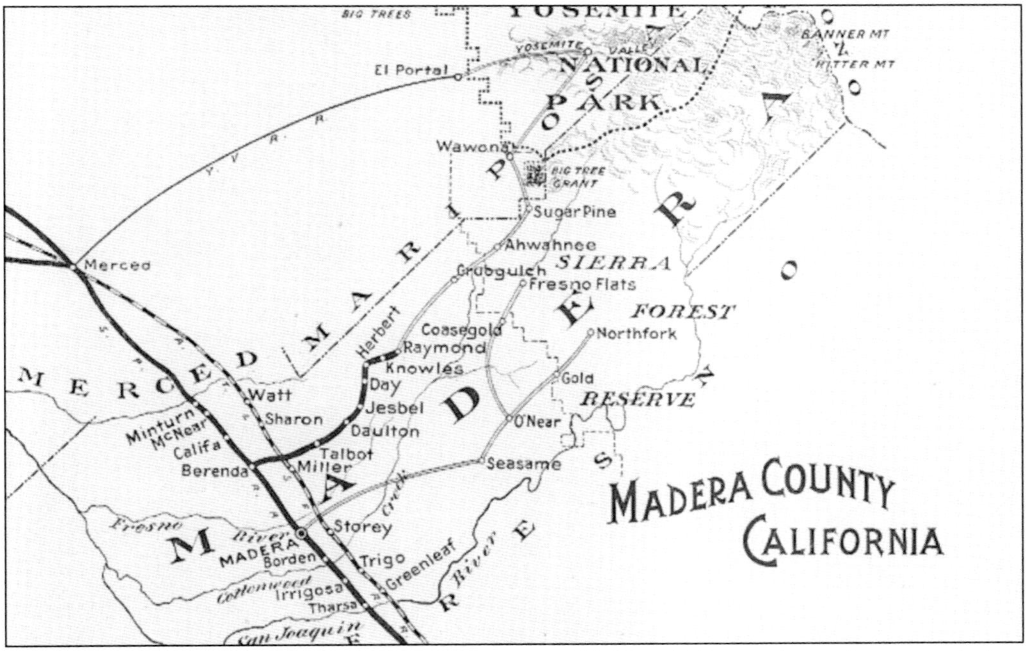

Madera County separated from Mariposa County in 1893. This 1911 map shows the county before Highway 49 became a modern route, with all the conveniences a paved roadway could bring. The link between Mariposa and Oakhurst was known as Bootjack Road until it became part of the Golden Chain Highway in 1969. While Fresno Flats (Oakhurst) was not as rich in gold as its neighbors (such as Coarsegold to the west), it is the official beginning of the "Mother Lode Highway." (Courtesy Madera County Library.)

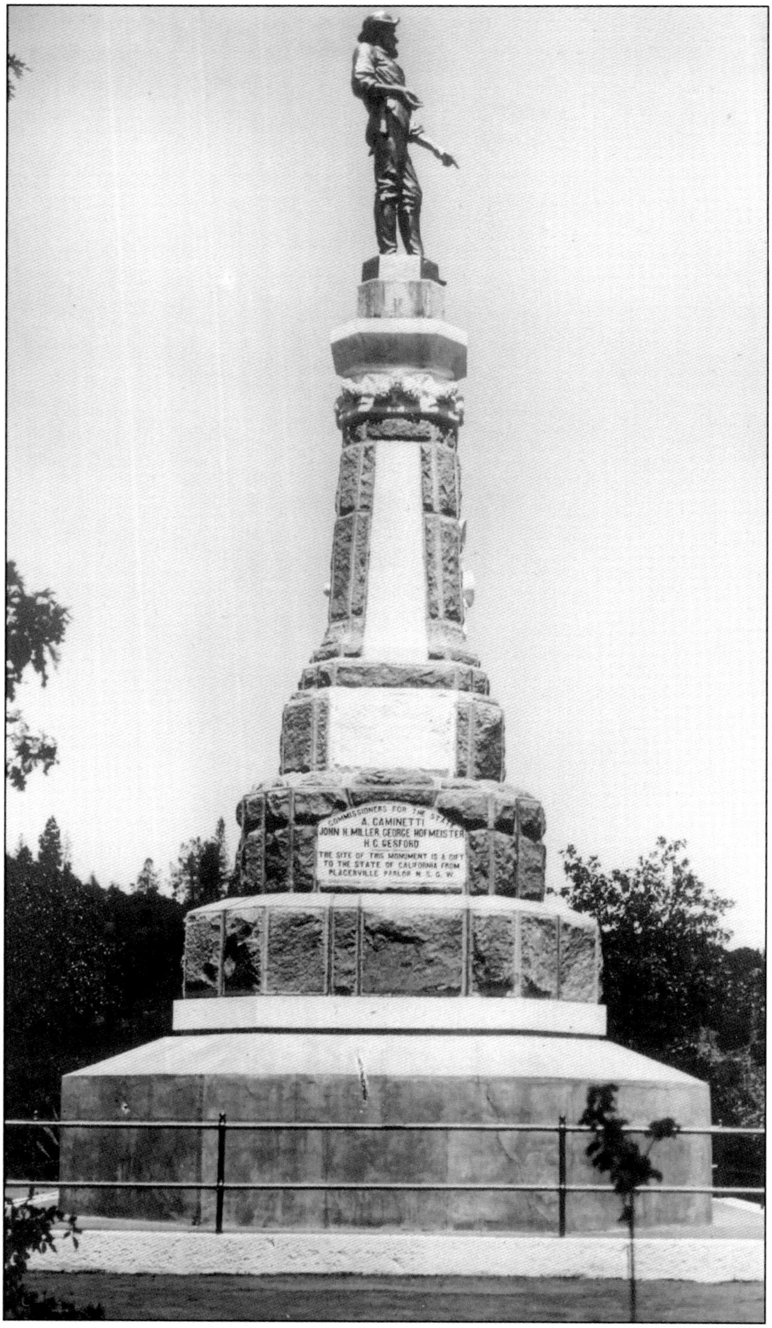

James W. Marshall's discovery of gold in the tailrace of Sutter's Mill on January 24, 1848, led to California's Gold Rush; this monument was erected near the discovery site in 1890 (for more see Chapter 4). At the southernmost tip of the gold fields was the community Fresno Flats; founded in 1850, it quickly established itself as a transportation hub and supply center to the northern mines. There were no brewers noted in Fresno Flats in the McKenny 1880 business directory, but of the nine businesses listed, two were liquor distributors—perhaps even selling beer from nearby Mariposa County breweries. The town's name was changed to Oakhurst in 1912. (Courtesy authors' collection.)

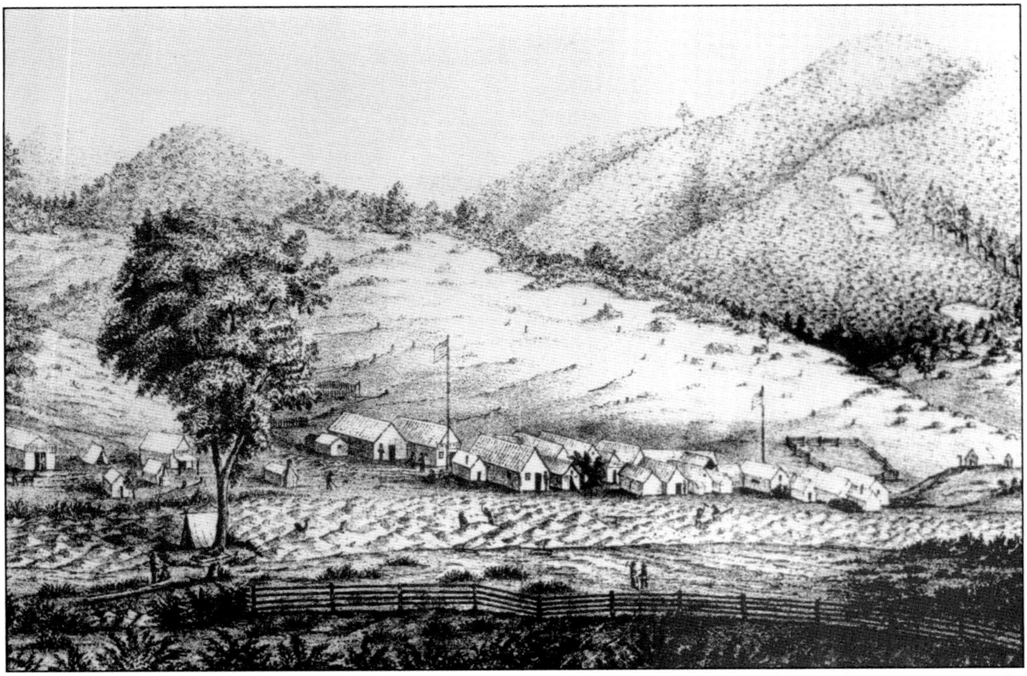

A thirsty miner moving into Mariposa County in the 1860s and 1870s would have found surprisingly few breweries. Of the several hundred occupations that men could hold in the Great Register of 1872, ranging from butcher, to artist, to simply "retired," by far the most common—nearly half—were miners. Of the rest of the men registered to vote in the county, only three listed themselves as brewers. Those worried about finding a wee nip, needed not fear: far more common than brewers on the 1872 register were "saloon keepers." One of the earliest breweries in the area, Gossner & Co. Brewery, would have been found in the town of Agua Fria, Mariposa's first county seat. Nothing remains of the town today, let alone the Gossner brewery. (Courtesy Leroy Radanovich.)

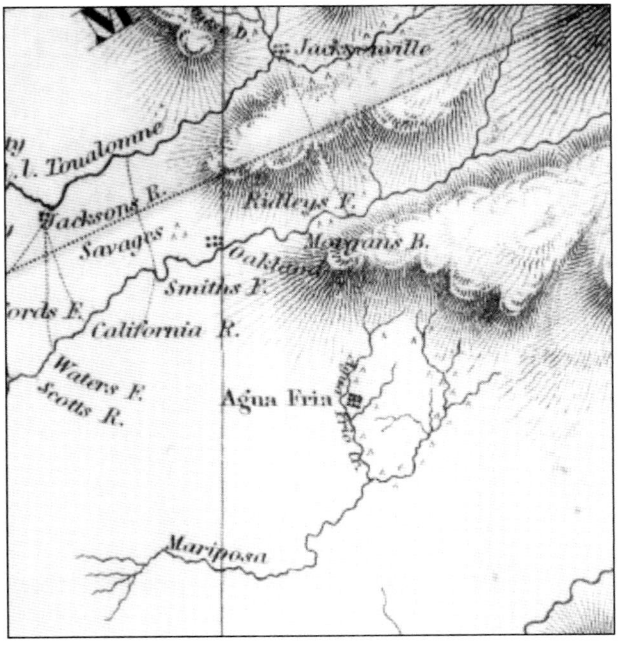

This early 1851 map of California's gold regions by C.D. Gibbes depicts the town of Agua Fria, the county seat at the time the map was drafted. Interestingly, the town of Mariposa to the east—which quickly replaced Agua Fria as county seat—is not depicted on the map, perhaps because the town flooded in the winter of 1849–1850 and was moved to higher ground.

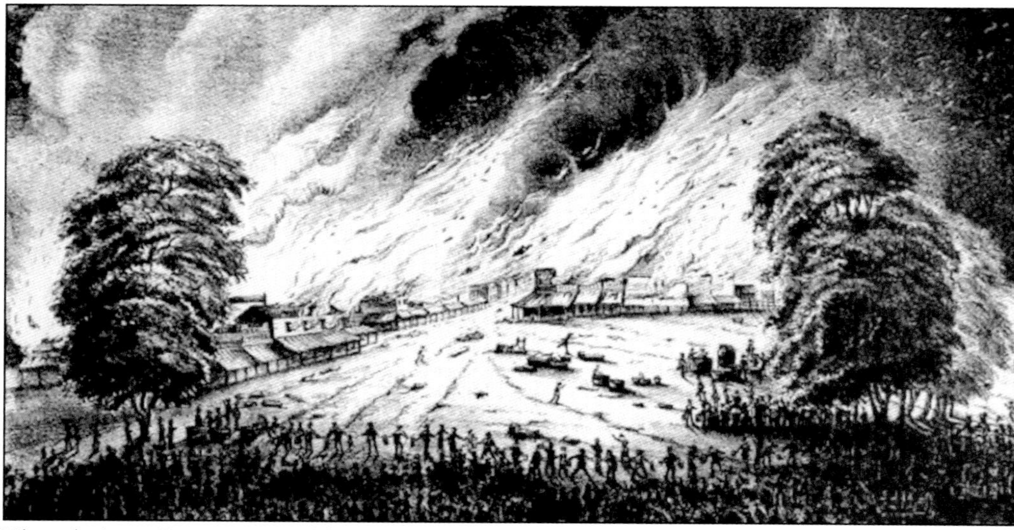

Though Agua Fria means "cold water" in Spanish, that was not enough to help the town in 1866. When Agua Fria burned that year, the Gossner (also Glossner) & Co. Brewery lost $9,000, and was only insured for $3,000 of that loss. The town was never rebuilt, and its brewers did not rebuild. While there is no firm proof that Gossner relocated, a Joseph Goesner is listed as a brewer in Hornitos, west of Agua Fria, on the 1872 Great Register. This etching actually depicts another early California community burning in the midst of a conflagration. (Courtesy Yuba County Library.)

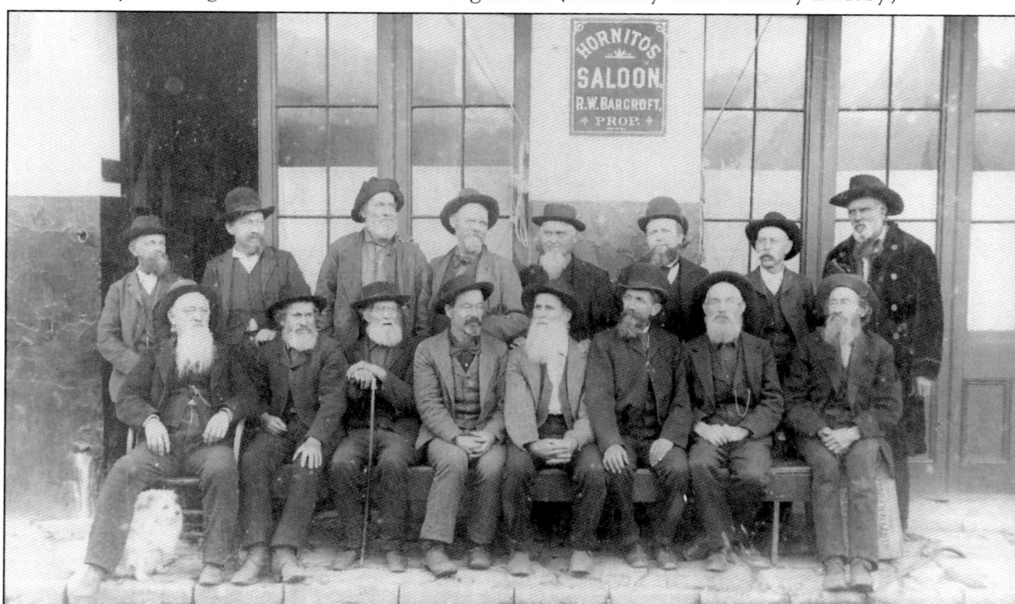

Hornitos started life as a prosperous mining camp at the very beginning of the Gold Rush but by the time these hopeful individuals paid to have themselves listed in McKenny's *Pacific Coast Directory of 1880–1881*, there were only 400 people left in town. Seen here are the "old-timers" of Hornitos seated in front of the Hornitos Saloon c. 1890. Pictured from left to right are (first row) saloon proprietor Ralph Barcroft, Al Sylvester, Sam Collier, Joe Spagnoli, Nat Bailey, Tom Thorn, Robert Arthur, and Tom "Spanish Tom" Williams; (second row) Henry Nelson, Thomas Smith, John Branson, Dennis William, Ben Shepperd, G. Gagliardo, Jim Craighn, and Mose Rodgers. (Courtesy Mariposa Museum and History Center.)

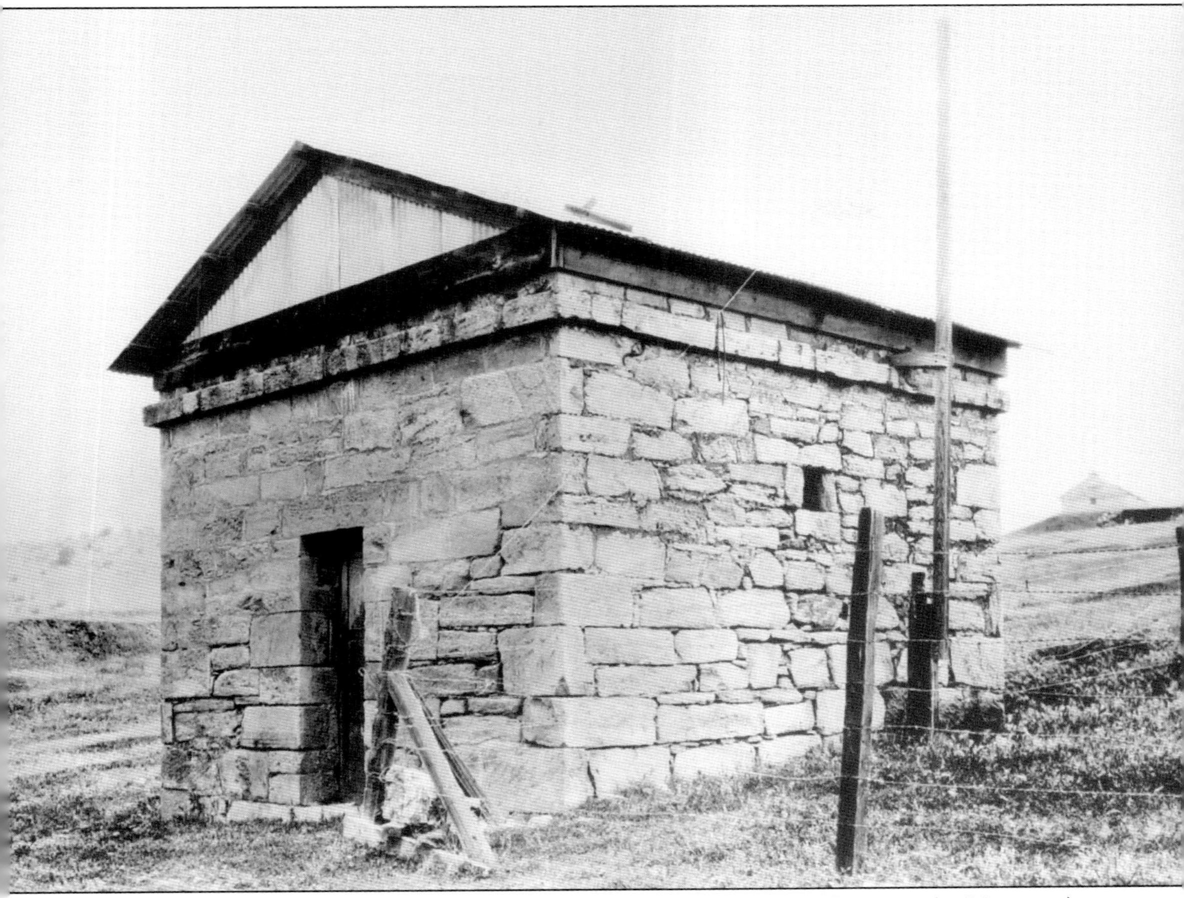

An A. La Grand is listed in Hornitos as owning a brewery in 1867. Henry Lessman (or Messman) appears to have taken La Grand's place as town brewer by 1872 and continued to operate until at least 1881. In the 1886–1887 business directory for Hornitos, it is Mrs. Lessman who is listed as the brewer. In comparison to the 1890 photograph on the previous page, only Barcroft (liquors), Arthur (blacksmith), and Gagliardo (general merchandise) are listed in the directory from the earlier decade. If any of these men had too much beer at Barcroft's saloon, they might find themselves spending the night in the Hornitos jail, pictured here c. 1934. (Courtesy authors' collection.)

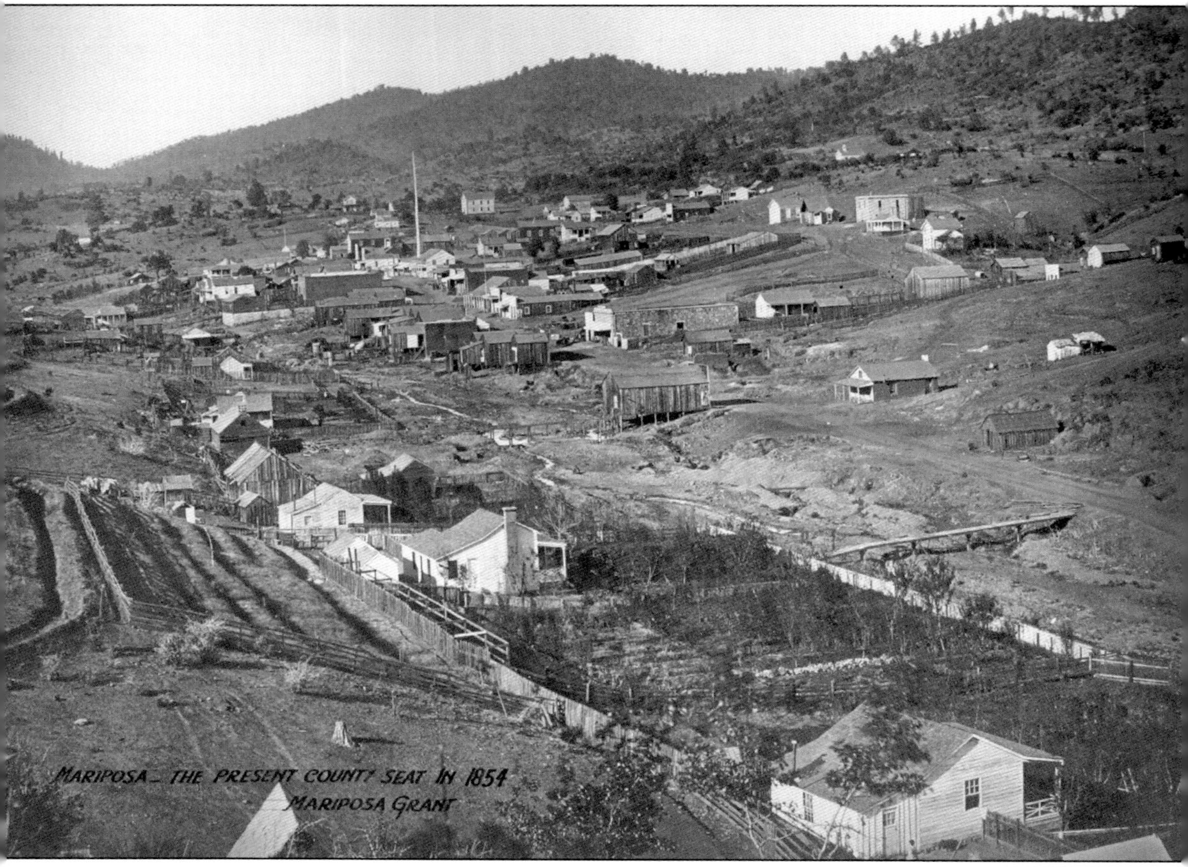

An early view of the town of Mariposa is seen in this 1860s photograph. John Weiler operated a brewery in town from at least 1872 (possibly as early as the 1860s) through the early 1880s. Like most of the brewers in this book, Weiler was from Germany. Born in 1829, he died in Mariposa in October 1892 at the age of 63; his obituary does not mention his brewing business. He married Esther Repetto-Quierolo (Weiler was her second husband) of Bear Valley, on September 20, 1874. They had four children, all born in Mariposa. Little is known about the day-to-day operations of Weiler's brewery, though the relative longevity of his business attests to its success. (Courtesy Mariposa Museum and History Center.)

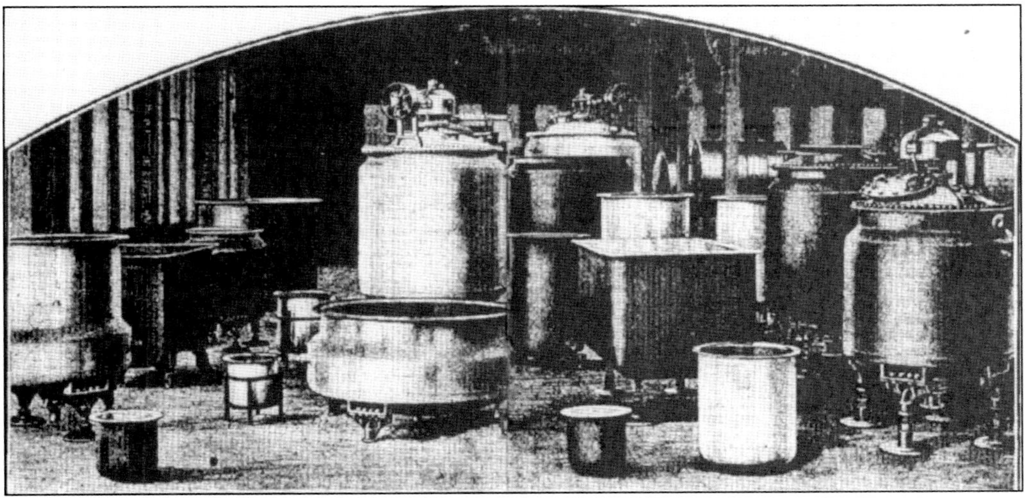

These images, from Rich & Co.'s *The Brewer's Hand Book*, depict what might have been found in a 19th-century brewery, such as Weiler's. Above is a variety of large kettles for brewing and, pictured on the right, a large wooden keg for storage. Smaller kegs would have been used for transporting the lagers. It is important to note that Weiler's name was also misspelled as Weller's. Censuses, directories, and other registers were often full of phonetic spellings of an individual's name, especially with some of the more difficult to pronounce or spell surnames. At the same time, immigrant families would often change their names to a more typically American spelling.

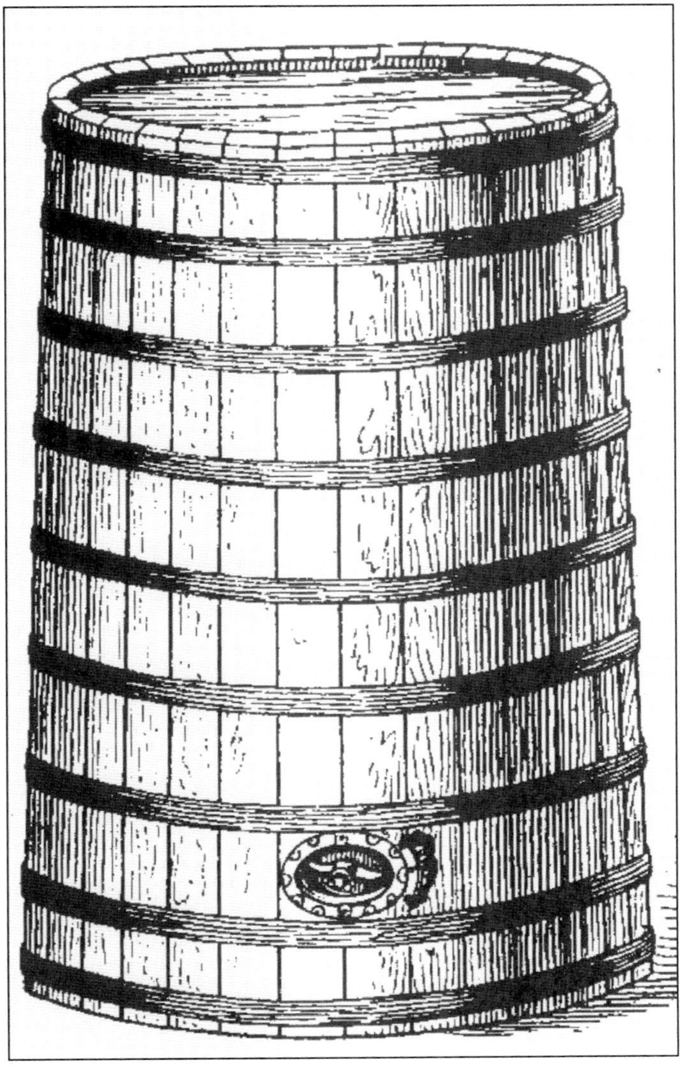

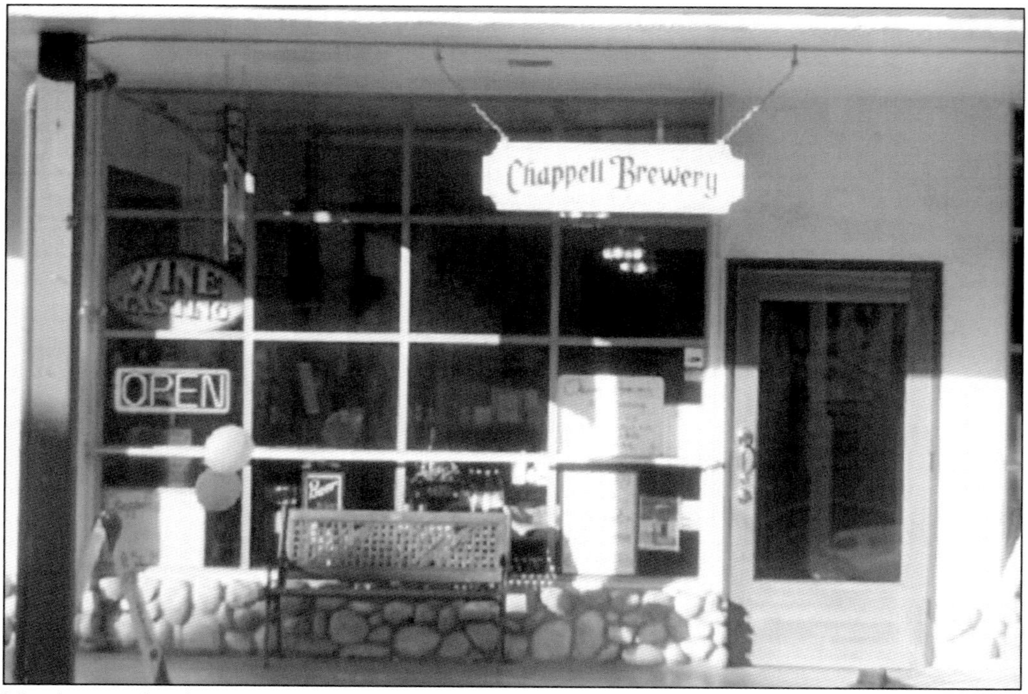

Until recently, the Mariposa Brewing Company operated in Mariposa. Currently Chappell Brewery, a "nano brewery," operates from a small facility on the town's Main Street following its Gold Rush predecessors. The store front is shown above, the brewing facilities are below. (Courtesy Chappell Brewery.)

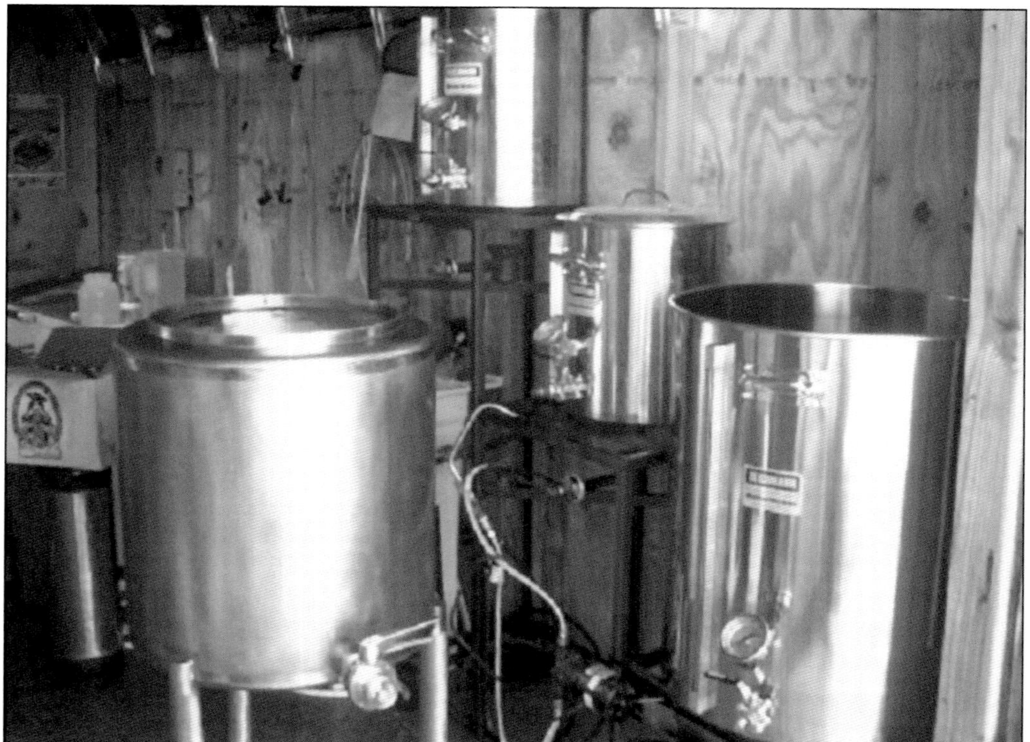

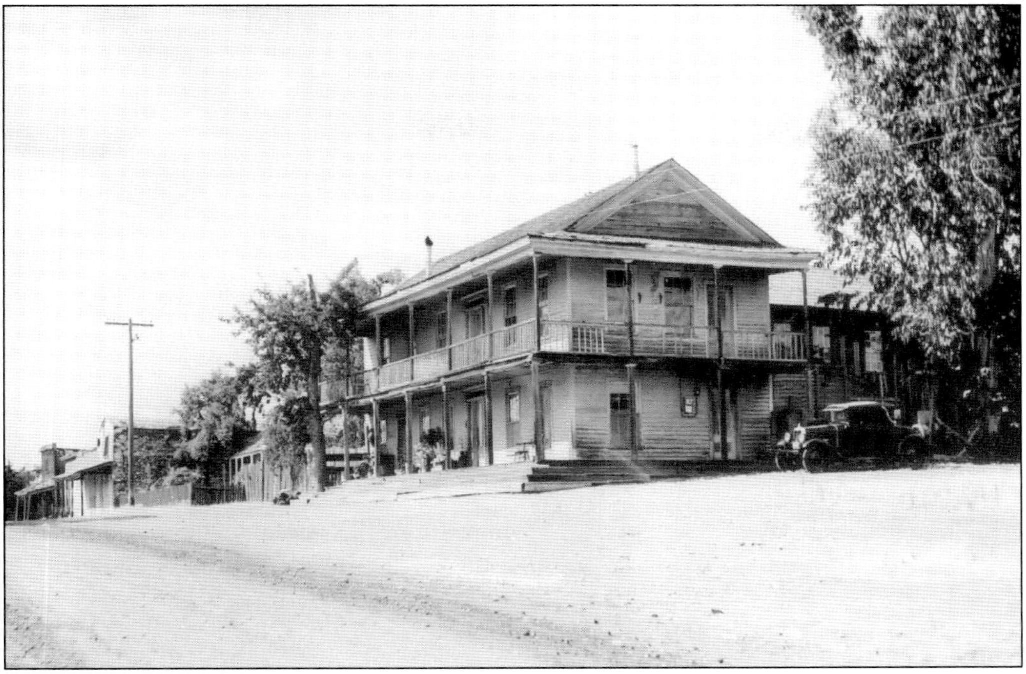

Beyond Mariposa were the towns of Bear Valley, Bagby, and Coulterville, though no brewers or breweries appear on registers in the two decades between the mid-1860s and mid-1880s. Once again, there were no shortages of liquor distributors or saloon keepers. Pictured above around 1936 is the Oso House Hotel, along the main road in Bear Valley. While Coulterville and Bear Valley are still communities today, Bagby (below), along the McClure Reservoir, was flooded and no longer exists. (Courtesy authors' collection.)

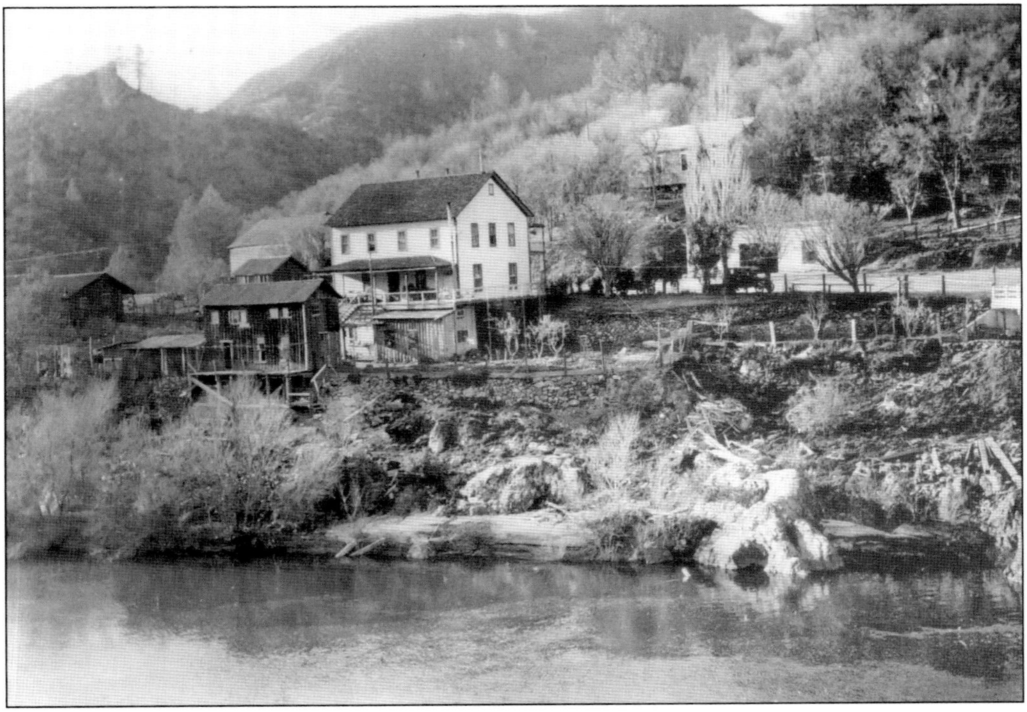

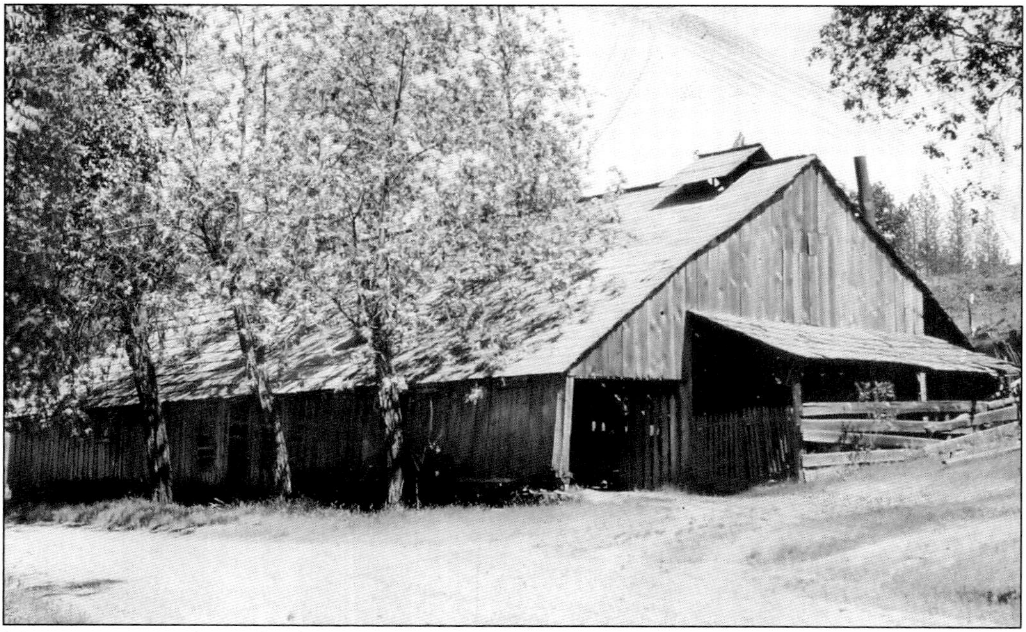

Moving past Coulterville through northern Mariposa County, one arrives at the junction of Highways 49 and 120 in Tuolumne County. Turning east along Highway 120, the road to Yosemite, one would have come across the small community of Garotte. The simple wooden structure depicted here housed Muller's Brewery, an early operation in that town. (Courtesy Tuolumne County Museum.)

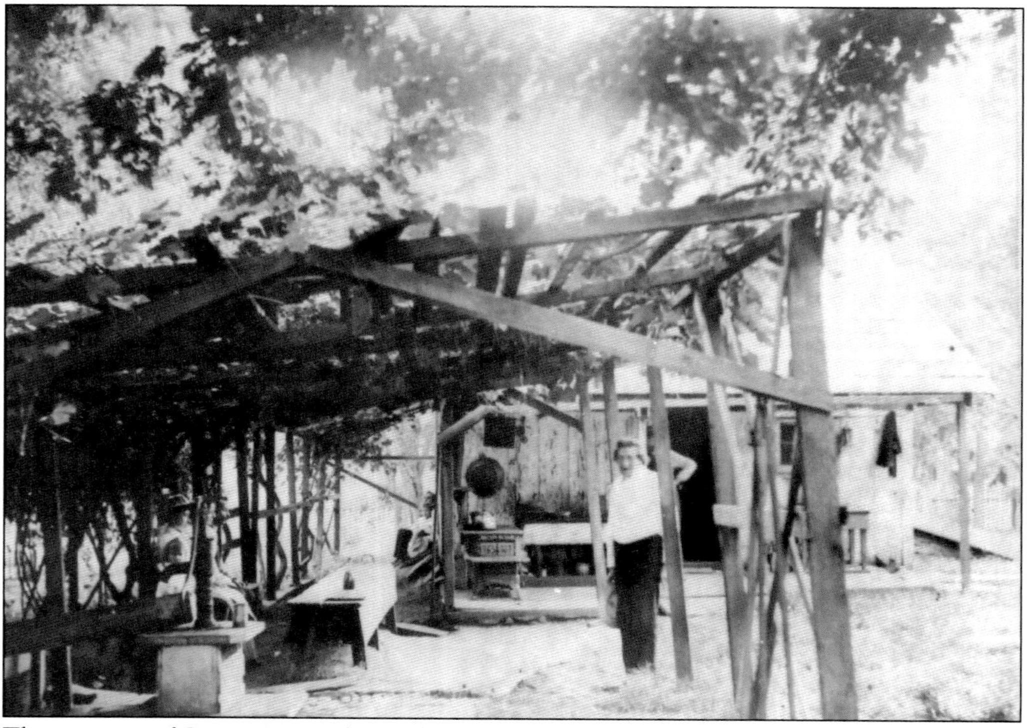

This is a view of George Macomber under the arbor at the Macomber Orchard. The Macombers produced champagne, cider, vinegar, and pickles. (Courtesy Tuolumne County Museum.)

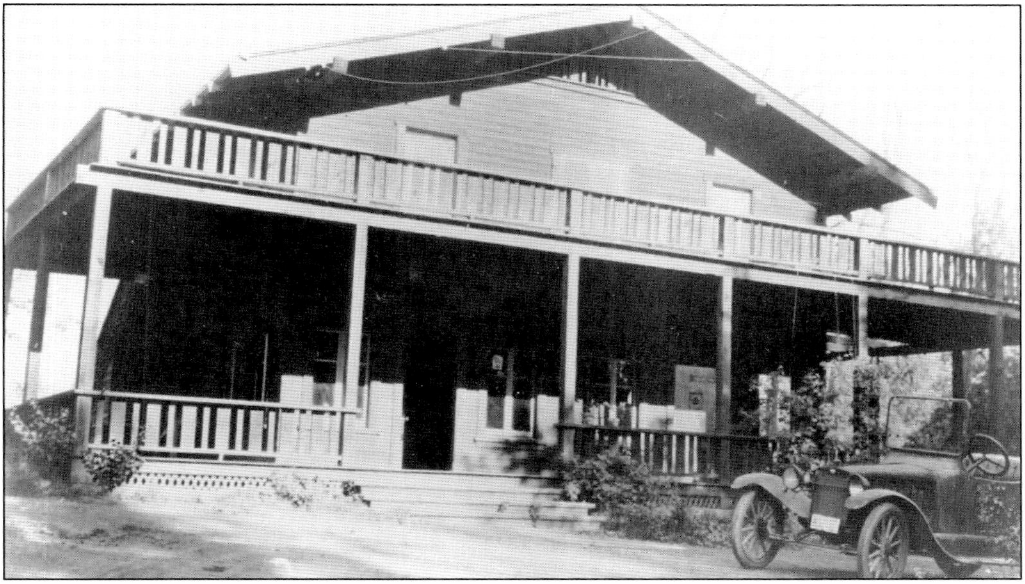

The Macombers lived in this house at their orchard. It is now part of the San Andreas High School. The vehicle in the foreground is a Saxon automobile. (Courtesy Tuolumne County Museum.)

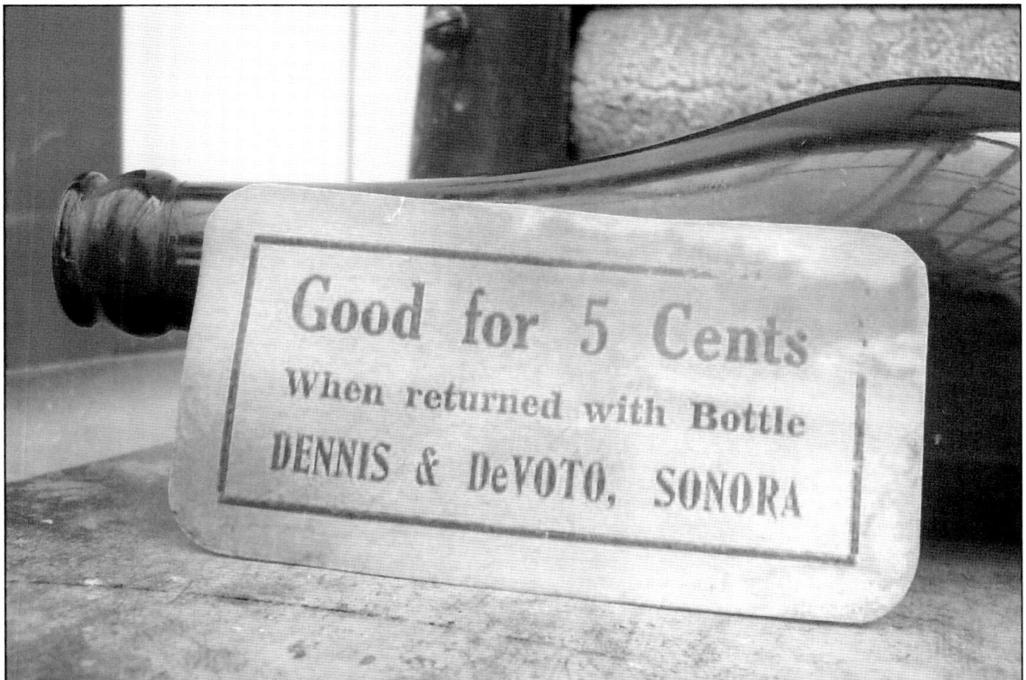

Recycling is not a modern concept; breweries, soda works, and other merchants often encouraged their customers to return their empties, saving both brewery and customer money. Shown here is a paper token from the Dennis & DeVoto mercantile in Sonora promising 5¢ if "returned with Bottle." Sonora had one brewery listed in 1880—"John Bauman, proprietor"—and with a population of 2,200, the town boasted 15 saloons and two liquor stores. Bauman was born in Germany in 1833 and immigrated to the United States in 1852; he arrived in California in 1856. (Courtesy authors' collection.)

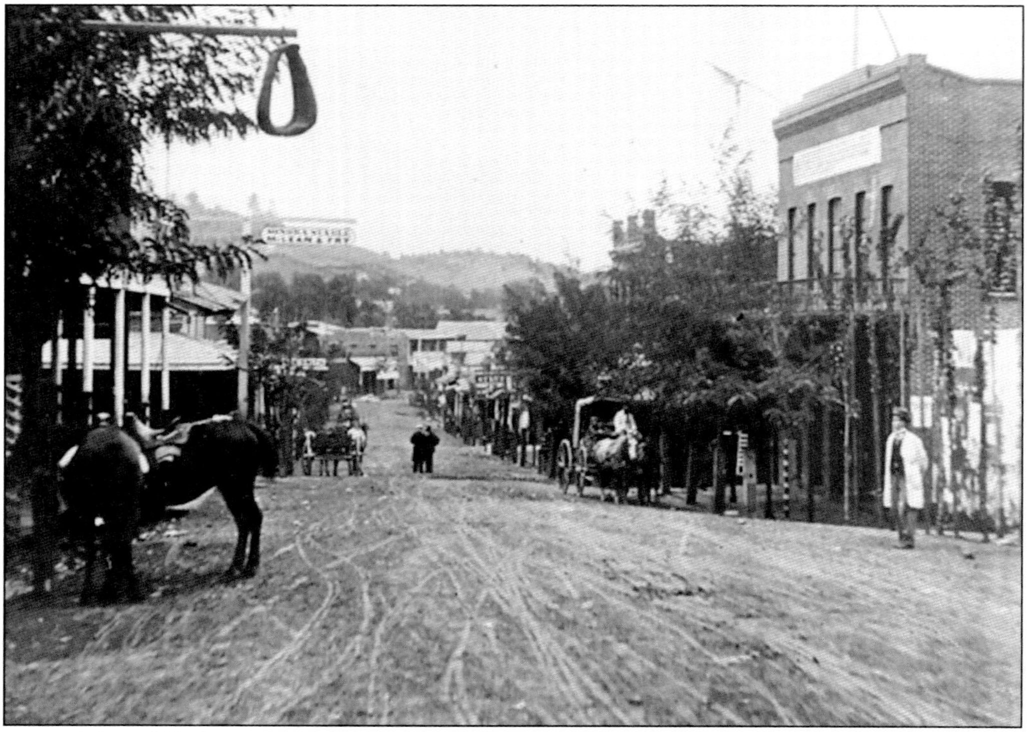

Sonora's busy Washington Street is seen in this 1870s photograph. By the time this photograph was taken, Bauman had been operating a brewery in town for nearly a decade. He started operating the Philadelphia Brewery in 1861, working there until 1865. He purchase the Sonora Brewery the next year, operating until at least the mid-1890s, when he was winning statewide awards for his lager, porter, and beer. According to the 1882 county history: "The brewery building is 60 x 120 feet, built of brick and stone. It contains all the necessary appliances for manufacturing beer and other beverages; and if the brewery were run up to its full capacity, it would turn out fifteen hundred barrels of beer per year." (Courtesy Society of California Pioneers.)

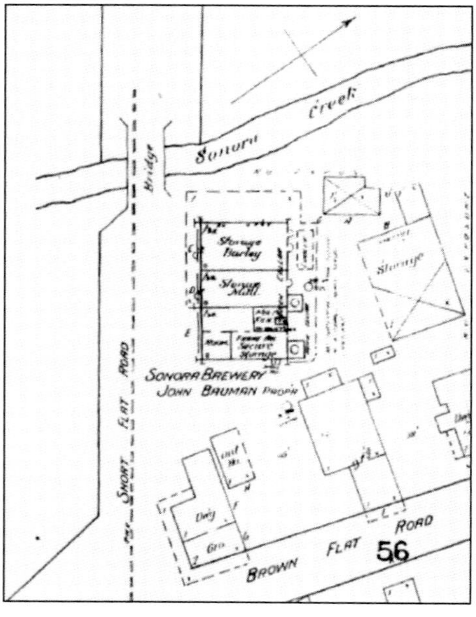

This 1890 Sanborn map shows the Sonora Brewery on the corner of Short Flat and Brown Flat roads, just over the bridge east of Sonora Creek. The map shows two large storage rooms, one for barley, a small cooler, secure storage, as well as a beer cellar. Cellars, or lower stories, were common features in breweries, where gravity was used to move the final product more easily. The map does not indicate a public bar, though a space simply marked "room" may have sufficed.

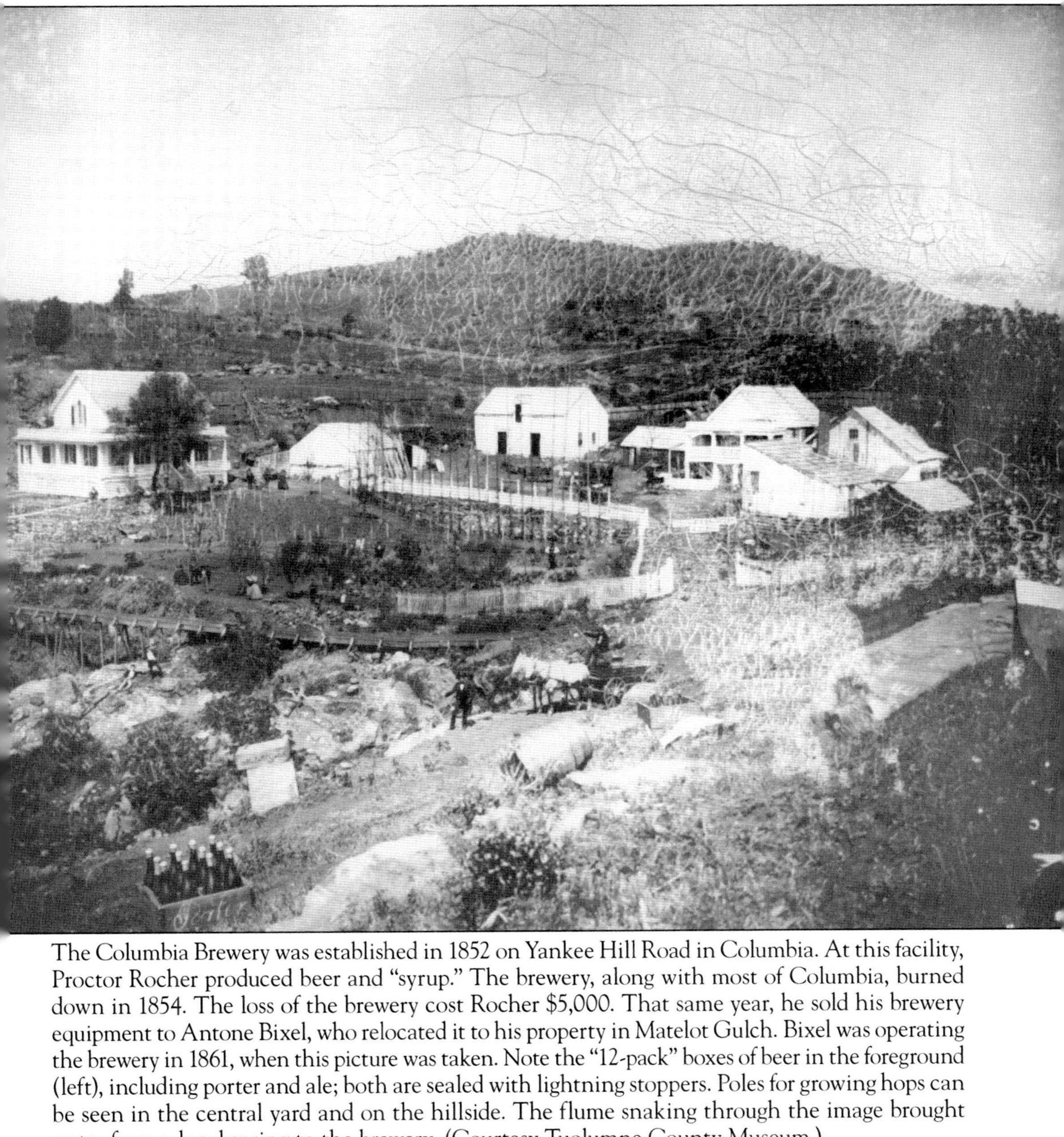

The Columbia Brewery was established in 1852 on Yankee Hill Road in Columbia. At this facility, Proctor Rocher produced beer and "syrup." The brewery, along with most of Columbia, burned down in 1854. The loss of the brewery cost Rocher $5,000. That same year, he sold his brewery equipment to Antone Bixel, who relocated it to his property in Matelot Gulch. Bixel was operating the brewery in 1861, when this picture was taken. Note the "12-pack" boxes of beer in the foreground (left), including porter and ale; both are sealed with lightning stoppers. Poles for growing hops can be seen in the central yard and on the hillside. The flume snaking through the image brought water from a local spring to the brewery. (Courtesy Tuolumne County Museum.)

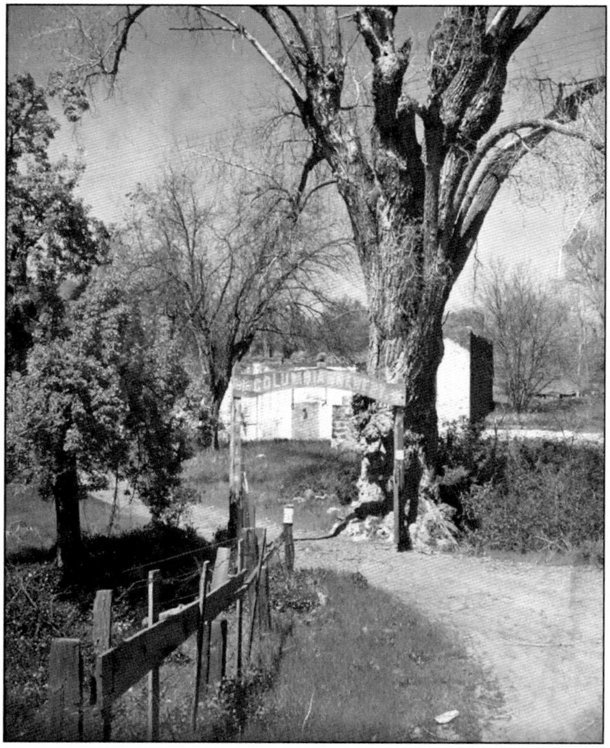

Antone Bixel operated the Columbia Brewery as a sole proprietor for the first few years. In 1856, his brother Joseph arrived from Germany, via Ohio, to join him. The ruins of the brewery can be seen in the background. A more detailed photograph of the brewery ruins is seen below. (Both, courtesy Tuolumne County Museum.)

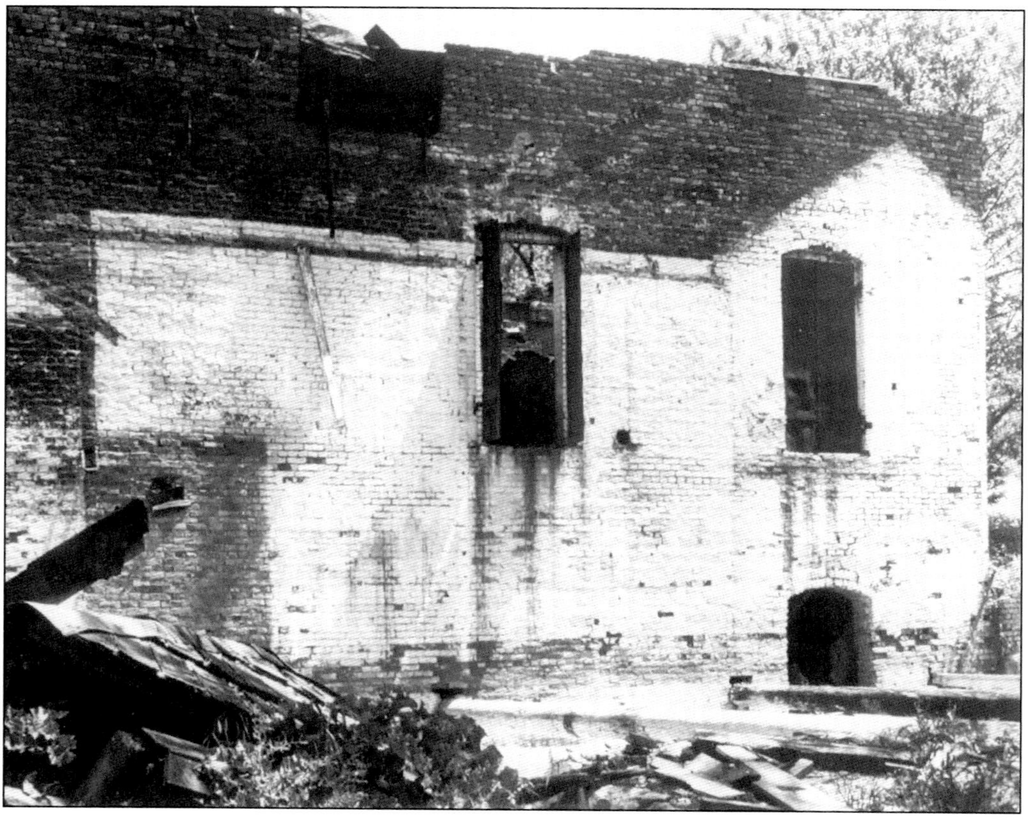

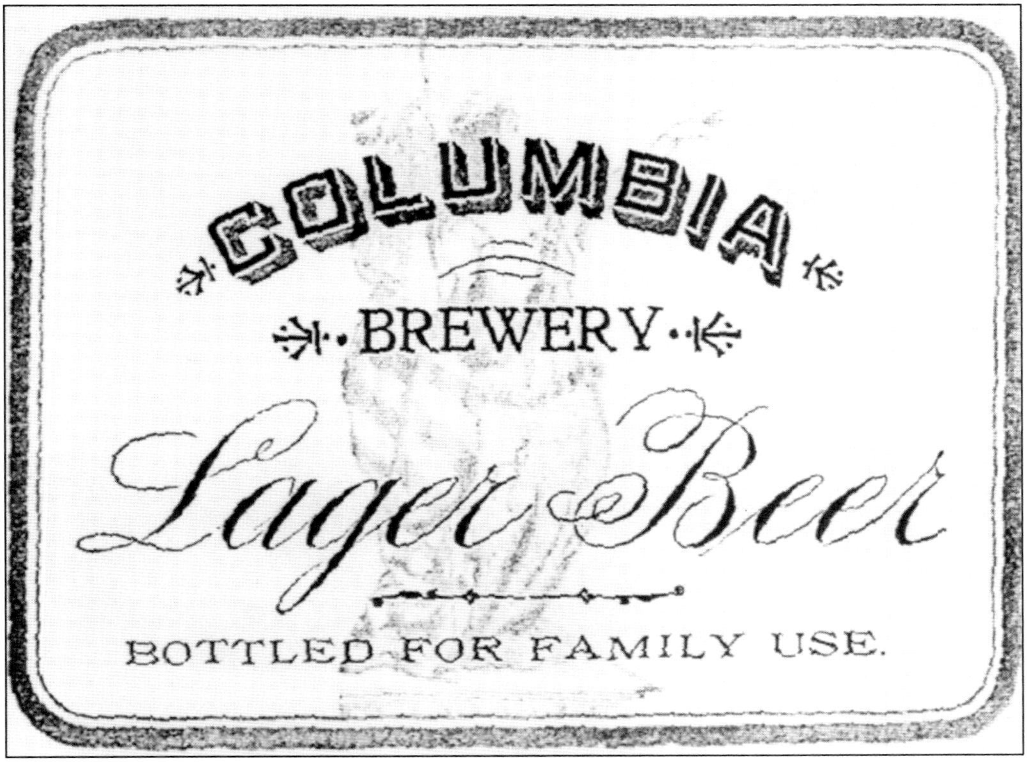

This label from the Columbia Brewery was created for their bottled lager beer, a very popular drink during the years the brewery operated. The label reads "Bottled for Family Use," indicating it was not for resale. (Courtesy Columbia Archives.)

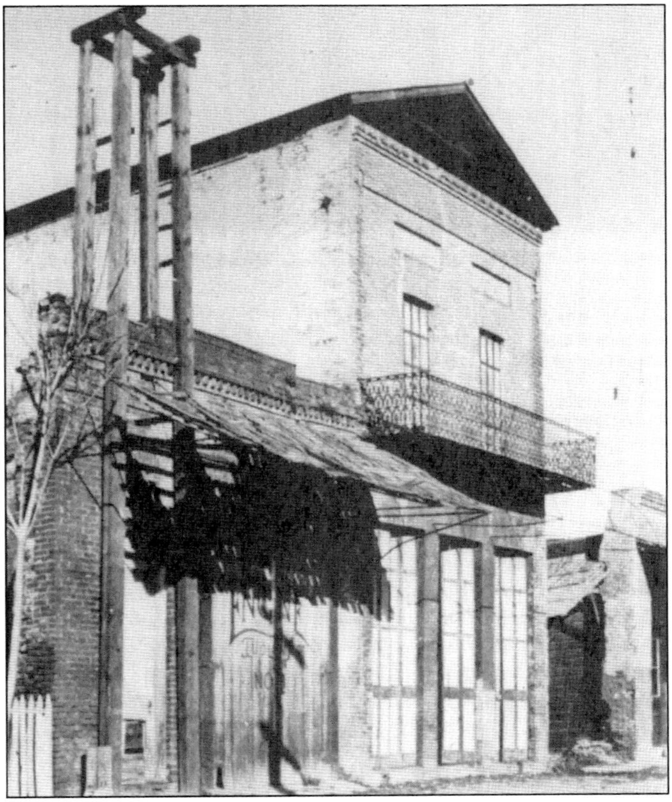

In downtown Columbia, the two-story brick Springfield Brewery can be seen standing next to the Tuolumne Engine House No. 1. Built in 1856 by John Duchow (and often referred to as the Duchow Building), he leased the lower floor to brewers C. Strake and J. Wedel in 1866. This 1948 image of the brewery contrasts with the restoration that the Main Street of Columbia State Historic Park has seen more recently. (Courtesy Division of Mines.)

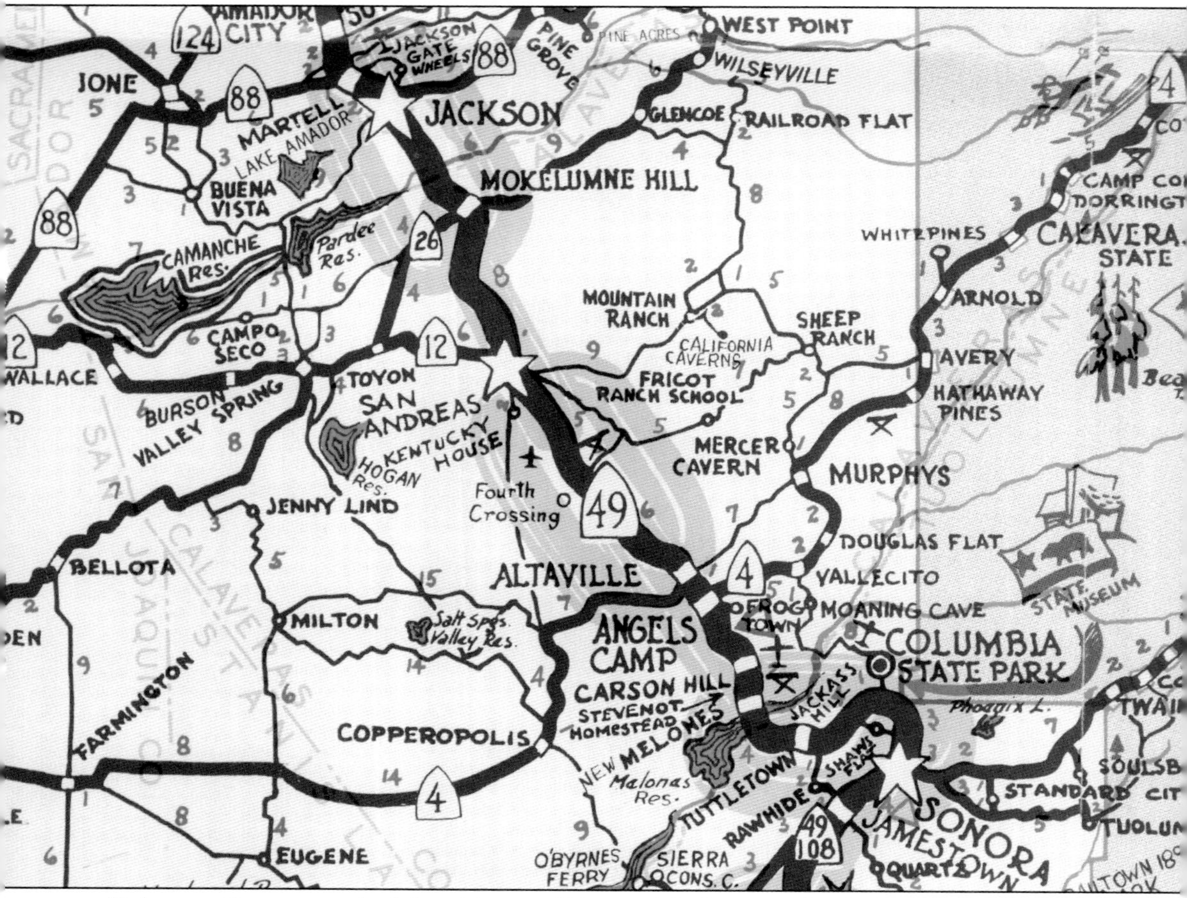

Calaveras County acquired the nickname "Home of the Jumping Frog" after Mark Twain wrote a short story about the county in 1865. Highway 49 runs northward from the Stanislaus River and New Melones Reservoir. Placer gold mining, and later industrial hardrock mining, occurred in all of the communities along this route, including Carson Hill, Angels Camp, Fourth Crossing, San Andreas, and Mokelumne Hill. Liquid gold was brewed at many of these communities as well. (Courtesy Golden Chain Council.)

Two

Calaveras County
Home of the Jumping Frog

"Of the demonstrably wise there are but two: those who commit suicide, and those who keep their reasoning faculties atrophied by drink."

—Mark Twain

Calaveras County is situated in the heart of the Motherlode, running from the crest of the Sierra Nevada Mountains to the floor of the Central Valley, and it is home to the famous giant sequoias of Big Trees National Park. Among the earliest explorers to visit the area were French trappers who arrived in the 1830s in search of beaver and other fur-bearing animals. Aside from these transient visitors, the region remained largely unexplored until the Gold Rush. In the matter of a few short months, thousands of miners entered the region to pursue its rich placer deposits. Soon, small towns with names like Altaville, Angles Camp, Campo Seco, Copperopolis, Mokelumne Hill, Murphys, San Andreas, and Sheep Ranch sprang up; all would become home to their own brewery.

Mokelumne Hill is one of the northernmost towns in Calaveras County, as well as one of the oldest. Situated on Highway 49 just south of the Mokelumne River, the town was once the county seat and home to two of the county's most well-known breweries. Farther south is San Andreas, which became the county seat in 1863, and was also home to several breweries. Finally, there is Angels Camp, near the southern end of the county. This small mining community was frequented by author and humorist Mark Twain, and it was the setting for Twain's tale of "The Celebrated Jumping Frog of Calaveras County." Nearby is the town of Murphys, and to the east, Arnold, currently home to Snowshoe Brewing Co., one of the Gold Country's modern microbreweries.

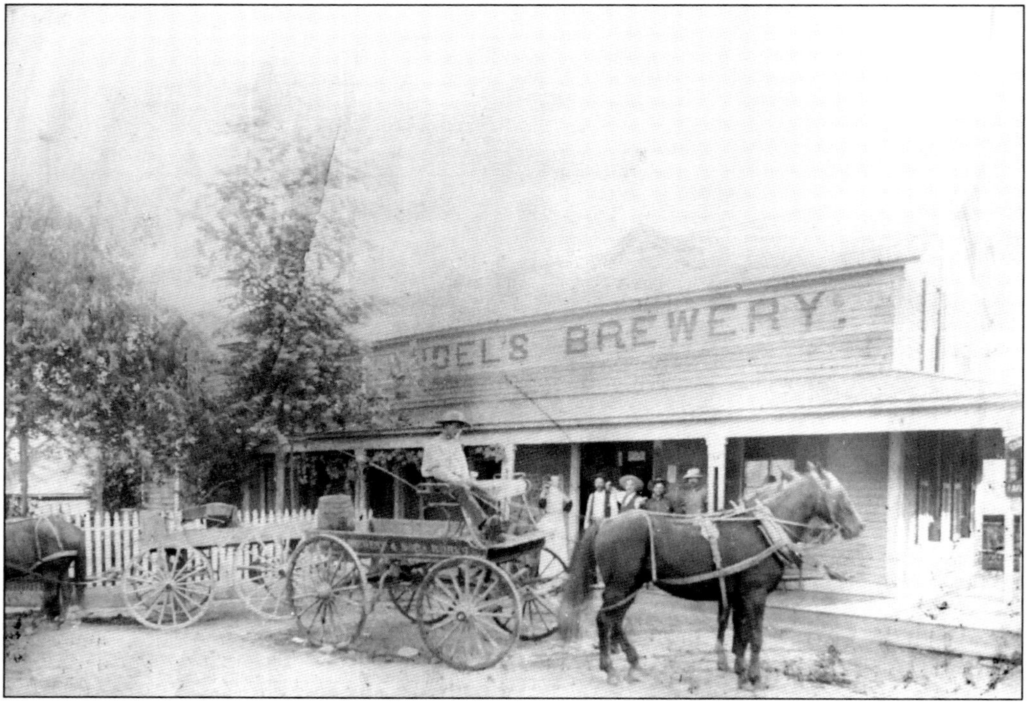

Angel's Brewery was located on South Main Street in Angels Camp. It also served as a soda works, something that helped to keep them in business for a few more years during Prohibition. The wagon is stenciled Angel's Brewery & Soda Works; at the reins is Fred Wilson. (Courtesy Calaveras County Archives.)

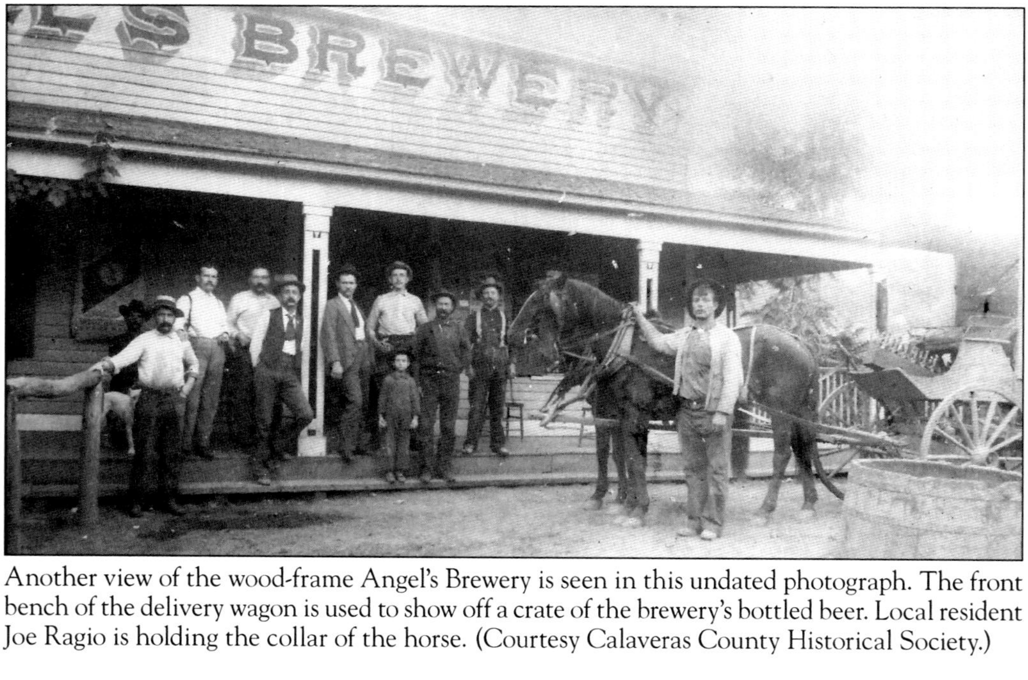

Another view of the wood-frame Angel's Brewery is seen in this undated photograph. The front bench of the delivery wagon is used to show off a crate of the brewery's bottled beer. Local resident Joe Ragio is holding the collar of the horse. (Courtesy Calaveras County Historical Society.)

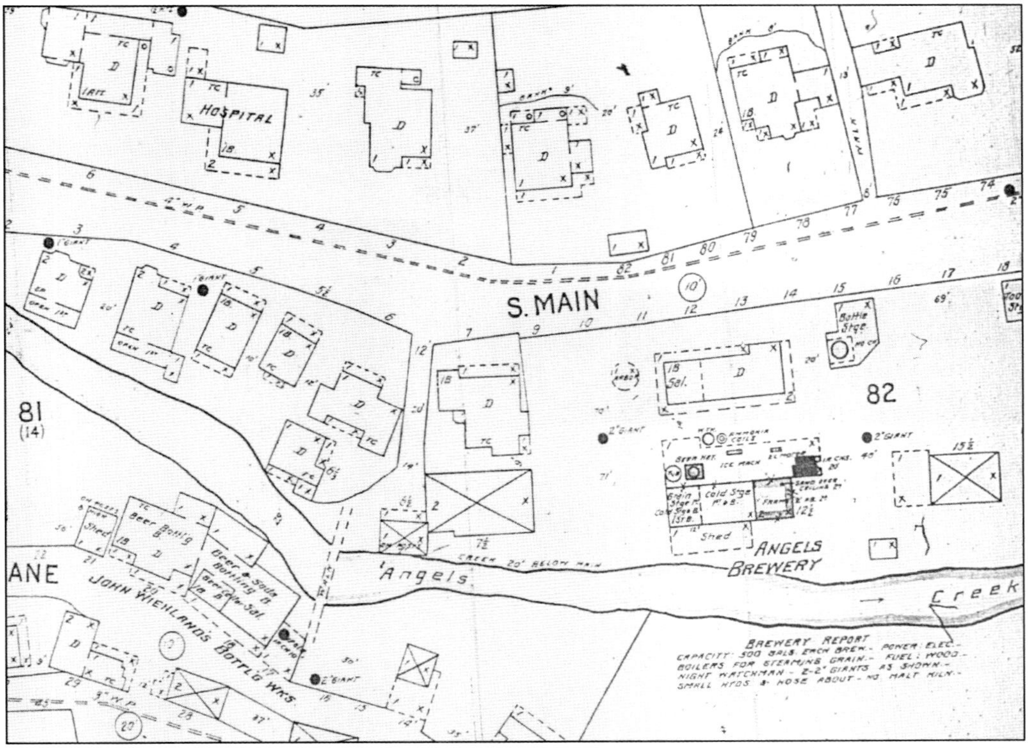

The 1905 Sanborn map above shows the geographical relationship of Angel's Brewery and John Weiland's Bottling Plant. Angel's Brewery produced beer and soda on the premises, while the Weiland plant bottled beer produced elsewhere. For many years, Weiland's was one of the largest beer producers in the state. Much of its beer was produced at breweries in San Francisco and San Jose, and then shipped in kegs to regional bottling plants, including those in Angels Camp and Jamestown. Close inspection of Angel's Brewery in 1905 shows ammonia coils used in the production of ice. When Angel's Brewery was producing beer, it had a capacity of 500 gallons per brew. Seen below is a detail of the Angel's Brewery as mapped in 1922. By this time, "Ice" had been incorporated into the brewery's name, the beer kettle had been replaced by cold storage, and the saloon behind the building was gone.

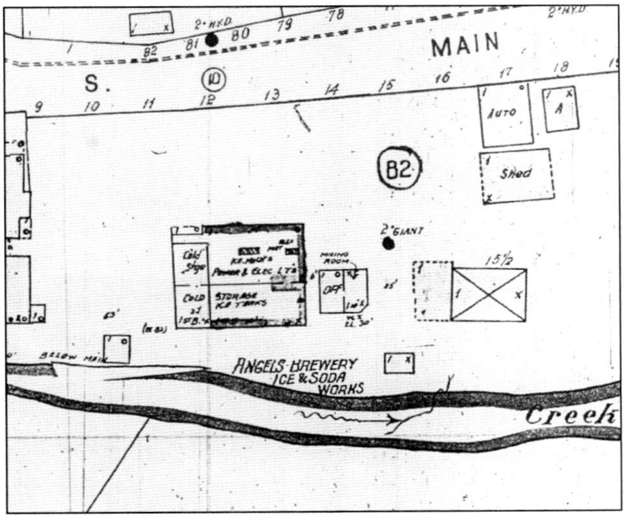

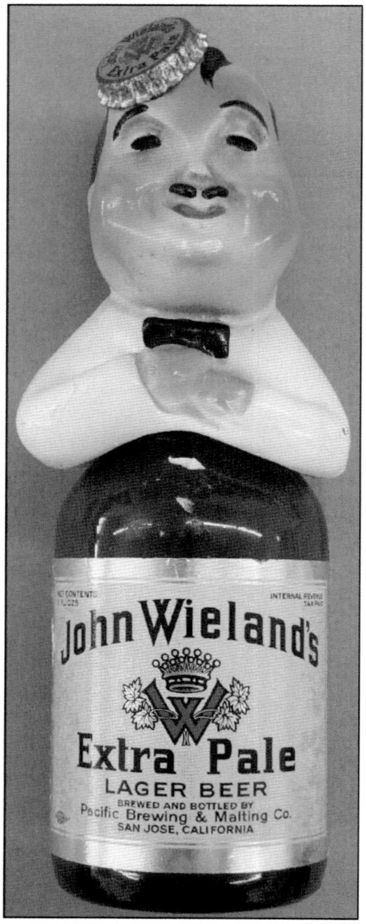

Like many breweries, Wieland's offered up promotional items to their customers. This festive beer topper is actually from the Wieland's brewery in San Jose. Similar items would have been distributed from other facilities, including their bottling plant in Angels Camp. The company also had a bottling plant in Jamestown, Tuolumne County. (Courtesy authors' collection.)

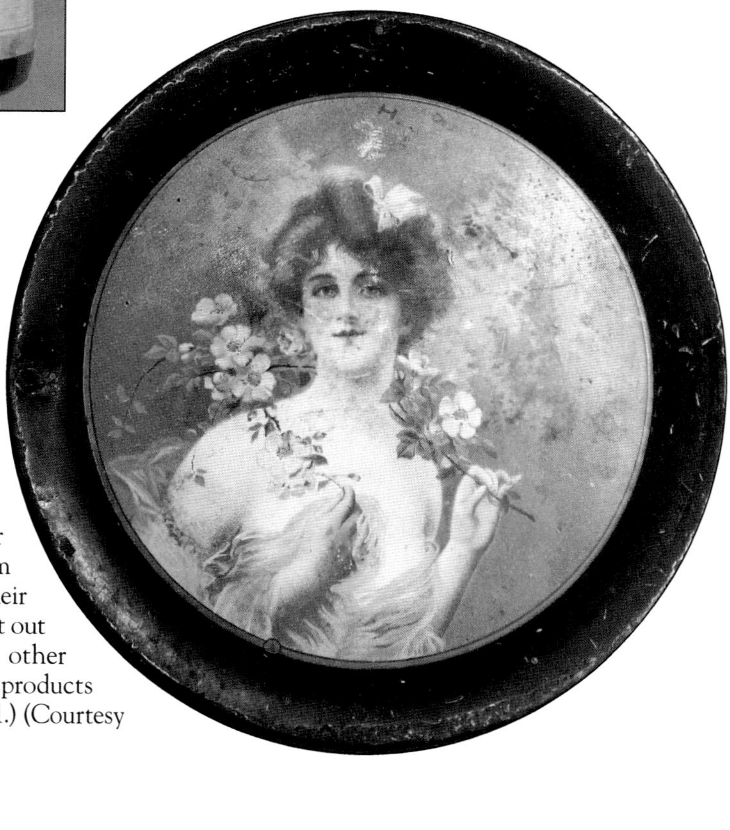

This tin coaster was another type of promotional item distributed by breweries to their clientele. Breweries also sent out trays, mugs, calendars, and other materials to promote their products (see the calendar on Page 121.) (Courtesy authors' collection.)

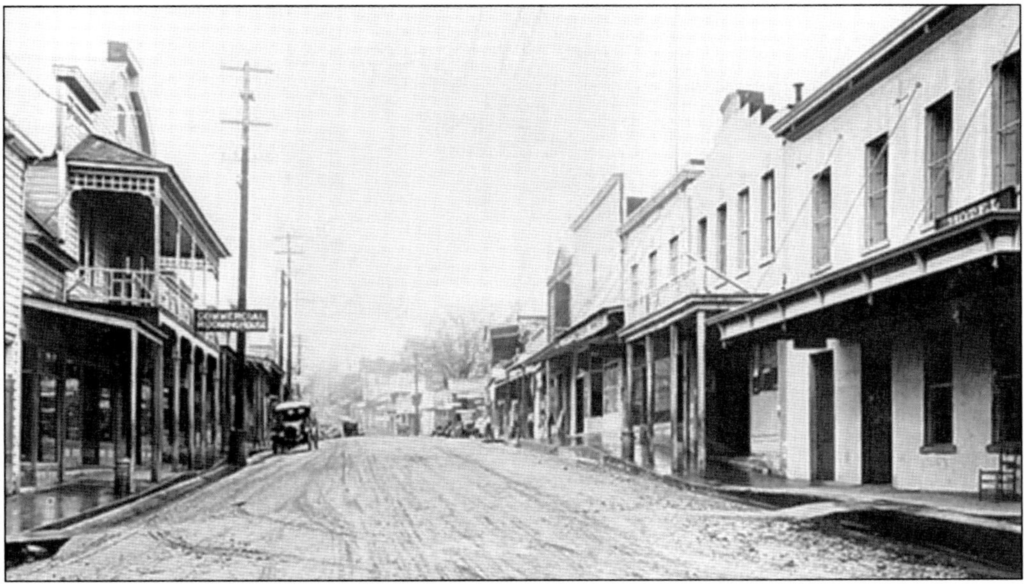

Seen here is the Main Street of Angels Camp in 1923, much as the town would have look when the Angel's Brewery was in operation. The brewery and the town were already three years into Prohibition. Ultimately, Angel's Brewery would not survive. (Courtesy authors' collection.)

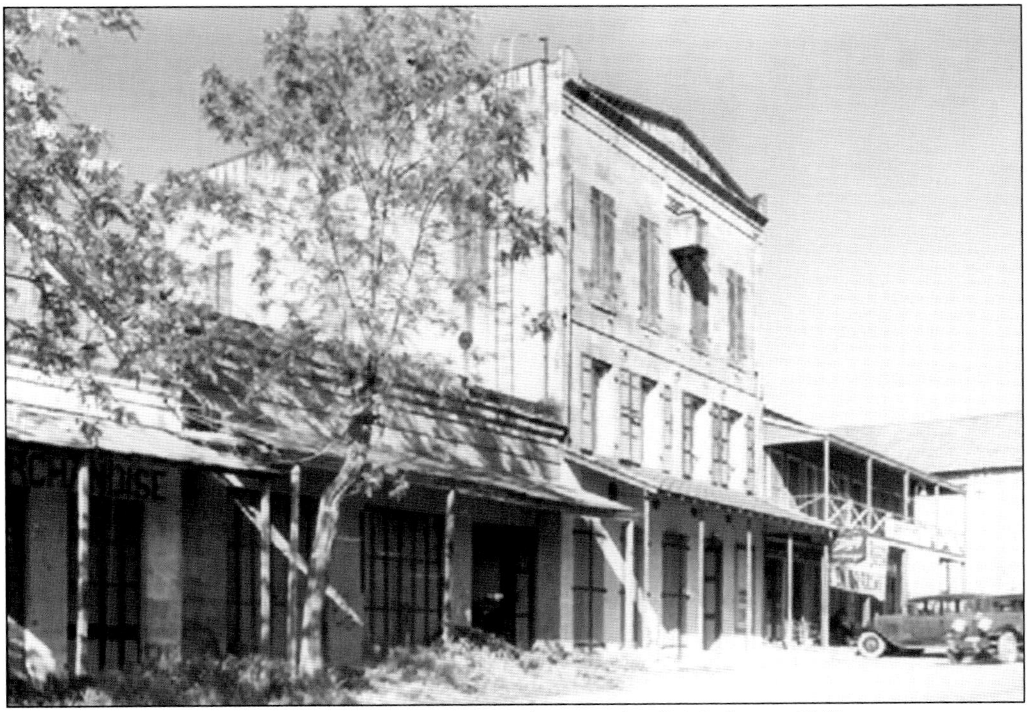

Looking like it had for nearly a century, this 1934 photograph of Mokelumne Hill captures portions of the business district of the town. An 1855 booster etching of Mokelumne Hill captured one of the earliest images of the J. Ch. Gebhardt & Staehler Brewery, located a few blocks to the north of these buildings. While a substantial structure is shown in the etching, it is a wood frame building, and Gebhardt would later build the beautiful stone building seen on the next page to house his brewery. (Courtesy authors' collection.)

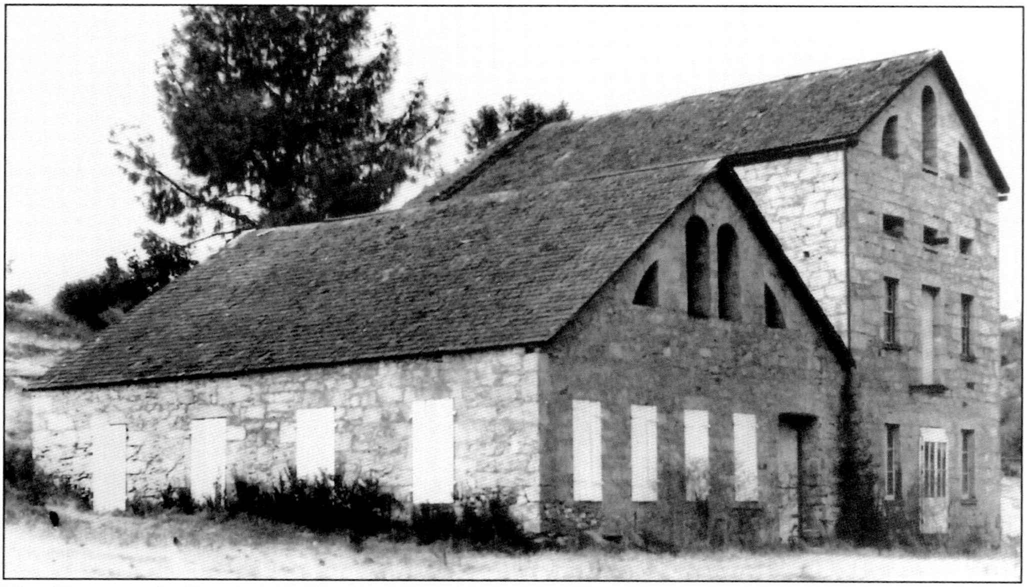

The Hemminghoffen & Suessdorf Brewery (also Hemminghofen and Himmighofen; also Suesdorf) was located on Church Street in Mokelumne Hill. This image shows the magnificent workmanship employed in its construction. The brewery was established by J.C. Gebhardt in 1855, with this substantial structure built by 1862. It was constructed of stone quarried on site, with walls two feet thick. It had a brew kettle that held 550 gallons and a mash tub capable of holding 2,000 gallons, both housed in the structure to the left. Once the wort was cooled, it was transferred to the fermentation room in the cellar. (Courtesy Calaveras County Archives.)

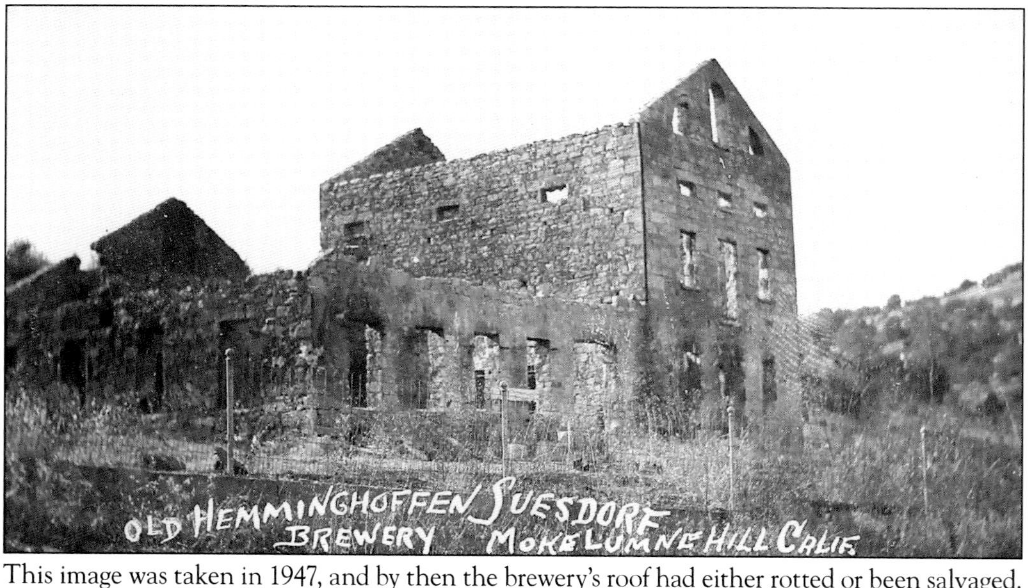

This image was taken in 1947, and by then the brewery's roof had either rotted or been salvaged. There was a tunnel extending from the basement into the hillside behind the brewery. It was four feet wide, six feet high (with an arched top), and 150 feet long. At the back of this tunnel was a ventilation shaft 80 feet deep. Several other "compartments" and shafts were attached to this tunnel. The three-story structure to the right housed the malt works. This included a storage room in the basement, a mill on the first floor, a malting room and drying kiln on the second floor, and a cooling room on the third floor. (Courtesy Calaveras County Archives.)

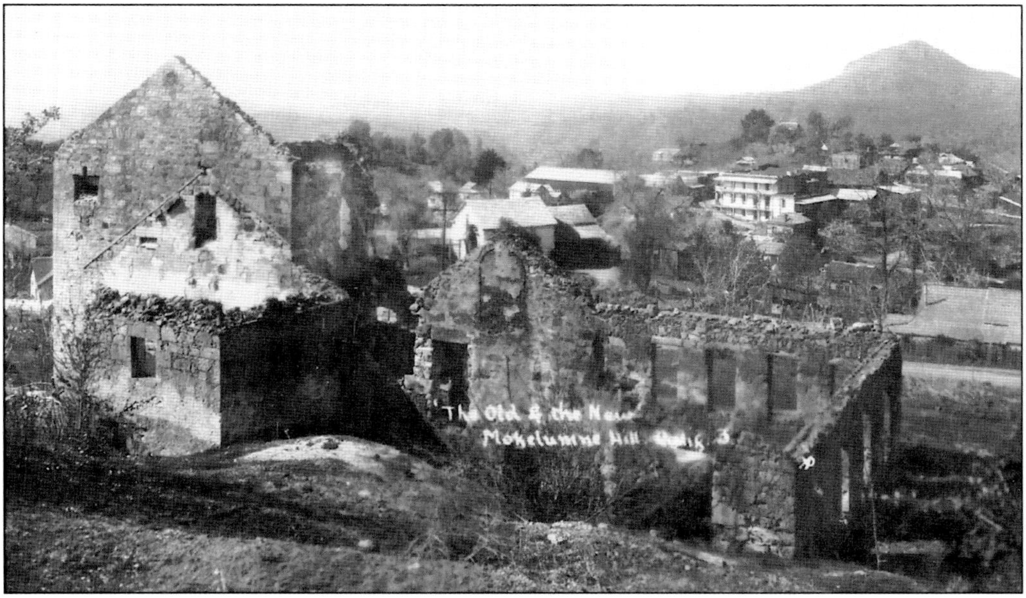

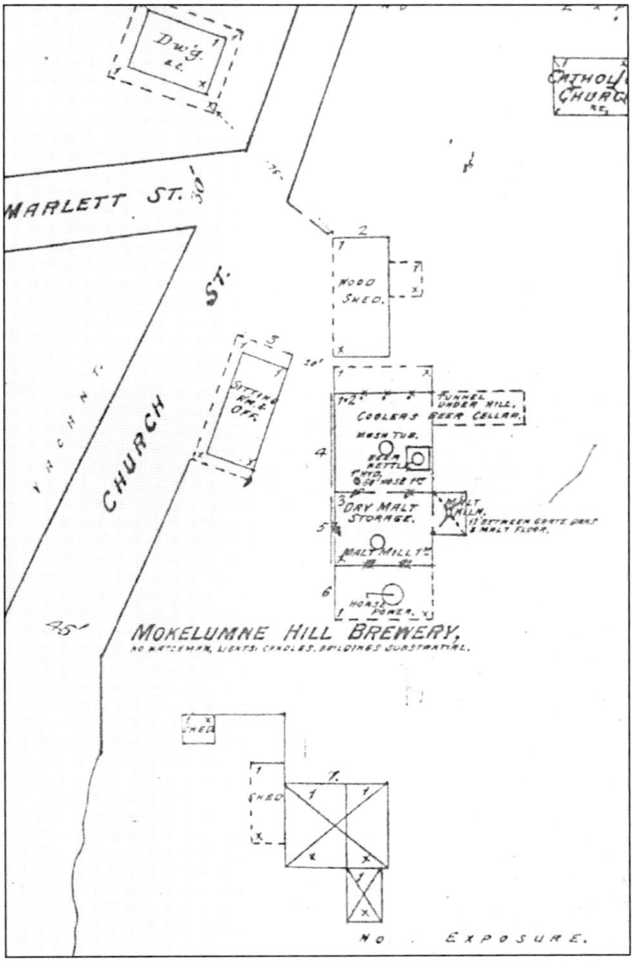

This image of the Hemminghoffen Brewery, known by then as the Mokelumne Hill Brewery, was taken some time after the previous image and shows the rapid decay of the building. Until 2000, the stone ruins of the brewery at the intersection of Church Street and Old School Way were slowly reused throughout Mokelumne Hill and in 2010 a modern home was built on the site. (Courtesy Calaveras County Archives.)

This is a portion of the 1890 Sanborn Fire Insurance Company map for Mokelumne Hill, which shows the general layout of the Mokelumne Hill Brewery during that time. Noted in particular are the malt kiln and floor, indicating they were producing their own malt. Also noted is the beer cellar tunnel extending into the hillside. This was originally a mine tunnel, which the brewery adapted for its own purposes. The Mokelumne Hill Brewery was also one of the first businesses to have electricity, having been wired by 1902.

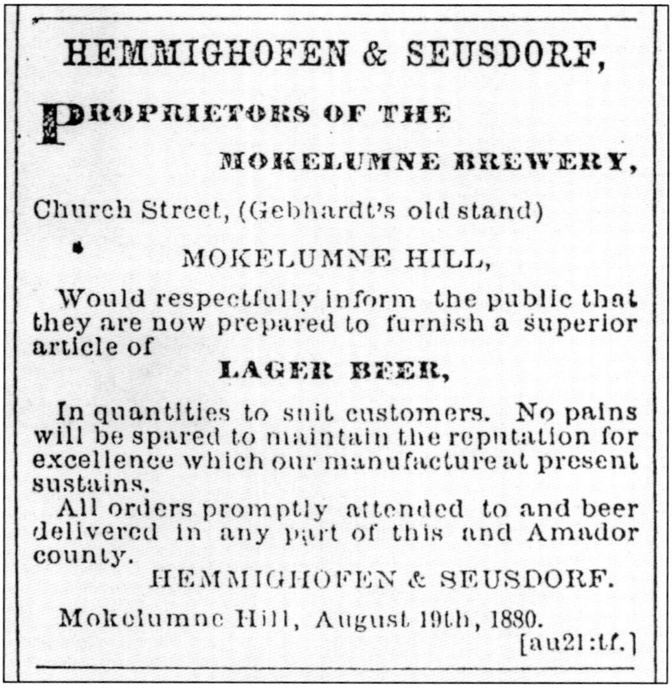
HEMMIGHOFEN & SEUSDORF,

PROPRIETORS OF THE

MOKELUMNE BREWERY,

Church Street, (Gebhardt's old stand)

MOKELUMNE HILL,

Would respectfully inform the public that they are now prepared to furnish a superior article of

LAGER BEER,

In quantities to suit customers. No pains will be spared to maintain the reputation for excellence which our manufacture at present sustains.

All orders promptly attended to and beer delivered in any part of this and Amador county.

HEMMIGHOFEN & SEUSDORF.

Mokelumne Hill, August 19th, 1880.

[au21:tf.]

In this 1880 advertisement, Hemminghoffen & Seussdorf announced that they would deliver their lager to any part of Calaveras and Amador Counties. This was not always a profitable venture. In 1878, having delivered a load of beer, Henry Hemminghoffen was robbed by a man brandishing a revolver. After some debate, Hemminghoffen "reluctantly contributed eleven dollars and six bits . . . to relieve the footpad's pressing financial necessities." Hemminghoffen was "mollified by consideration of the fact that forty or fifty dollars in gold laid undisturbed in his inside pants pocket."

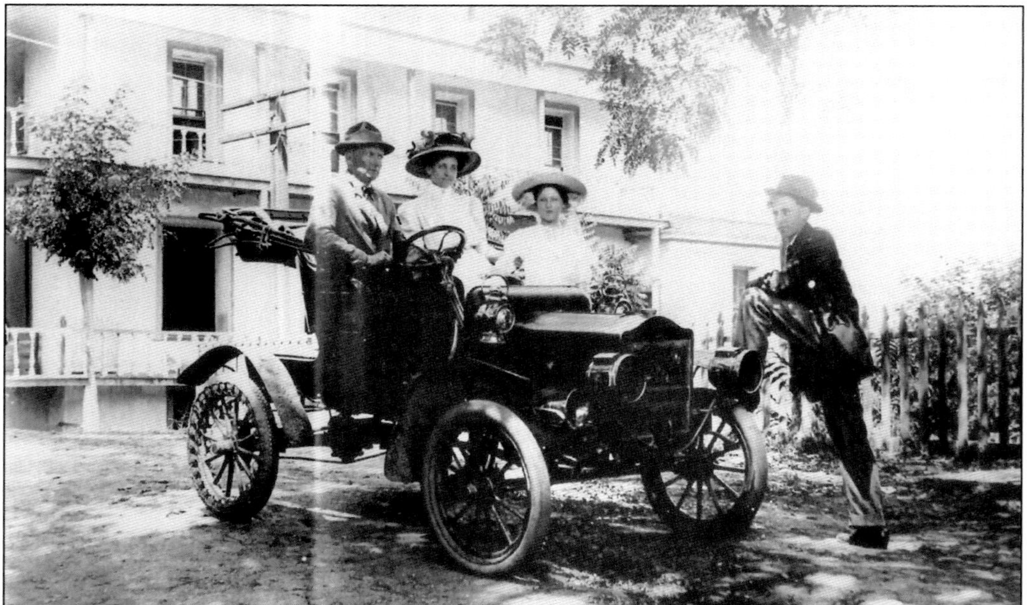

The Gebhardt Brewery eventually passed into the hands of the Suessdorf family, who operated what was then known as the Mokelumne Hill Brewery with Henry Hemminghoffen. Peter Suessdorf was born in Bavaria in 1832. Having come to the United States in 1855, he made his way to Mokelumne Hill about 1860, where he was engaged as a brewer. Peter and his wife, Madeline, had several children, including Frederick, who would go on to operate the Mokelumne Hill Brewery. Frederick Seussdorf is seen here with his foot on the tire of the Carter brand automobile. This c. 1910 image also shows Tom Peters, Luella Peters, and Hilda Peter Farnsworth. (Courtesy Calaveras County Archives.)

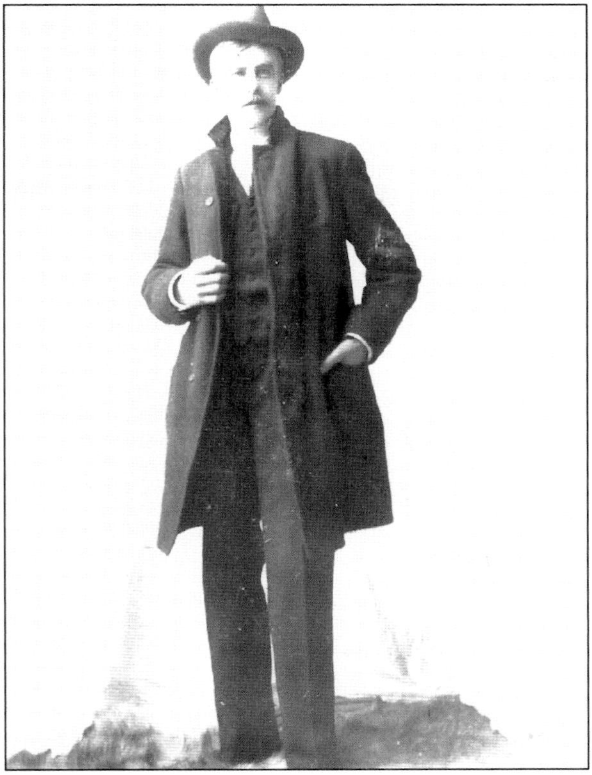

Pictured here in their wedding photographs are Frederik and Mae Seussdorf (née Kean). Fred was the son of Peter Suessdorf, who ran the Gebhardt Brewery (later the Mokelumne Hill Brewery). Frederick, or Fred, worked for his father at the brewery. (Courtesy Calaveras County Historical Society.)

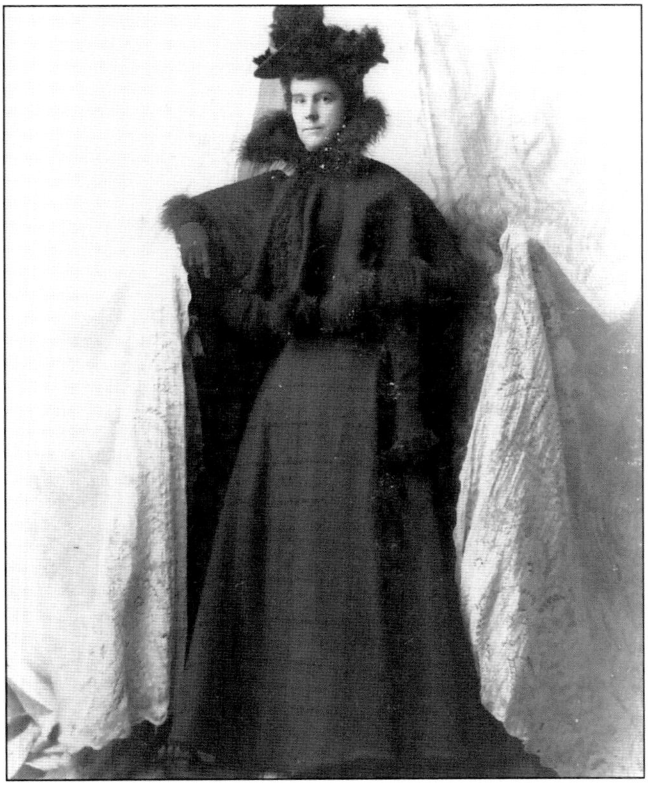

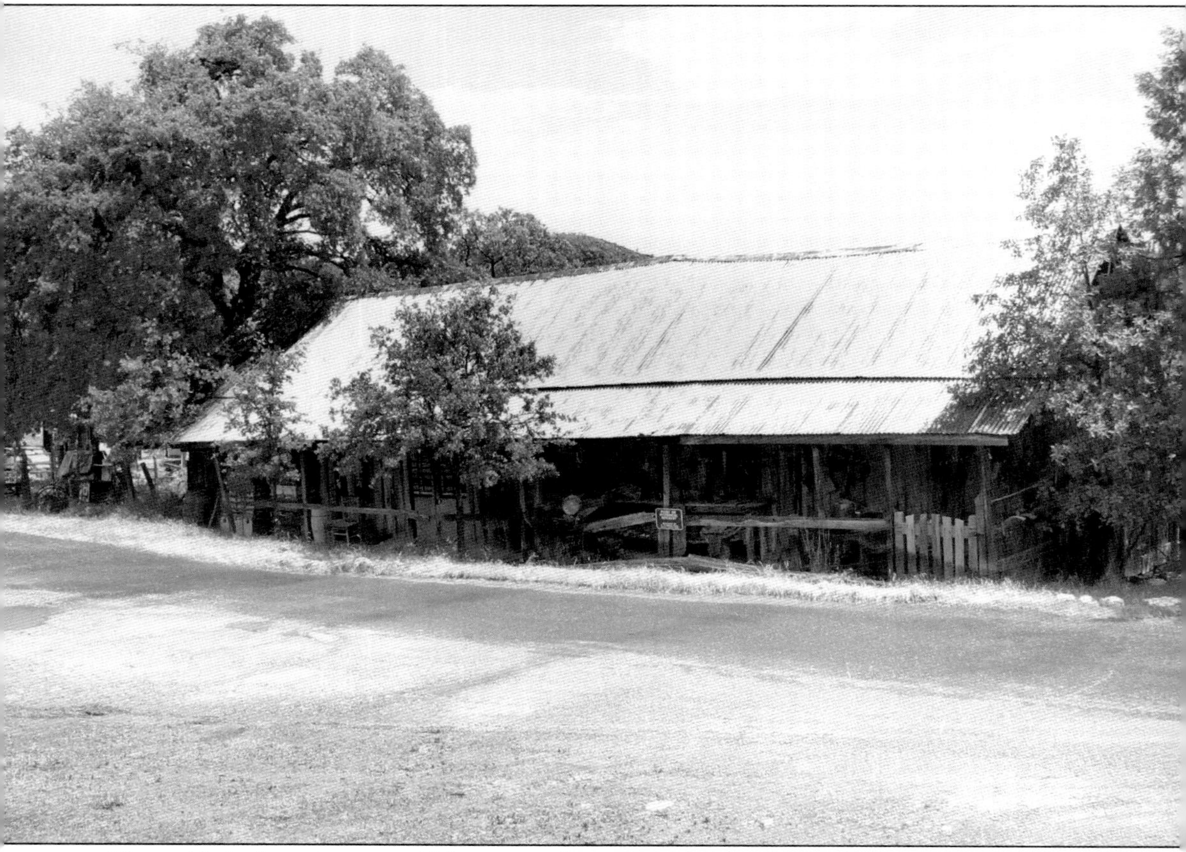

This is likely the only intact 19th-century brewery in California's Gold Country. It is located on Armstrong Road in the Calaveras County community of Sheep Ranch. Although it is currently in a state of disrepair, it reportedly retains most of its original brewing equipment. (Courtesy authors' collection.)

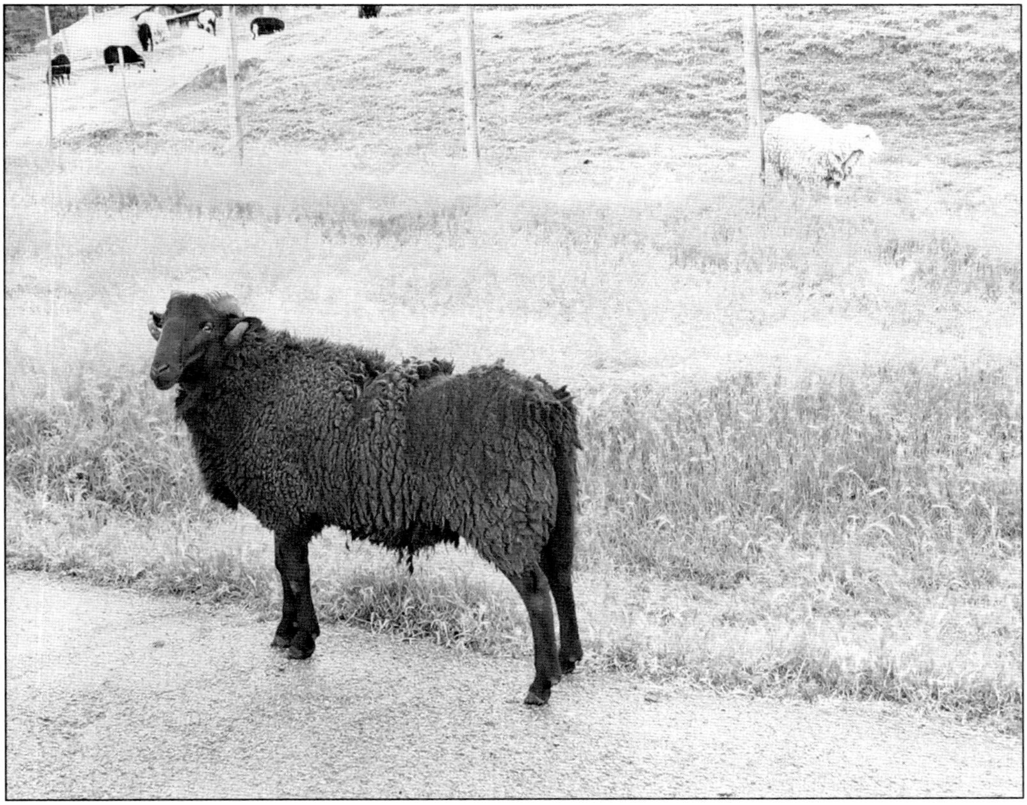

It is sometimes easy to see why this community was called Sheep Ranch, but at one time, this mining camp boasted a large enough population to support a brewery. The image below shows just some of the artifacts that have been preserved at the brewery, including a small wooden keg and shipping boxes. (Courtesy authors' collection.)

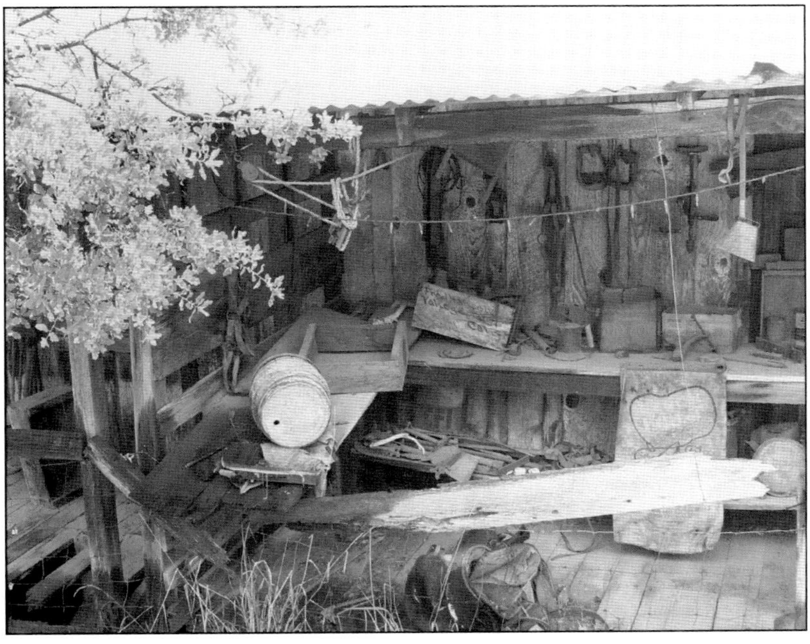

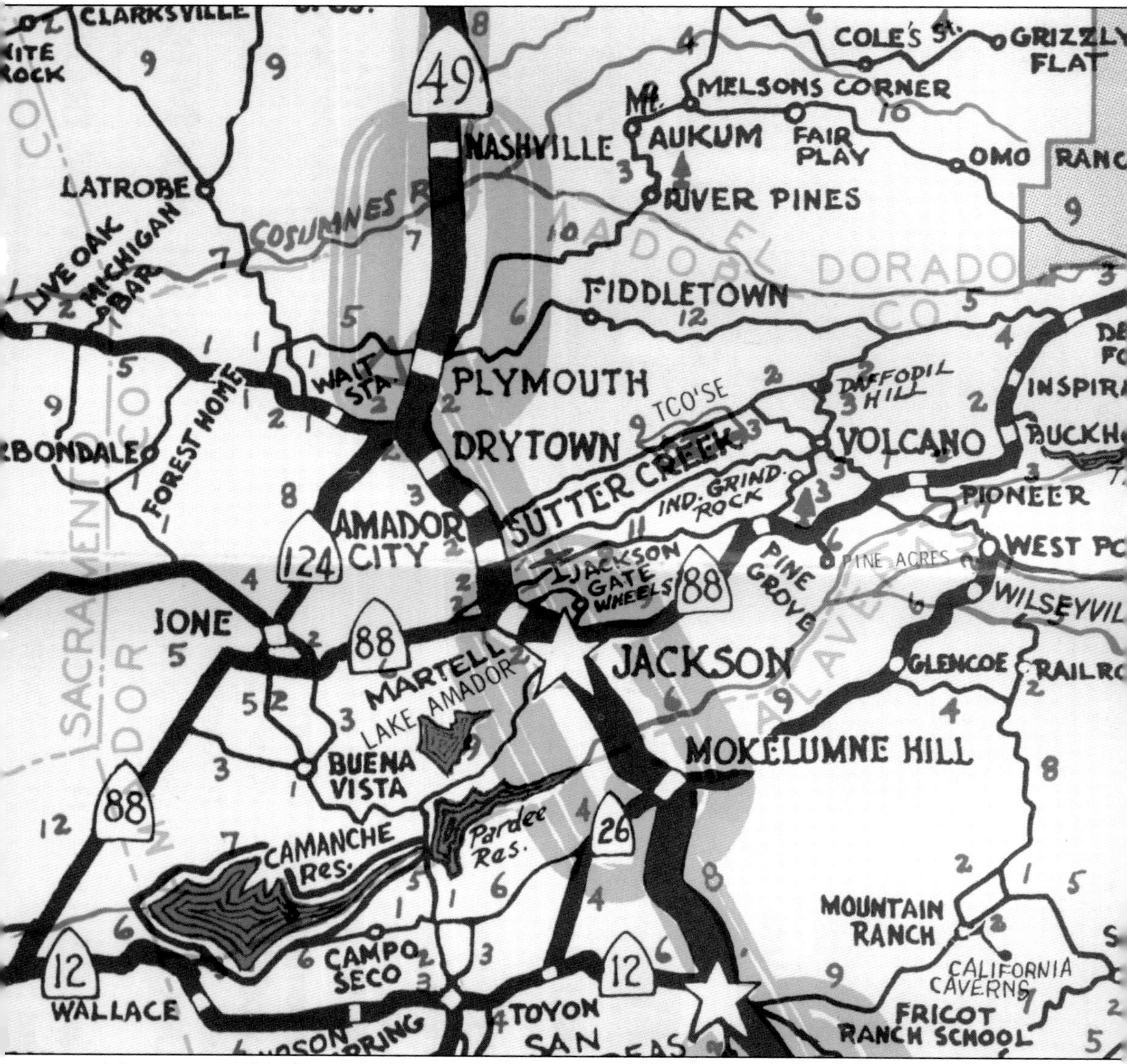

Moving past Mokelumne Hill, an early delivery driver for a local brewery would have had a steep drop down into the Mokelumne River Canyon, then a long climb back up into Amador County. Passing Big Bar on the river, he may have stopped in Butte City for a cold libation (perhaps one for the horses too), but the beer would not have been produced there. It was not until one reached Jackson and the Jackson Brewery that the largest brewery in Amador County was found. From Jackson, one would have continued on through Martell, to Sutter Creek, and eventually a road would have diverted off a few miles towards Fiddletown, or "Oleta," to those with more sophisticated leanings. (Courtesy Golden Chain Council.)

Three

AMADOR COUNTY
THE HEART OF THE MOTHERLODE

"Rescue, cave-in at Bunker Hill Mine; men trapped 24 Hours. Man drinking beer only one rescued."

—Description of mine rescue on February 18, 1912

Amador County, in the heart of the Motherlode, has a history of mining, beginning with the earliest diggings carved out with pick and shovel to capital-rich, industrialized hardrock mines. Gold mining earned the county millions in the century that the mines were active. While today many associate Amador with a long legacy of winemaking, the county had a rich brewing history as well. Unlike its viticulture industry, only a shadow of its brewing history remains—but it is a story interwoven with the daily lives of the county's residents, reflecting both cultural traditions, and with time and Prohibition, cultural prejudices.

Amador County was established in 1854, taking chunks from its neighbors to the north and south. Beginning in southern Amador County along Highway 49's Golden Chain, the first breweries encountered would have been in Jackson and the "Gate," then Sutter Creek; moving east and west off the main route, breweries were established in Volcano and Ione, then north again to Fiddletown. Of these many commercial enterprises, only the breweries in Ione, Volcano, and Fiddletown remain standing, but none have been working breweries for decades.

Following the ownership of Amador's breweries, like many in the Motherlode, can be problematic, as many were small, family-run operations, quickly changed hands, and often existed for only a handful of years. In one letter written in 1855, Lambert Littlefield mentions "I've started in the brewing business;" this was quickly followed by a second letter home that said, "I am no longer in the beer business." Jackson, probably more than any community in Amador County, had a rowdy reputation and, not surprisingly, the largest and longest-lived brewery.

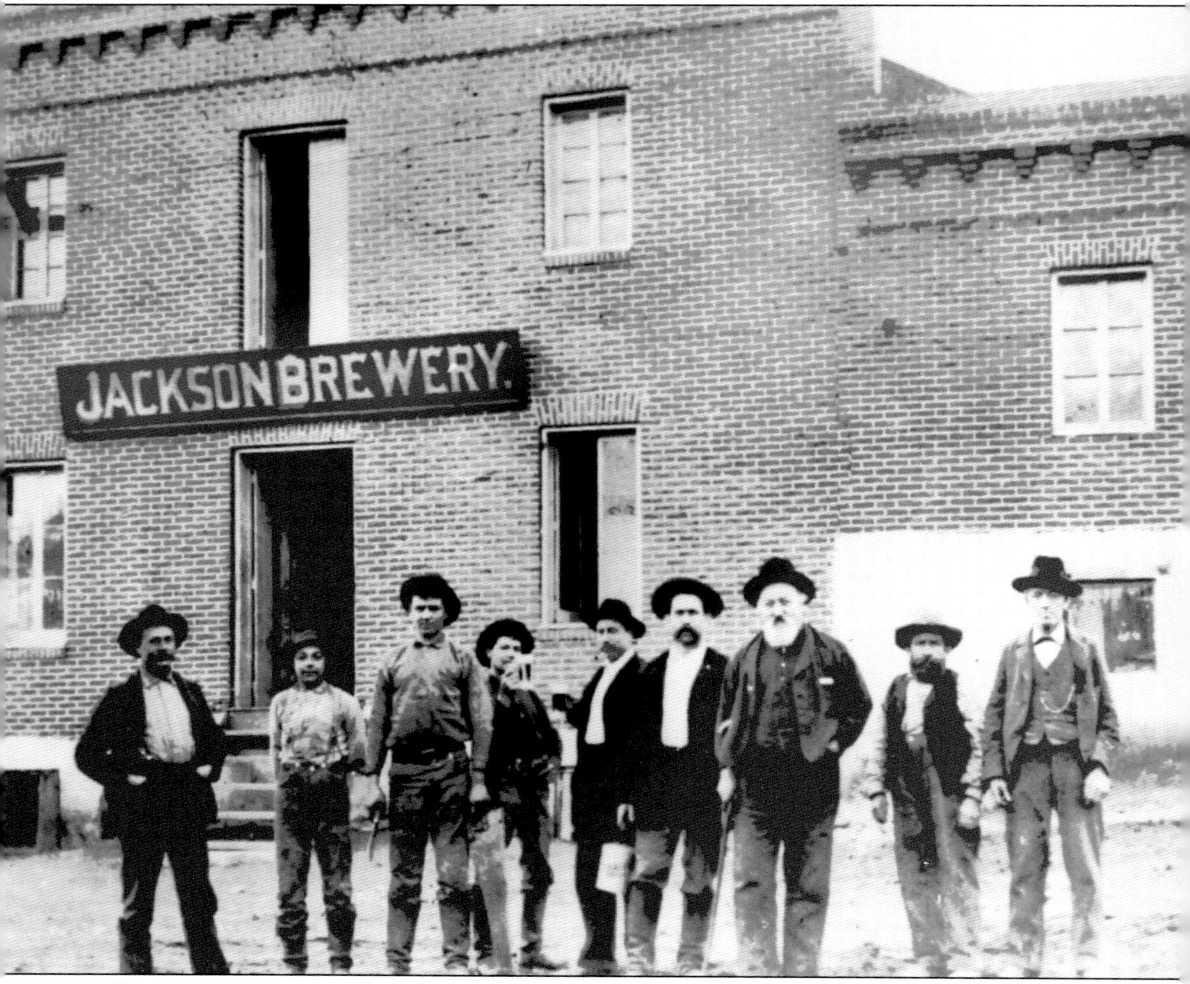

The Jackson Brewery and saloon was built in the mid-1850s by Augustus Trenschel, originally from Germany, who brewed lagers and beer into the late 1870s. Breweries often had a public saloon, offering patrons a cool pint and providing a social gathering spot for a community. This image shows the Jackson Brewery after John Strohm had taken ownership in the early 1890s. Strohm, mostly likely the individual on the far left, poses with his employees. Note the stoneware jug one employee holds and the cold pints others are enjoying. (Courtesy Amador County Archives.)

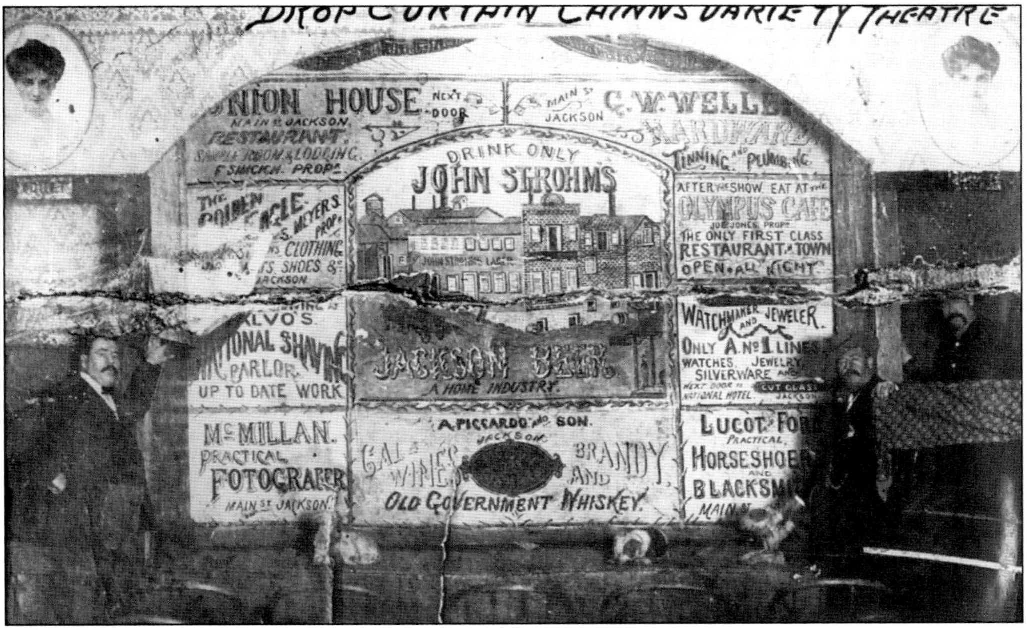

One could not be more direct with the audience than to say "Drink Only" John Strohm's Jackson Beer. This curtain backdrop for Jackson's Chinn's Theater provides one of the more detailed images of the Jackson Brewery, dating after the early 1890s, when Strohm was proprietor of the brewery. The painting shows three industrial brick buildings, when in truth only the two structures on the left were brick. (Courtesy Amador County Archives.)

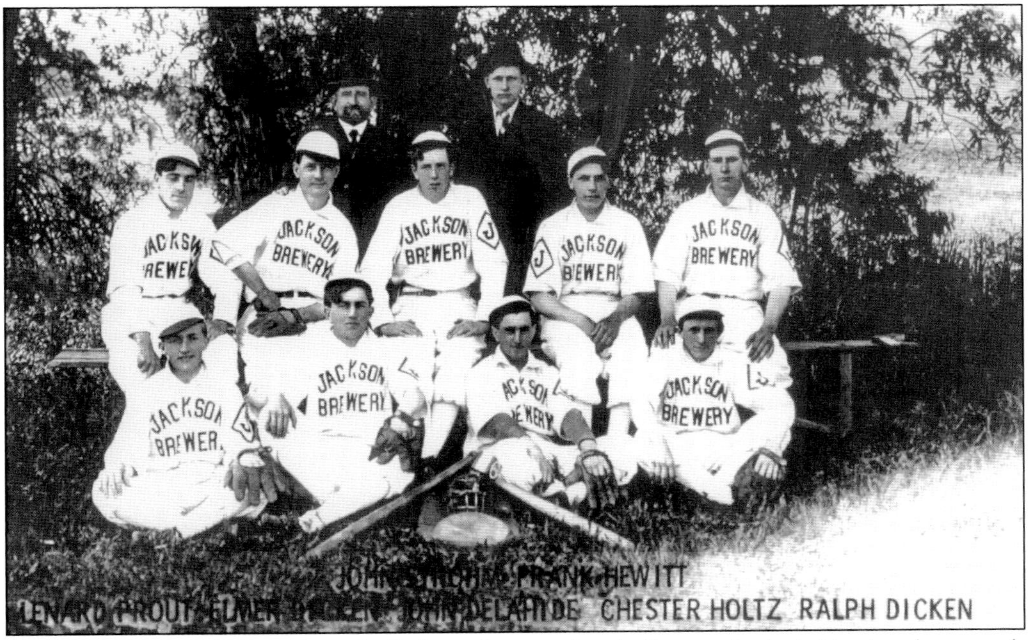

Pictured here on July 4, 1908, is the Jackson Brewery baseball team. Included in the photograph are John Strohm (back left with beard) and Frank Hewitt (to Strohm's right). The players, in no particular order, are Leonard Prouty, Elmer Dickens, John Delahide, Chester Holtz, Ralph Dickens, Lorentis Love, Bill Boro, Jim Carrera, and Dess Love. The Sutter Creek Brewery also had a baseball team, the Valley Brews. (Courtesy Amador County Archives.)

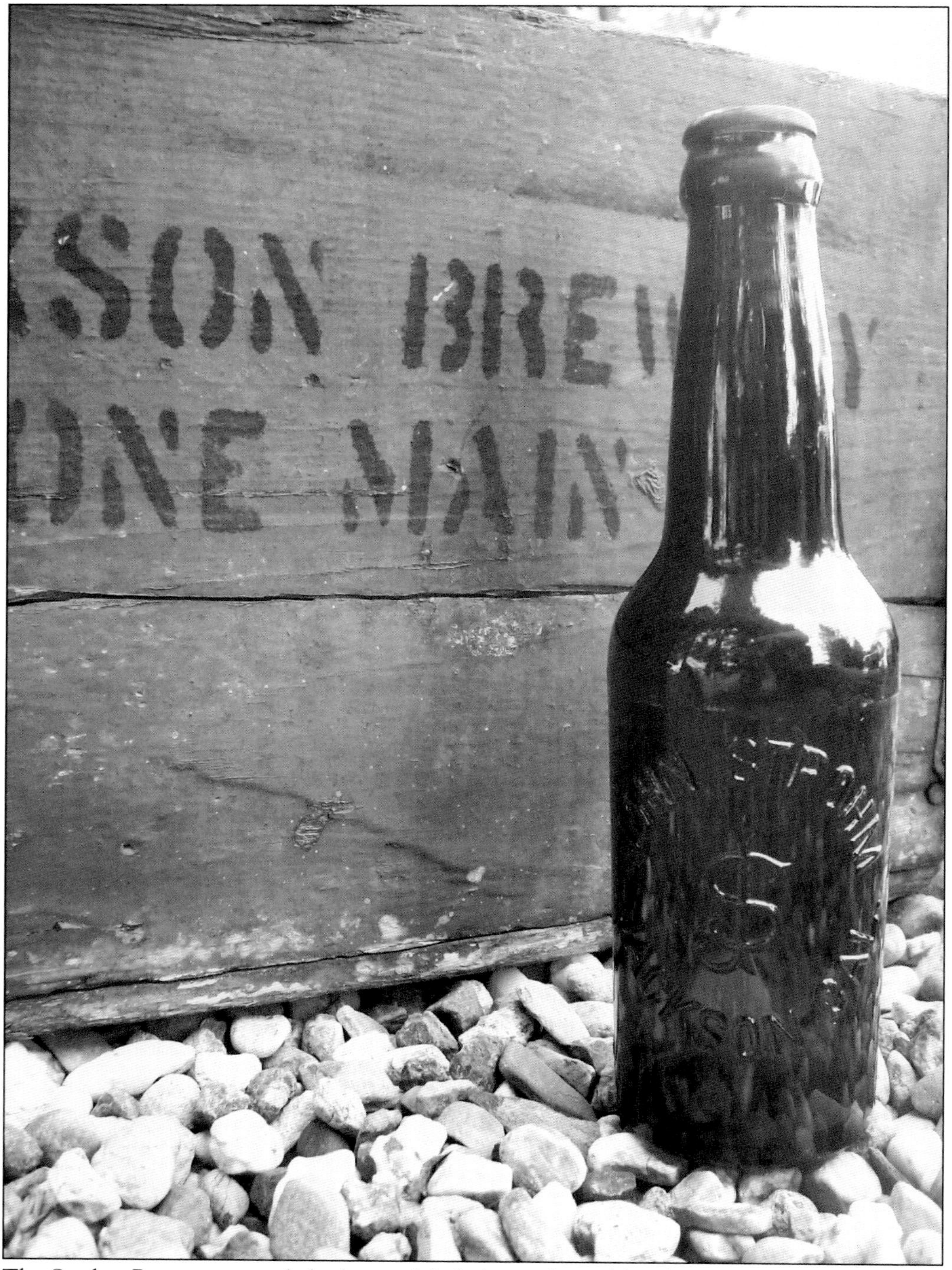

The Strohm Brewery not only had paper labels, but embossed bottles coming in a wide variety of sizes. Jugs and kegs were available if customers needed larger quantities. In the background is a Strohm Brewery crate, phone number 21, which would have been used to recycle empties. Crates like these can be seen in a detail of a local bar on Page 52. (Courtesy Michael Backovich.)

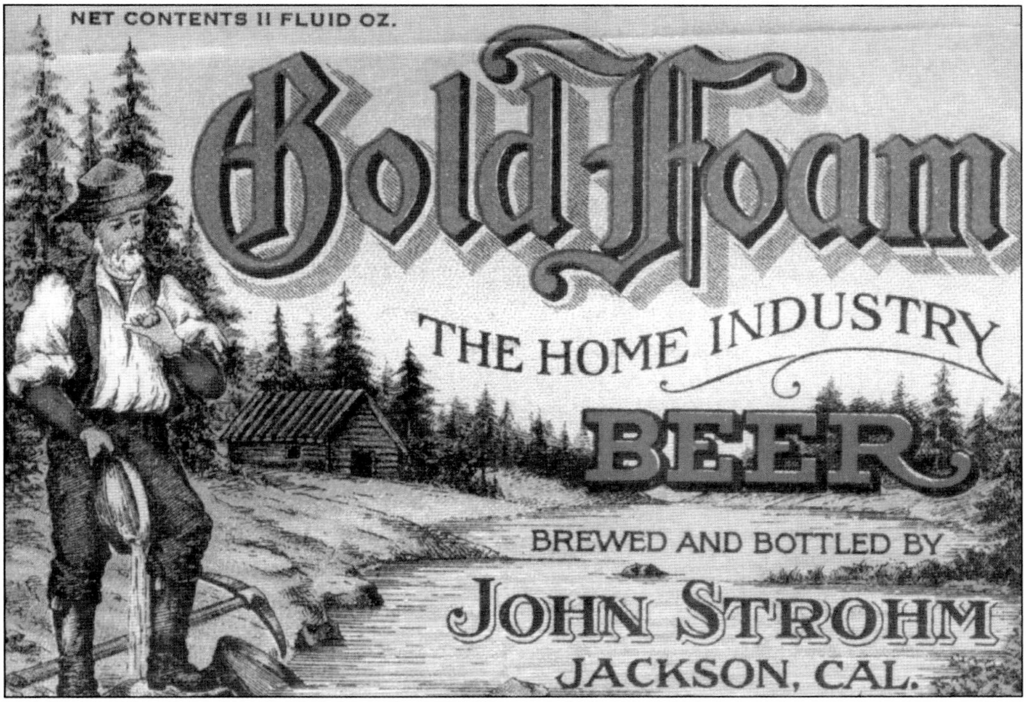

One of John's Strohm's many paper labels, "Gold Foam" is a direct reference to the history of the Motherlode, with its miner forty-niner and his pick and shovel, gold pan, and humble log cabin. While most of the embossed beer bottles reflect an earlier technology than use of paper labels, dating either can be problematic. (Courtesy Amador County Archives.)

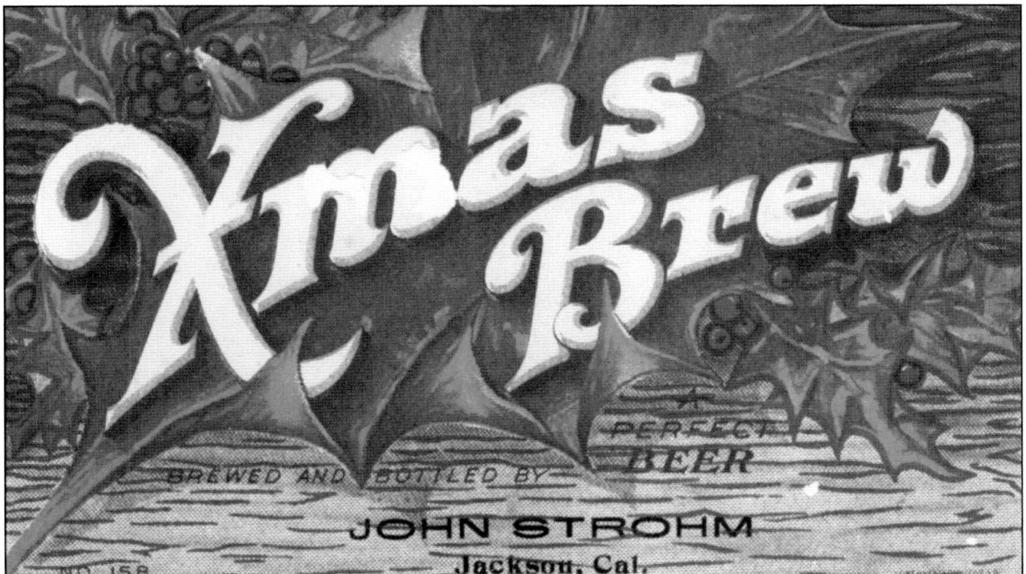

This Jackson Brewery label reads "Xmas Brew: A Perfect Beer" and is aptly decorated with festive sprigs of Christmas holly. It is wrong to assume modern marketing is any more creative than John Strohm and other brewers were a century ago. Christmas brews had traditional ties to what was seasonally available, as well as cultural ties to brewers of German heritage, for whom brewing remained an important aspect of their lives in America. (Courtesy Amador County Archives.)

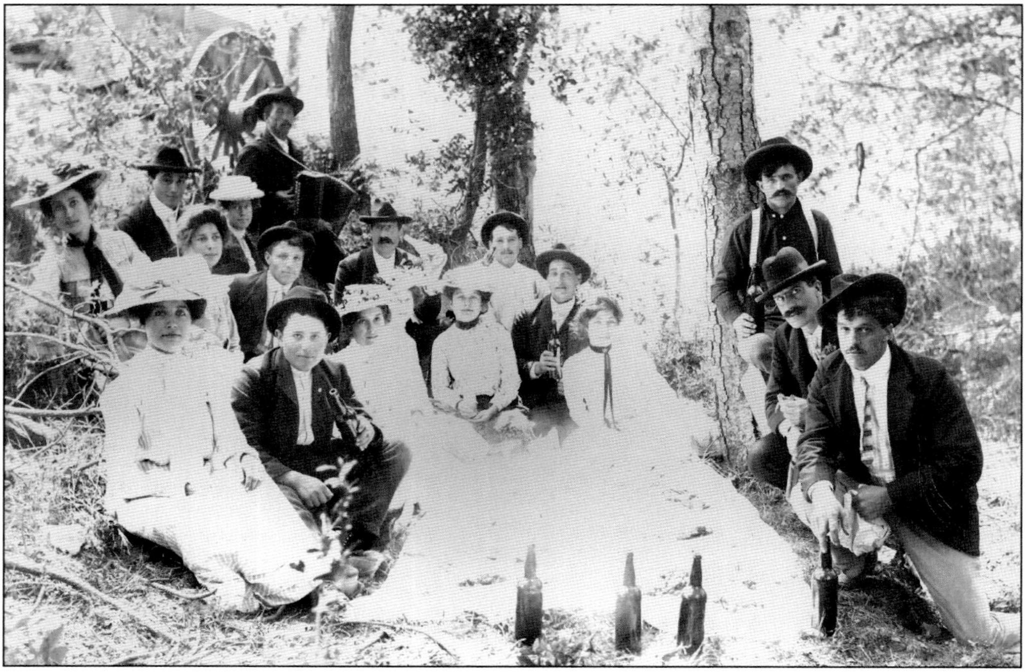

Amador's German community, like many in the state, socialized in a group loosely referred to as a Turn Verein, and perhaps the picnickers seen in this image were doing such. One description from the Amador County Federation of Women's Clubs County History, published in 1927, read, "The Turn Verein met here for singing, and balls were always given in this pavilion, the May Day Ball being especially fine. Shade trees of cedar and pine and live oak made a beautiful grove, and little summer houses were placed in close proximity toward town. This was a beer garden where men brought their families for an evening, and met their friends in friendly chat. On ball nights, one of the lager houses was set aside for the young children." (Courtesy Amador County Archives.)

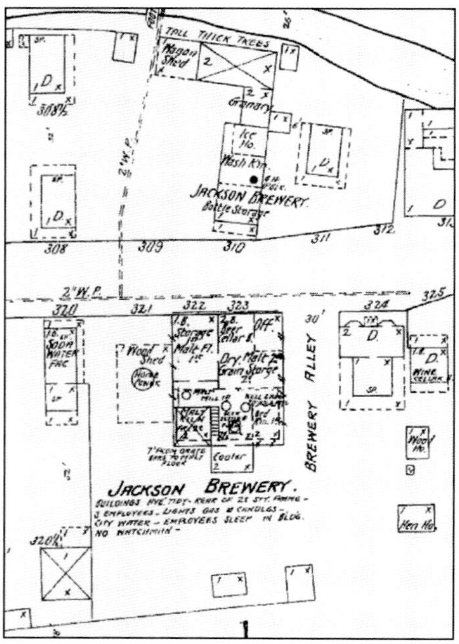

This 1898 Sanborn map of the Jackson Brewery provides many details about the layout of the brewery and the brewing process. One of the more interesting social aspects was the brewery's beer garden: "Across from the brewery, where the handsome homes of George Thomas and Mrs. Esther Dal Porto stand, was Trenchel's beer garden, cool and inviting under spreading trees." The topmost notation on the map reads "Tall thick trees," and it is easy to speculate that the beer garden was here.

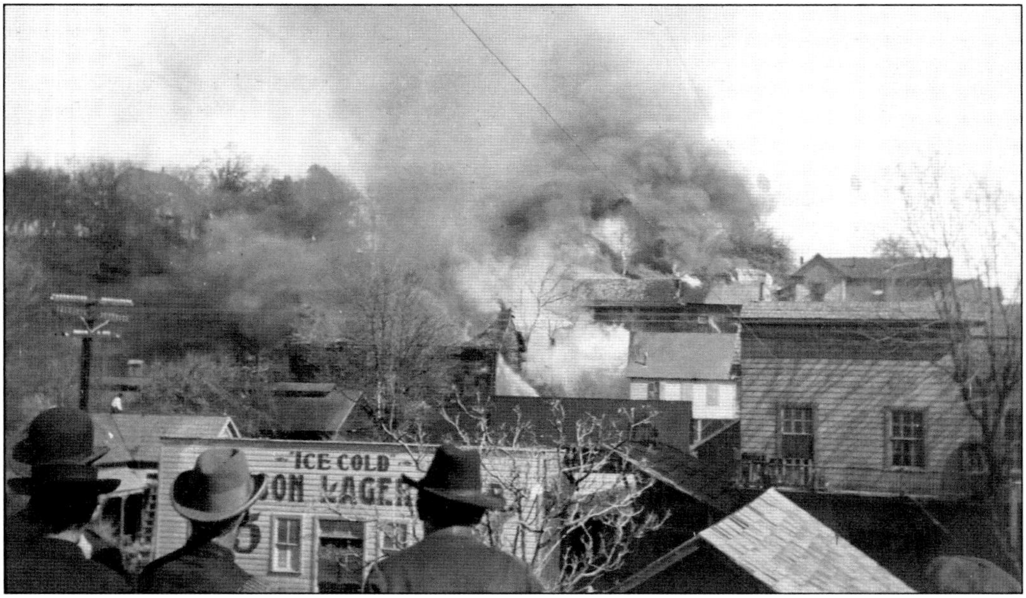

Men in bowlers look on as a fire burns in Jackson. With limited water supplies and technology, these fires could get out of hand rapidly. Many a brewery in Amador County burned down, or nearly so, including the Jackson Brewery. When the men were tired of watching the fire, they could step into the saloon and get an ice cold lager for only a nickel. In the end, the Jackson Brewery would not survive progress, though it would not be fire that destroyed the building. (Courtesy Amador County Archives.)

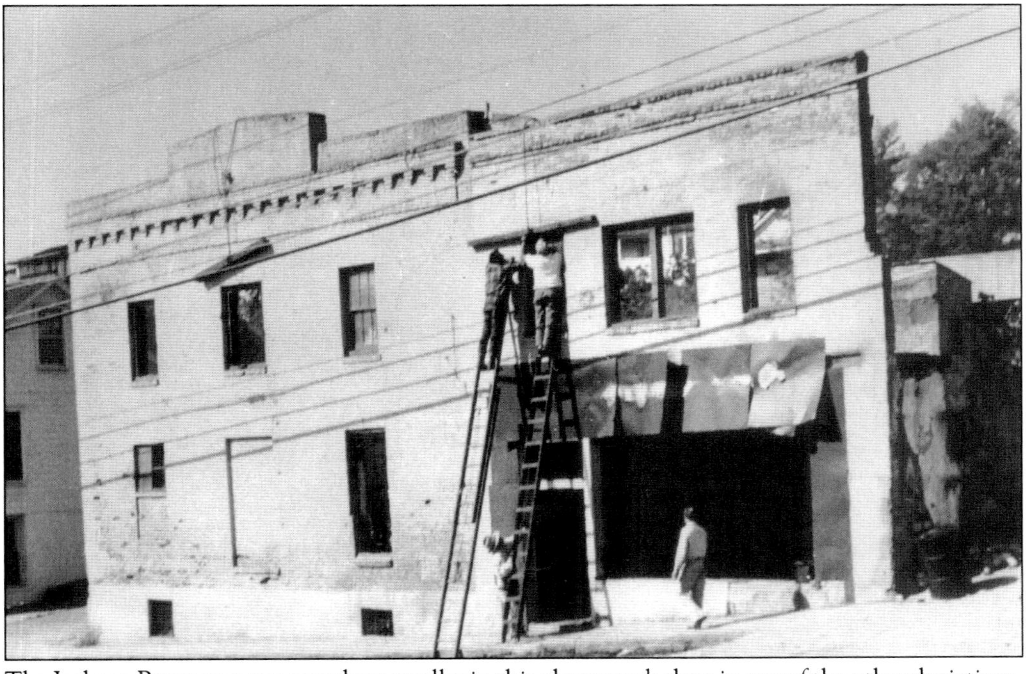

The Jackson Brewery seems somehow smaller in this photograph than in any of the other depictions. The faux roofline is again gone, and the shell of the brewery stands much like it originally did in the 1850s. Attempts to modernize the brewery (as seen with the large showroom window) failed, and in 1958, the brewery was torn down. (Courtesy Amador County Archives.)

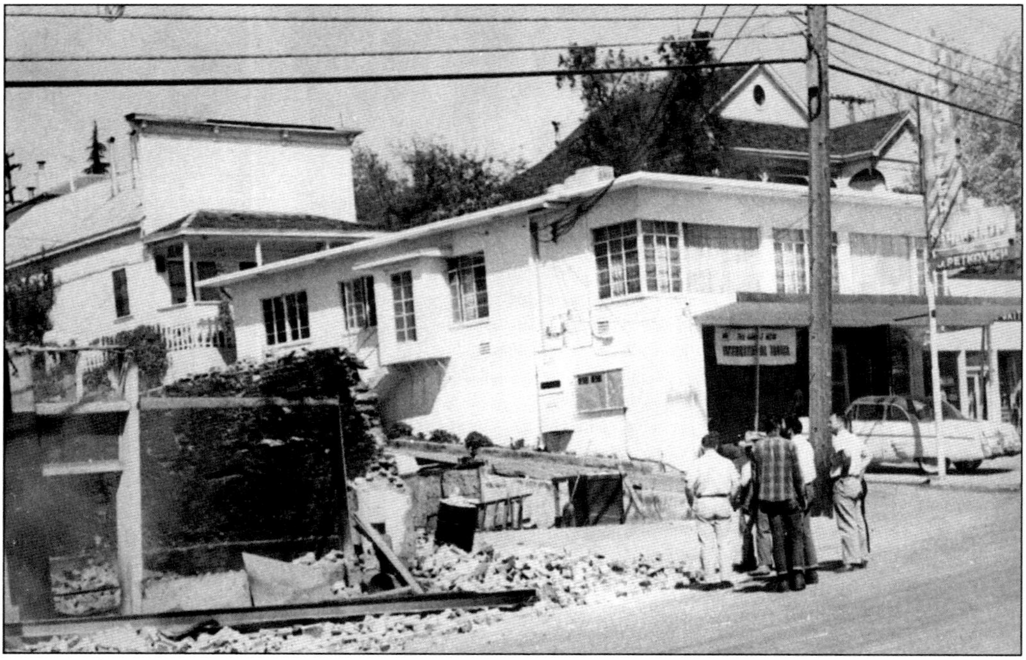

A second image shows the destruction of the Jackson Brewery, which had served the community fresh beer for almost a century. The massive stone wall of the brewery contrasts with what was once its public brick facade. (Courtesy Amador County Archives.)

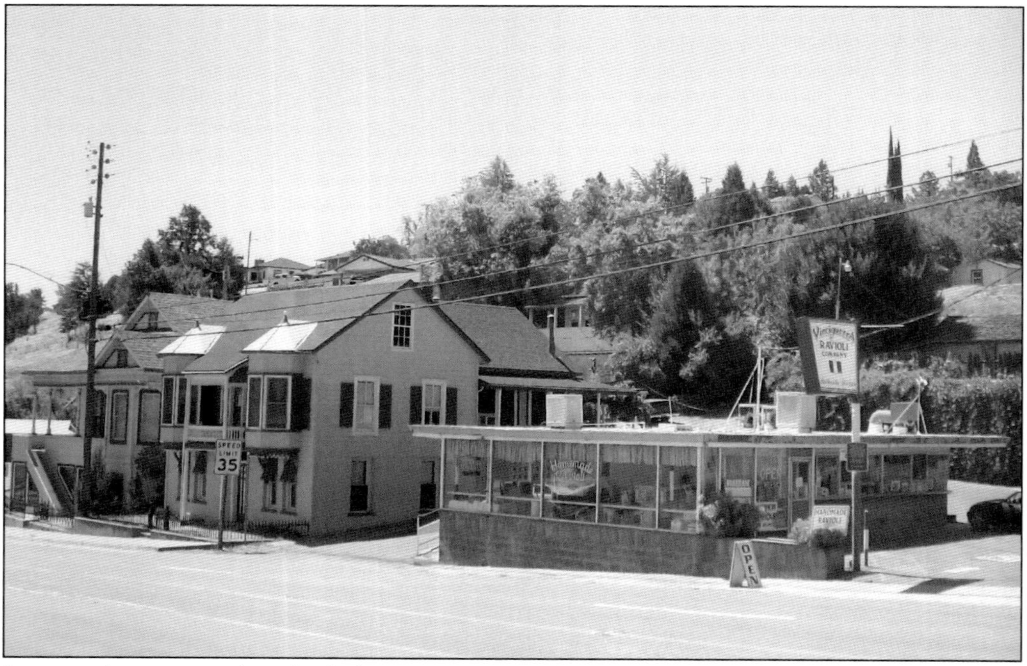

It is somehow ironic that the Jackson Brewery would come to be replaced by a drive-in dinner serving soda pop and malts, when the brewery, like so many others, was not able to make the transition from brewery to creamery/soda shop successfully during Prohibition. Almost a century after being built, the site of the Jackson Brewery provide a new social gathering spot for the county's teenagers when the Gallis Drive-in was built. (Courtesy authors' collection.)

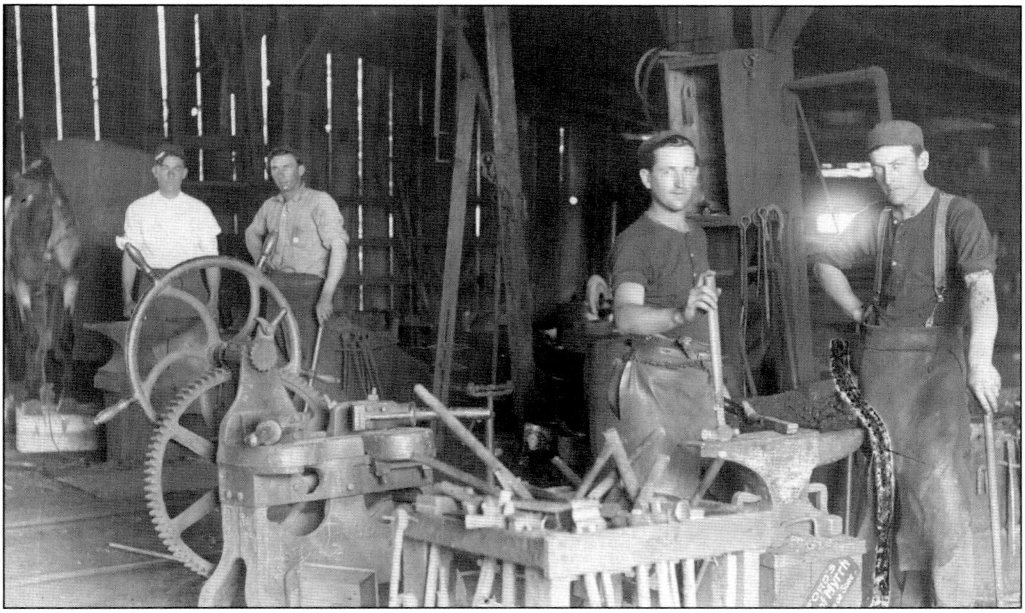

Brewery customers were miners, laborers, men, and women. The blacksmiths working here at the Knight Foundry shops on Eureka Street in Sutter Creek would have found their work hot and dirty. A glass of beer at the Sutter Creek Brewery's bar would have been quite refreshing and was only a few blocks away. (Courtesy Amador County Archives.)

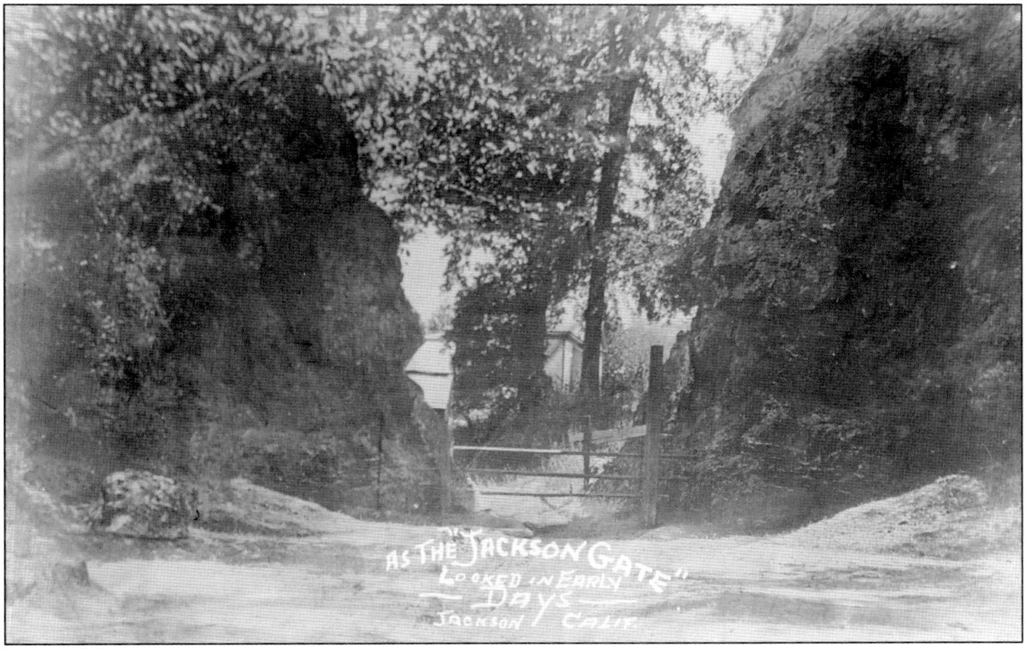

Jackson Gate was named for the natural rock formation along the North Fork of Jackson Creek. While this photograph was supposedly taken in 1850, it was a promotional photograph intended to capture the region's historical nature and was more likely taken in the 1930s. Two other breweries were mentioned in historical documents for "Village of the Gate," including the Strasbourg Brewery and the Maykeefer Brewery, although both may be the same as Börger's Gate Brewery. (Courtesy Amador County Archives.)

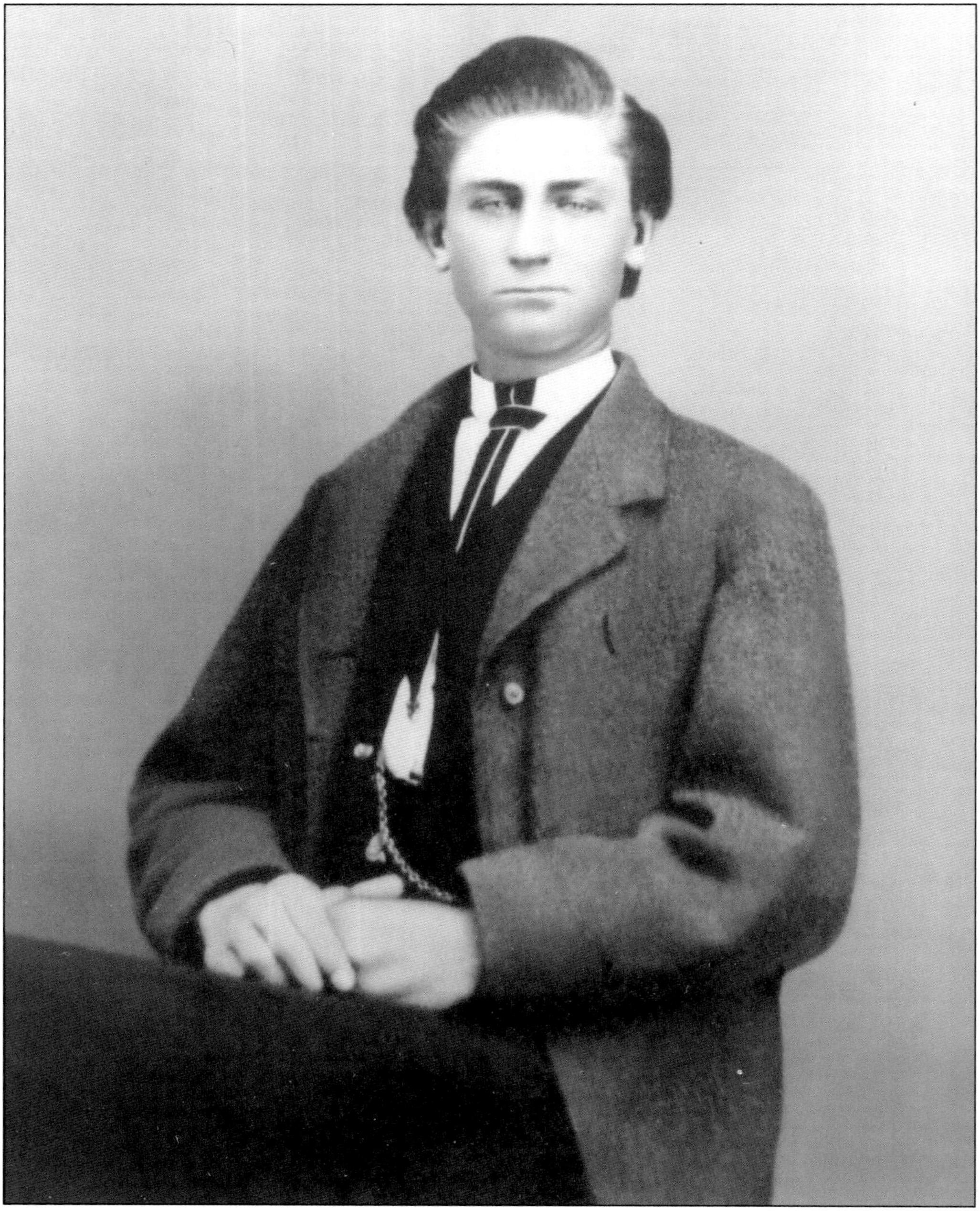

While the Jackson Brewery remains the longest running and most well documented of Jackson's breweries, several other breweries were producing beer in Jackson in the mid-19th century. One of the earliest belonged to Prussian (later Germany) native Phillip Börger, pictured here about the time he would have arrived in California in 1850. He operated out of his barn in the community of Jackson Gate, or the "Gate." Jackson Gate was one of the earliest settled areas around Jackson and the roadway provided a major link between Sutter Creek and Jackson. Phillip Börger opened the winery in 1863. Of the demise of Borger's brewery, the 1881 county history states: "July 10 1867. Philip Burger's [sic] brewery, near the Gate, consumed by fire. Loss, two thousand dollars." After his facilities burned in 1867, there is no evidence that he returned to brewing in Amador County. (Courtesy Amador County Archives.)

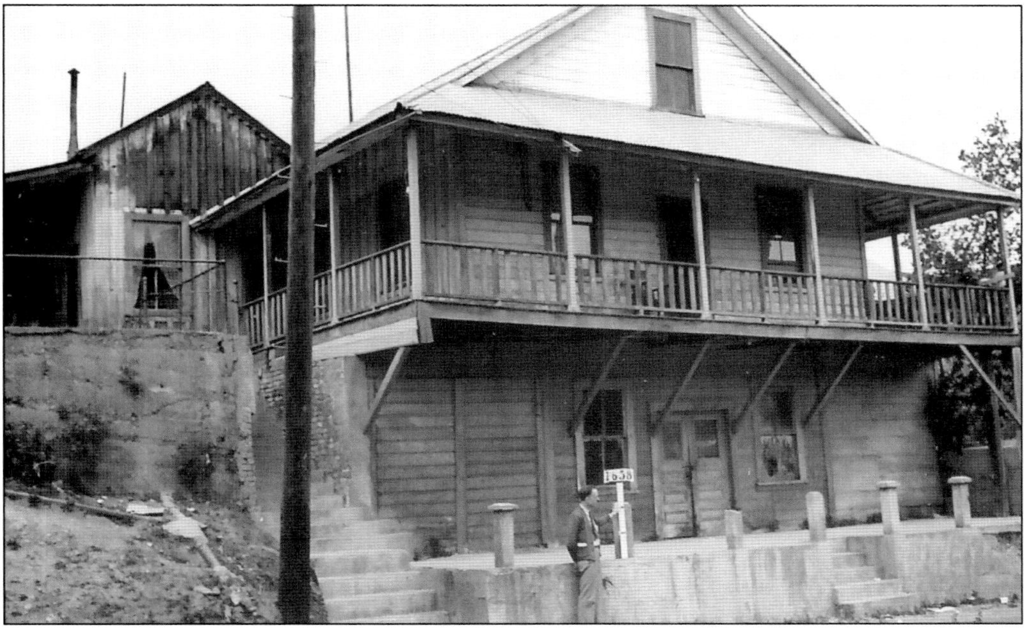

Driving down Jackson Gate Road, one finds a road lined with boardinghouses that provided homes to the laborers—a ready customer base—from the Kennedy and Argonaut hardrock gold mines. Beer was likely served with board, possibly from breweries just a stone's throw away. This building had a bar and/or mercantile downstairs, and rumors have it that a brothel operated upstairs, which most likely provided beer to the customers, among other things. (Courtesy Larry Cenotto.)

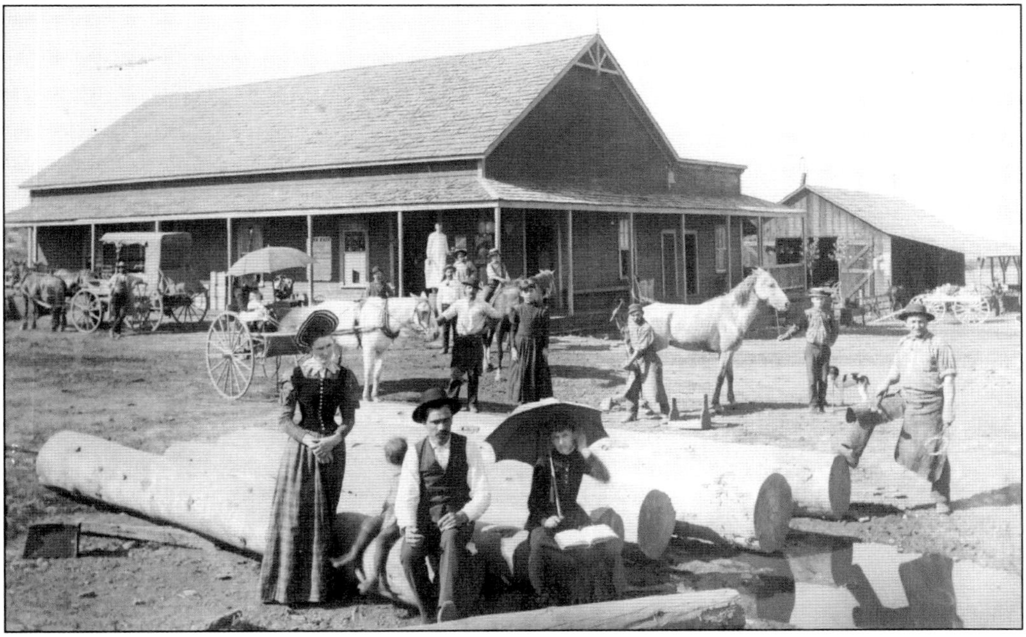

On the road to Sutter Creek, at the junction between the road to Ione and the road coming out of the Gate, was Martell Station. Once again, a Buffalo Brewing Company advertisement can be seen in the details. Another oft-mentioned regional competitor for local breweries was the El Dorado Brewery in Stockton, west of Amador County. Martell Station still stands at the juncture of Highway 49 and Jackson Gate Road. (Courtesy Amador County Archives.)

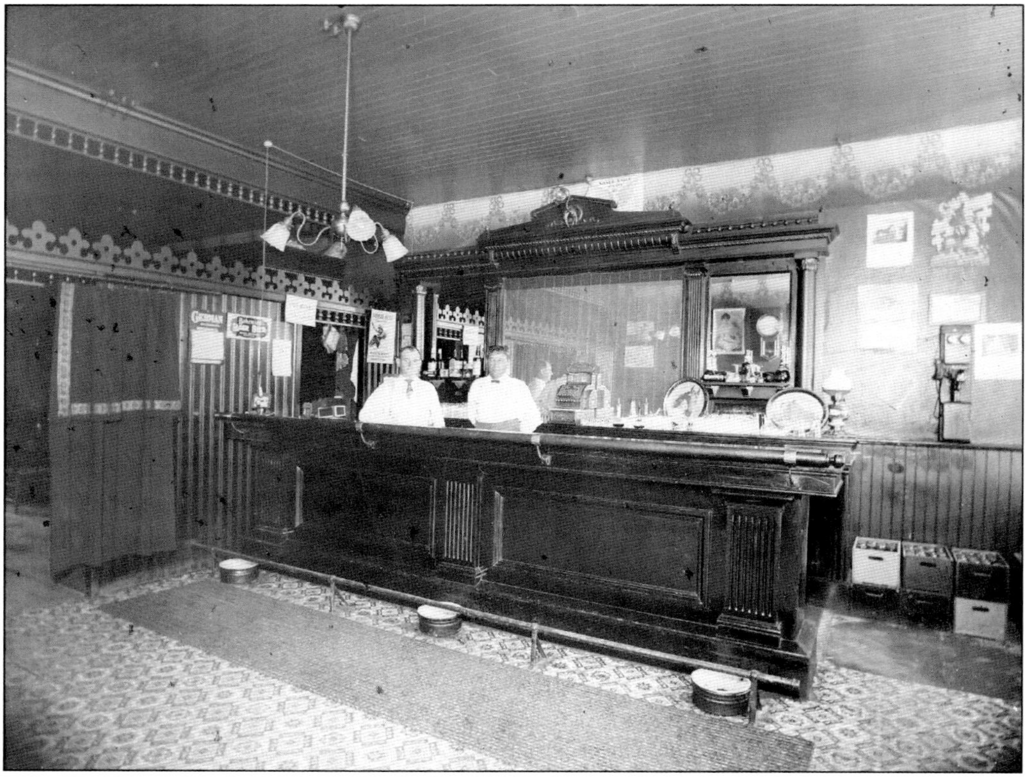

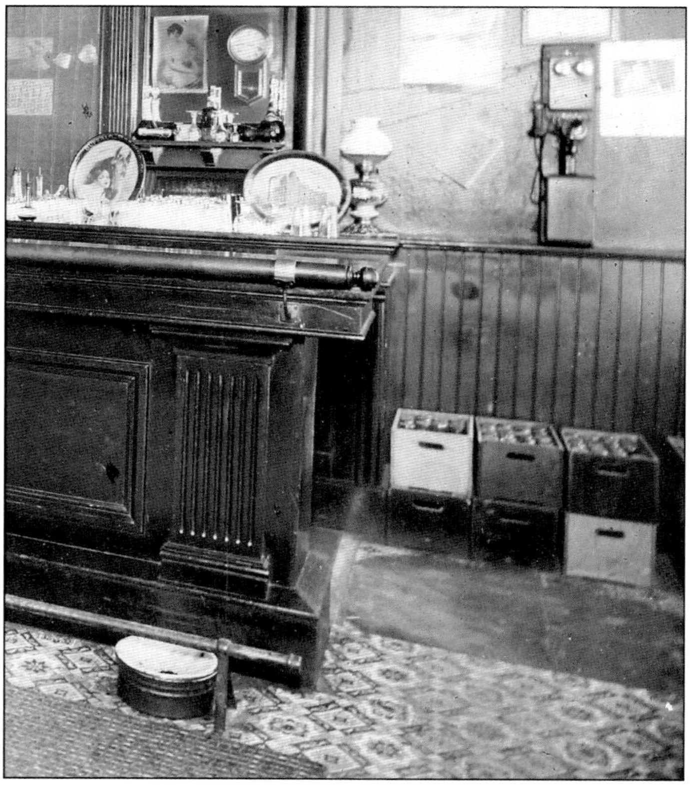

A picture is worth a thousand words, and this photograph of a local bar tells a story of brewing in its details. Pictured on the left is a detail showing storage of empties (as with the Strohm box on Page 44). Also seen is a Buffalo Brewing metal advertisement serving tray. The Buffalo Brewing Company was a large, regional producer based in Sacramento, in direct competition with Amador's breweries. (Courtesy Amador County Archives.)

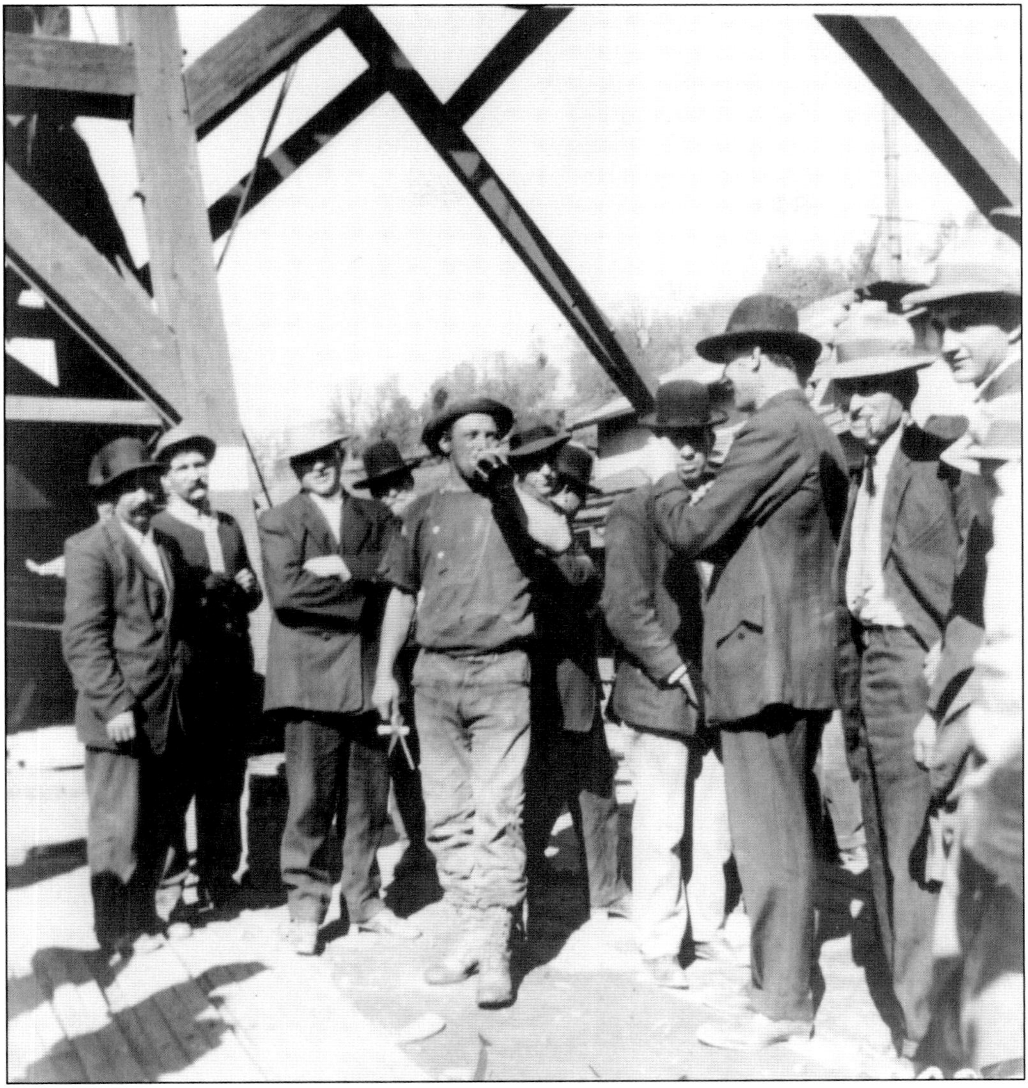

The caption for this 1912 photograph may be a little misleading—"Rescue, cave-in at Bunker Hill Mine; men trapped 24 Hours. Man drinking beer only one rescued." It seems unlikely it was beer that the man in center of the photograph is happily drinking that saved his life, but there was definitely a tie between miners and beer that began in the earliest days of the Gold Rush. The thousands of miners who poured into California—and Amador County in particular—provided a ready market for the limited number of brewers who brought their trade with them from other states (and in many cases, other countries). (Courtesy Amador County Archives.)

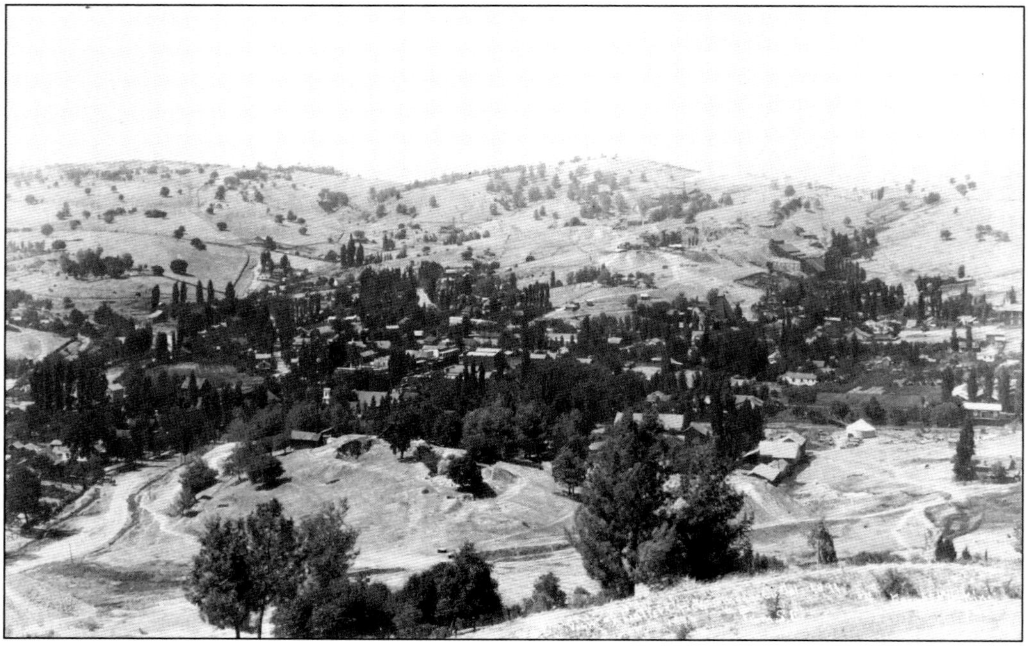

If one were unhappy with the quality of beer served by the breweries in Jackson, one could travel north to Sutter Creek, seen in this early overview of the town, and imbibe a pint and a pickled egg at the Sutter Creek Brewery. An image of the brewery can be seen on the book's cover (please see the full image on Page 118). While the Sutter Creek Brewery was the most enduring in the city, the earliest references to a brewery in town (and in the county) is to a Sarsaparilla Beer Brewery, possibly in Sutter Creek in 1853. (Courtesy Amador County Archives.)

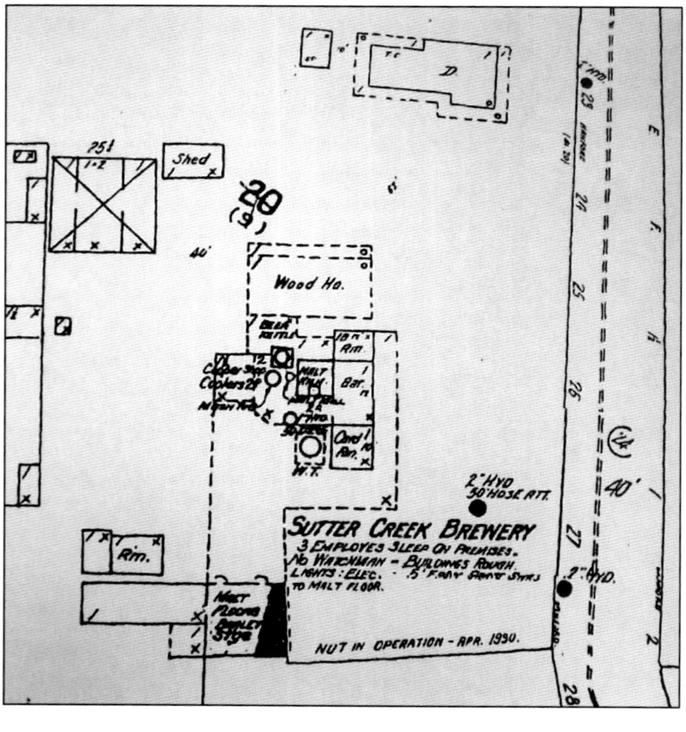

Sanborn maps were created for insurance purposes, giving a detailed layout of the Sutter Creek Brewery between 1890 through Prohibition in 1930. The mapping shows that the layout of the brewery changed little during this 40-year period. Another anecdote illustrates the daily importance of beer in everyday life of a town's residents: When she was 10 years old, Ann Backovich would walk across the street to the Sutter Creek Brewery, buy a pail of fresh beer, and walk it back home. (Courtesy Amador County Archives.)

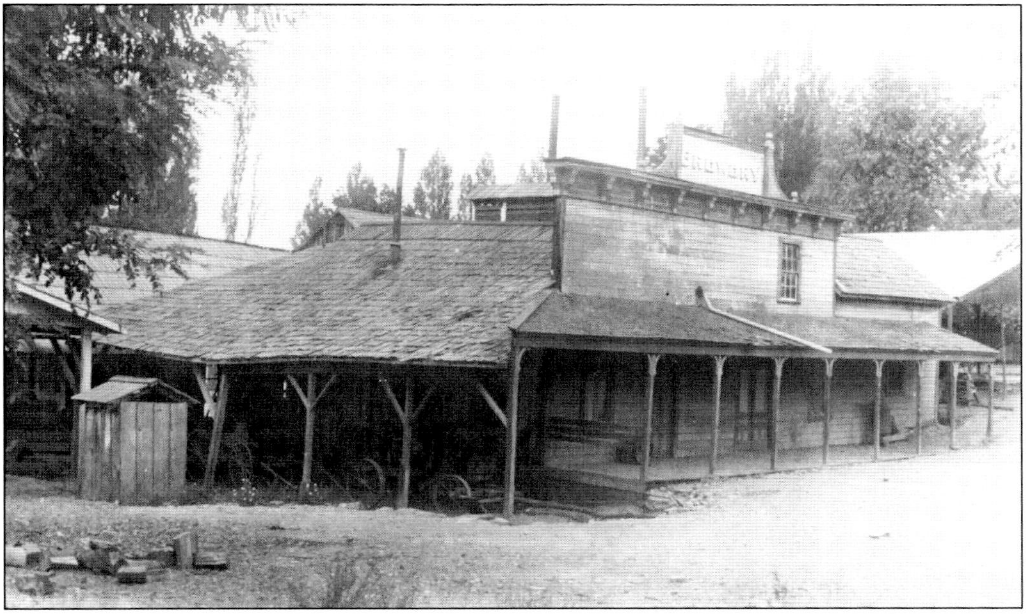

The earliest reference to the Sutter Creek Brewery is in 1861. By 1866, Leopold Rabolt had acquired the brewery. Rabolt committed suicide in 1891, perhaps in part due to the death of his wife two years earlier. John Raddatz and Albert Ludwig purchased the brewery that same year and began an extensive remodel; the cover image of this book reflects those improvements. The image above is how the Old Rabolt brewery looked just before that remodel. Raddatz continued to operate the brewery until Prohibition. The Sutter Creek Brewery was torn down sometime after 1932; the stone granary on Hanford Street is all that remains today. (Courtesy Amador County Archives.)

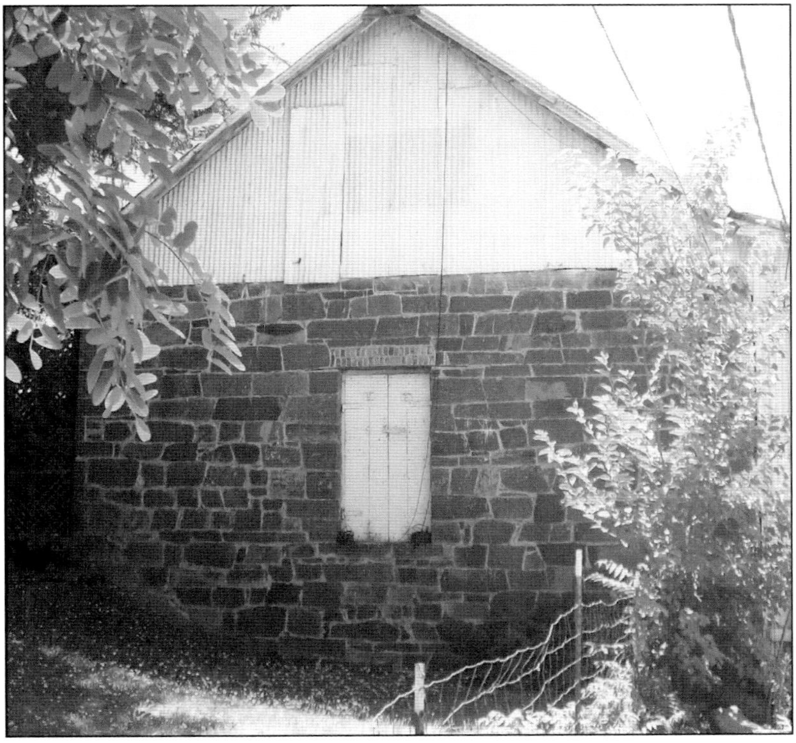

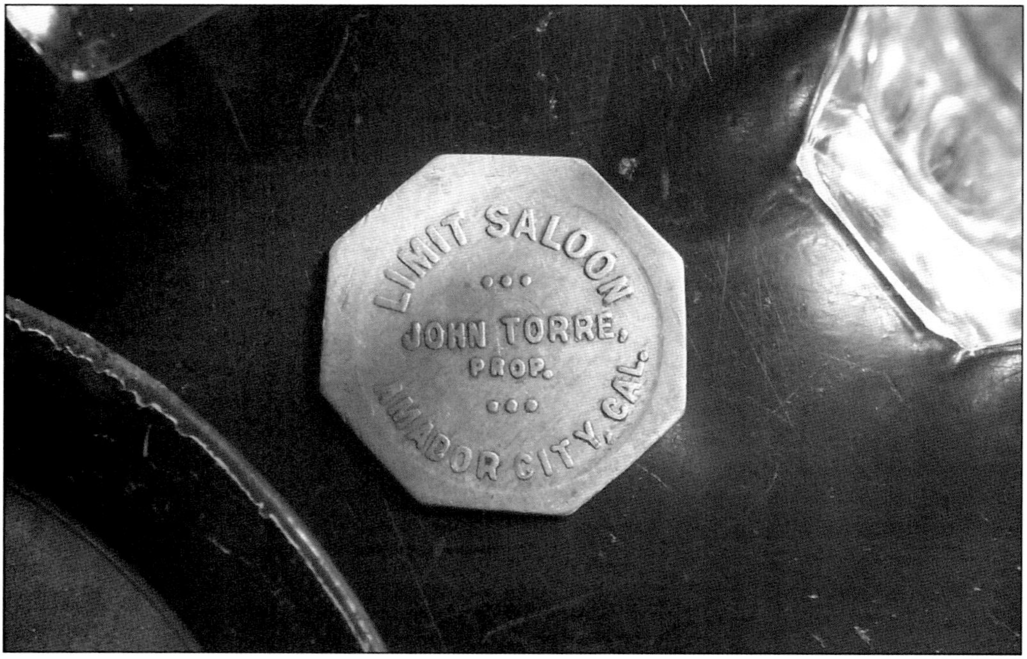

One way of encouraging patrons to imbibe at a particular bar was to offer drink tokens. Seen here is the front and back of a token for the Limit Saloon, also referred to as the Torre Saloon, in Amador City. The token was "Good for 1 Drink," and often the drinks being served were a pint of local beer. The Limit Saloon, known for its Saturday night dances, still stands on old Highway 49. (Courtesy authors' collection.)

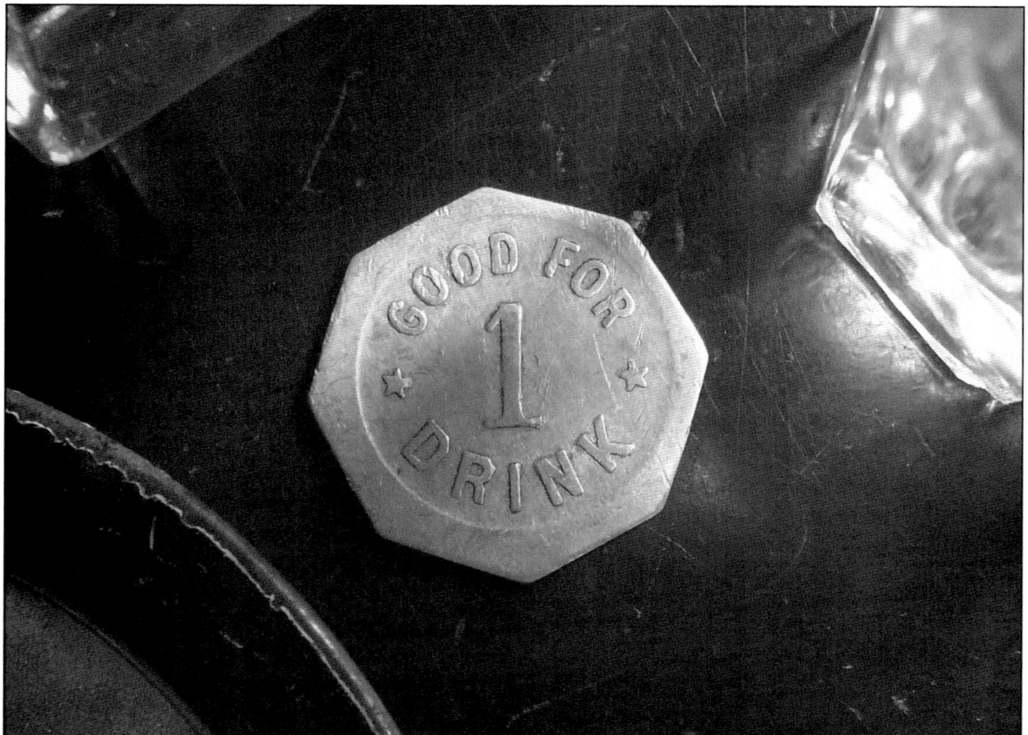

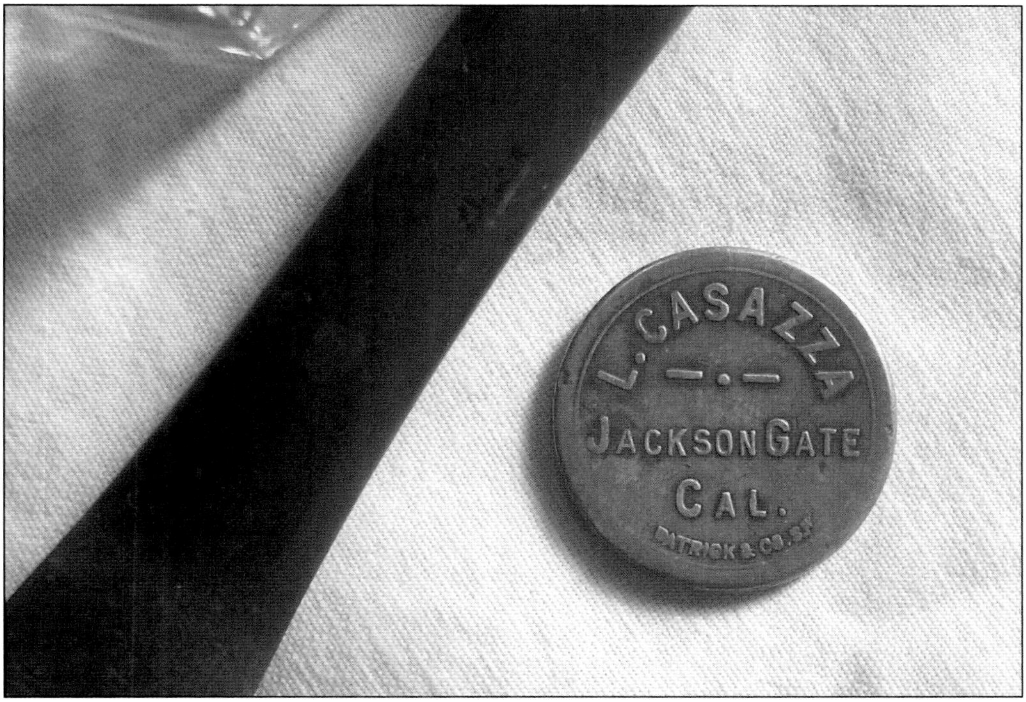

These pictures provide two more views of the front and back of a drink token from L. Casazza's Jackson Gate establishment. The token was "Good for One 10¢ Drink"—though what that could buy, one could never be sure. It is reasonable to think that Casazza purchased stock from breweries in Jackson and the Gate. (Courtesy authors' collection.)

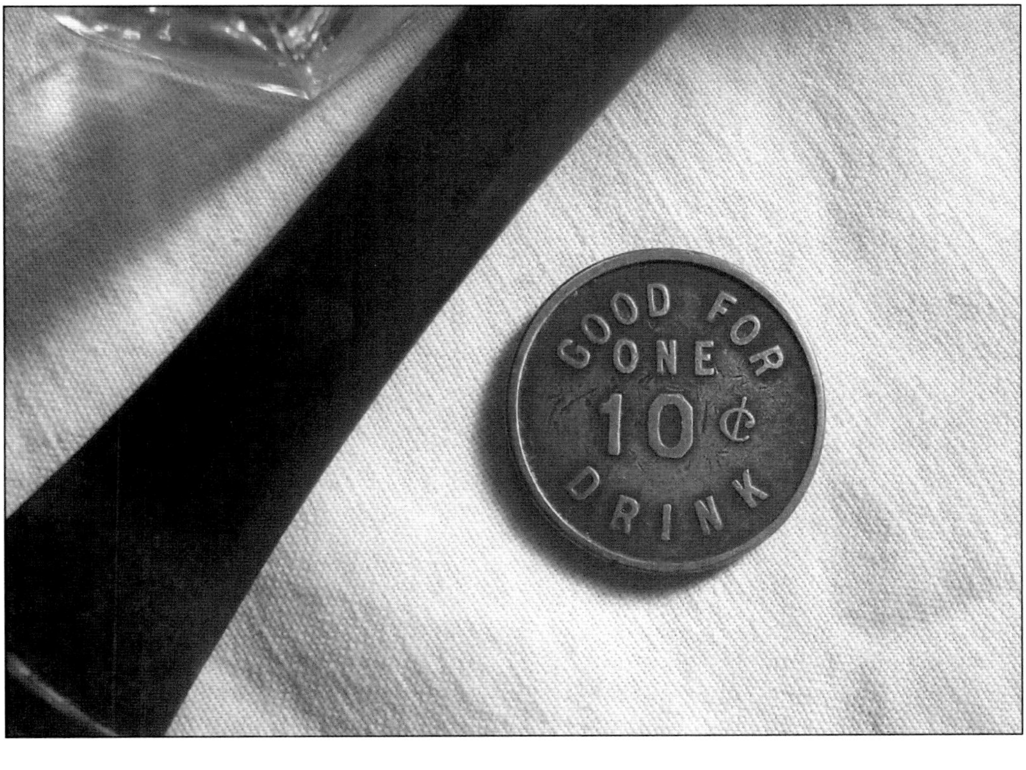

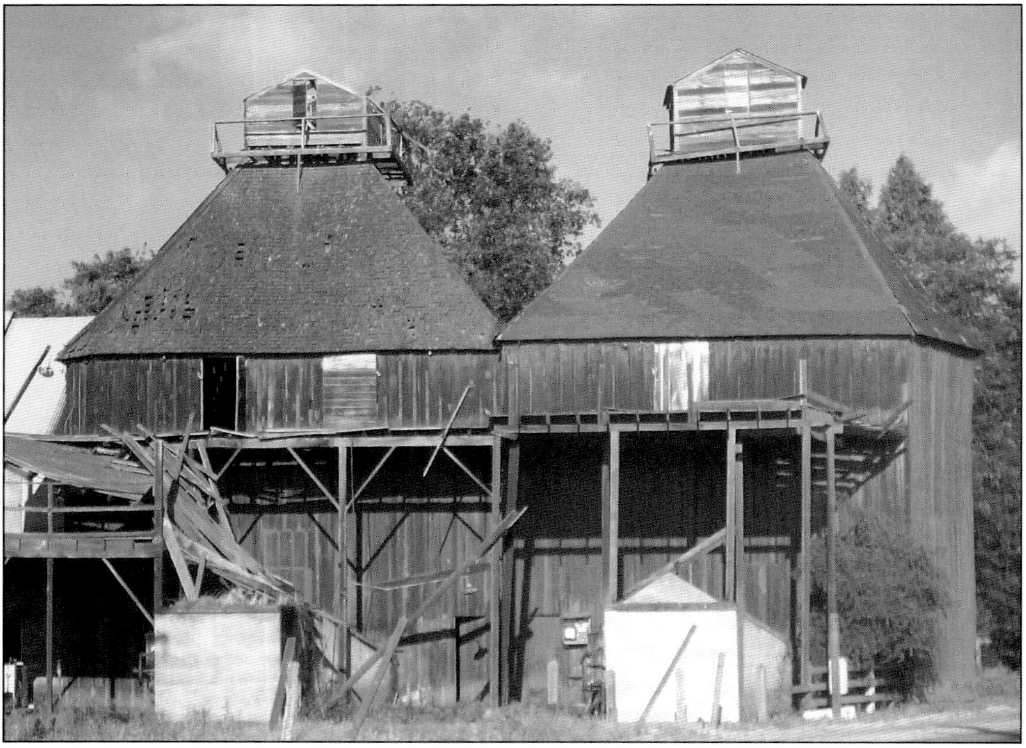

Aside from grains (which some brewers farmed, as was the case with the family who ran the Ione Brewery), hops were the other critical ingredient in brewing beer. These images show hop barns in Sloughhouse on Jackson Highway, where they were grown in Sacramento County. California's climate lends itself well to the growing of hops, and a wide variety of hops were grown in the state. The specialized barns were constructed to house and dry the hops once picked; these barns represent one of the few surviving examples of this type of structure in California. (Courtesy authors' collection.)

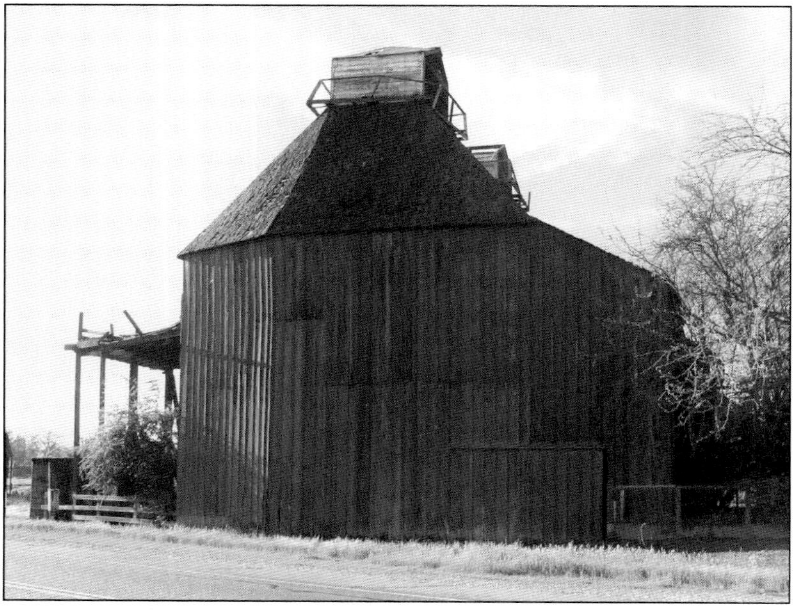

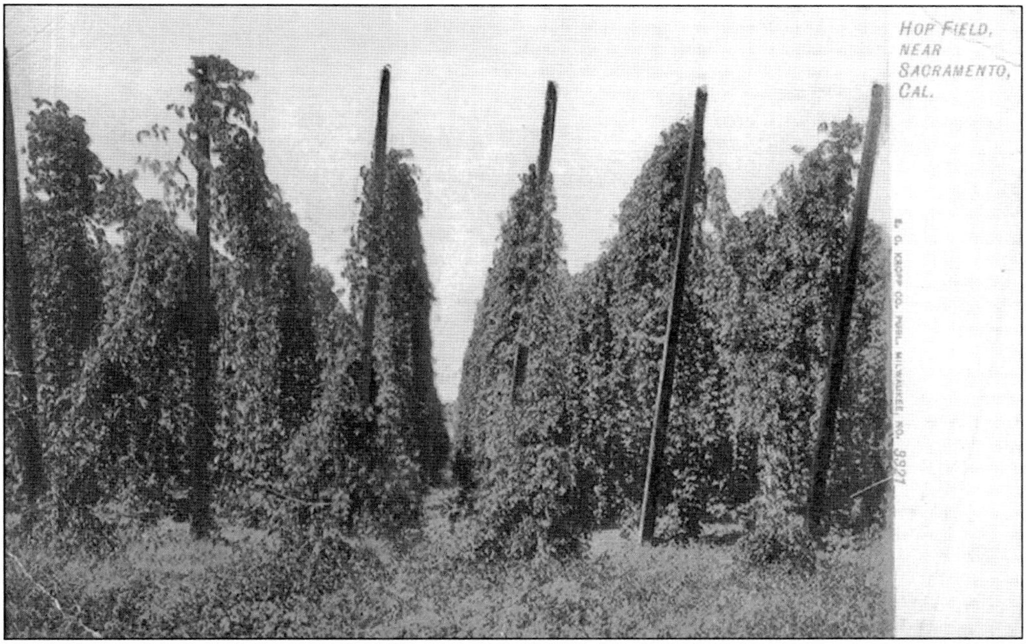

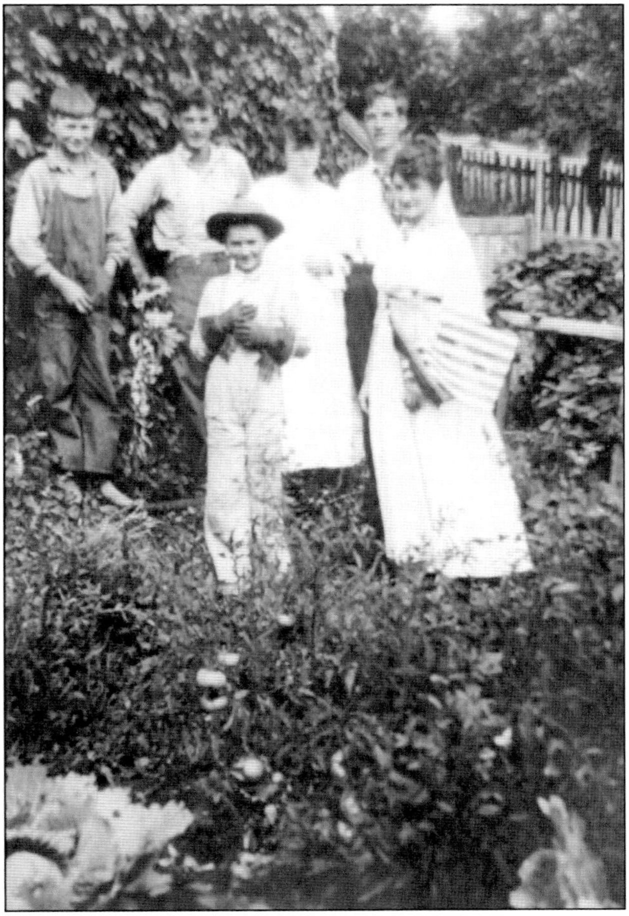

Hops were grown up tall trellises, as seen in this early-20th-century postcard, and until relatively recently, hops were grown in Sloughhouse. It was common for farm laborers, including women, to travel to the Sacramento Valley for the hops harvest season. (Courtesy authors' collection.)

Local farmers also raised the crops that supplied the breweries with grains and hops. Henry Garibaldi recalled that after delivering his load of barely to the Sutter Creek Brewery, he would stop in the bar, and for a nickel he could buy a glass of fresh beer, a pickled egg, and half a sandwich. This would have been the time of Raddatz's period of ownership, around 1912. Brewing beer at home was very common in rural communities, and hops can be seen growing up in the background of this c. 1915 portrait of the Farnham family of Fiddletown. (Courtesy Amador County Archives.)

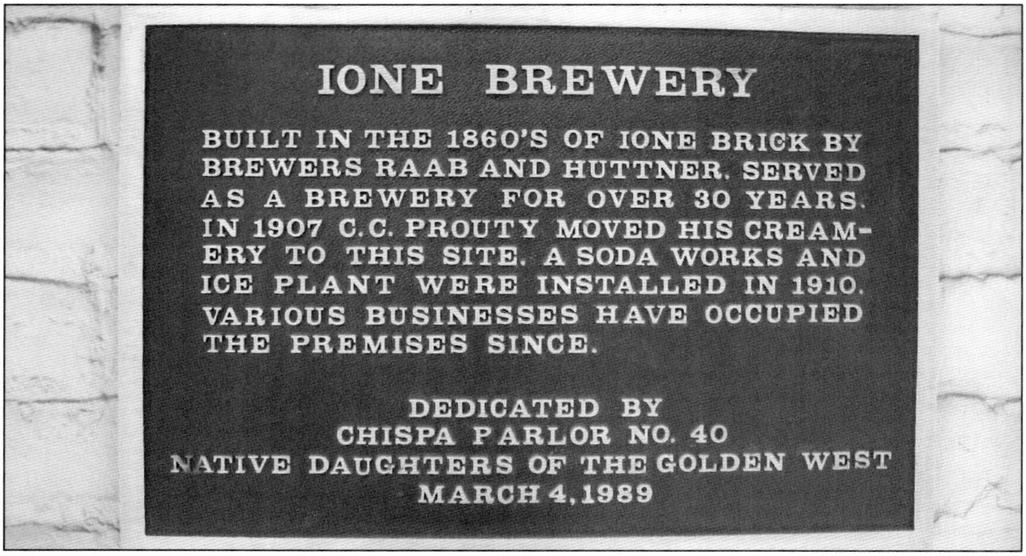

Only one brewery operated in Ione, beginning in the 1860s with Frederick Raab and Frederick Huttner, both of German descent. The operation was either called the Ione Brewery or Ione City Brewery. The building still stands today. Pictured also is the building's commemorative plaque. The Landgraf family purchased the building in the 1970s and were responsible for its restoration. (Courtesy authors' collection.)

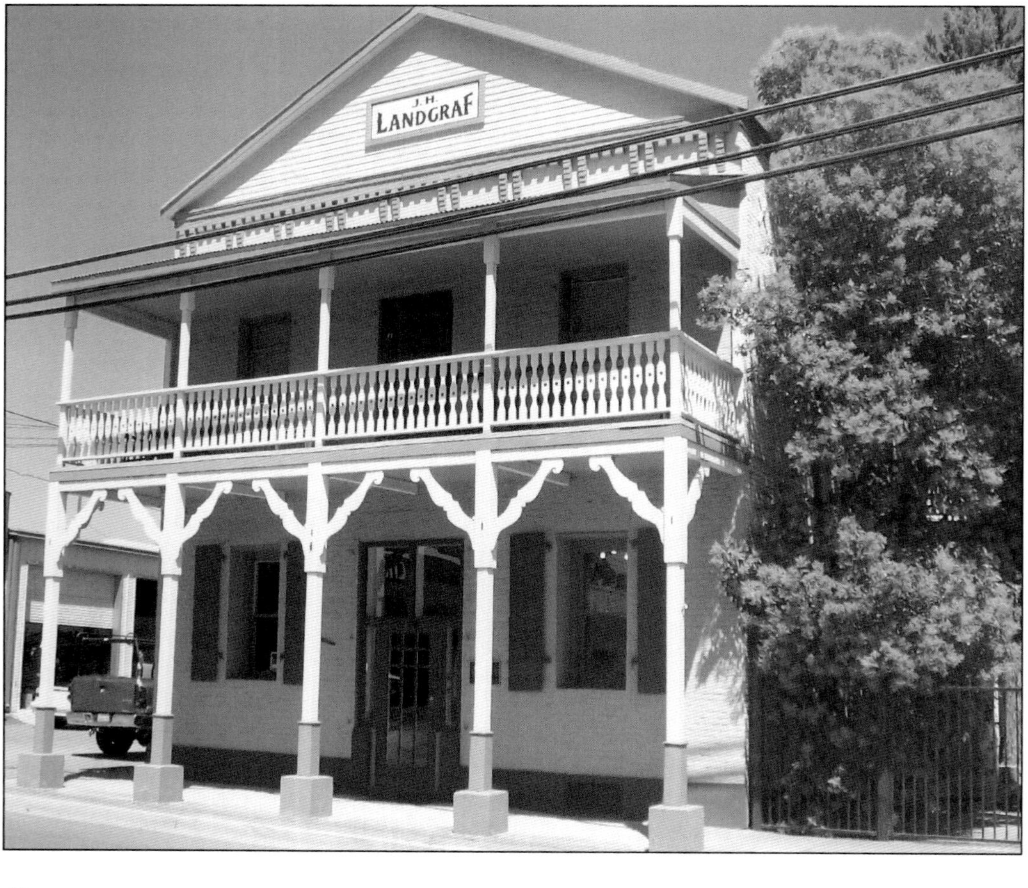

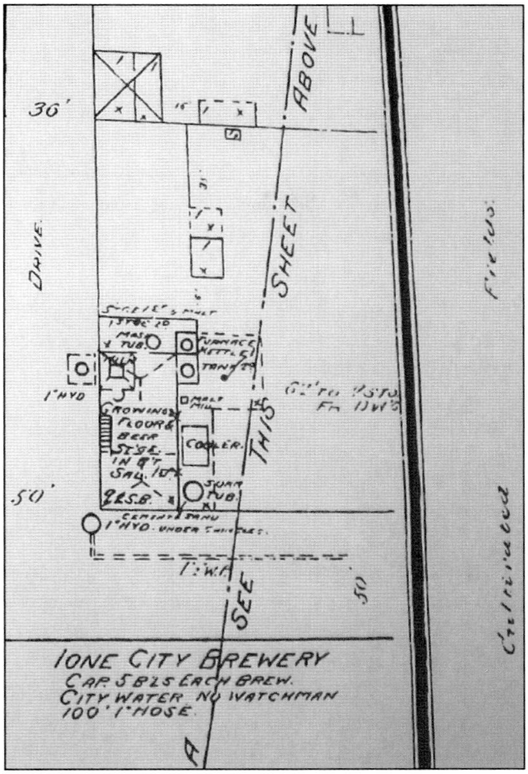

Traveling west, the town of Ione sat on the very edge of the goldfields, and was once—and remains today—one of the largest communities in the region. This Sanborn map depicts the brewery during its operations as the Ione City Brewery. At this point in time, the brewery had the capacity of five barrels for each brew. A growing floor, beer storage, mash tubs, furnaces and kettles—all the tools of a brewers' trade—can be seen depicted in the map. After Raab and Huttner's ownership, it was purchased by C.C. Prouty in 1907 and turned into an icehouse.

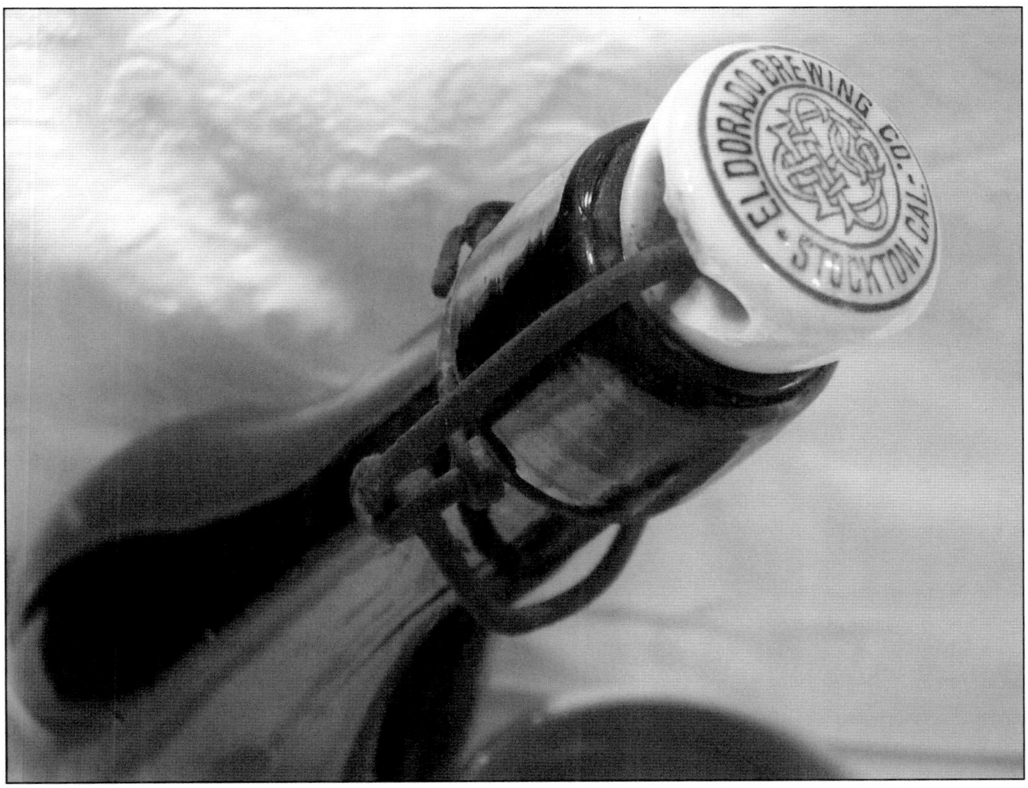

Shown here is a ceramic bottle closure, called a "lightning stopper." The stopper, working on a wire hinge similar to a canning jar, was invented by Karl Hutter in 1875. It was one of the more popular bottle closures until Prohibition. The "crown cap" bottle cap that most are familiar with today was not patented until 1892; it became the closure of choice after Prohibition ended. (Courtesy authors' collection.)

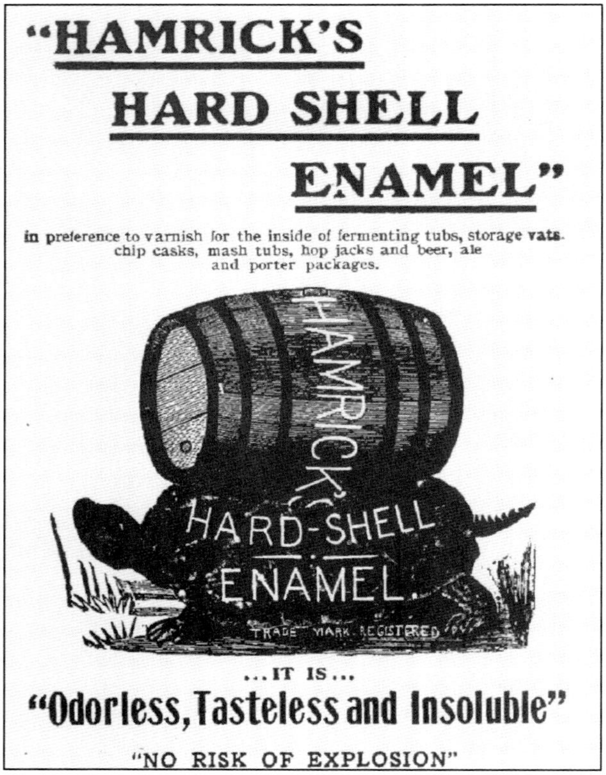

Along with stoppers, bungs, corks, and all manner of equipment, brewers like Raab and Huttner would have ordered products and equipment for their operations. Hamrick's kegs promised "No Risk of Explosion" as advertised in the 1918 Western Brewer supplement, *Brewer's Handbook*, self-described as "the standard directory of the American brewing industry." Incidentally, the Sutter Creek Brewery is the only Amador County brewery listed in the handbook.

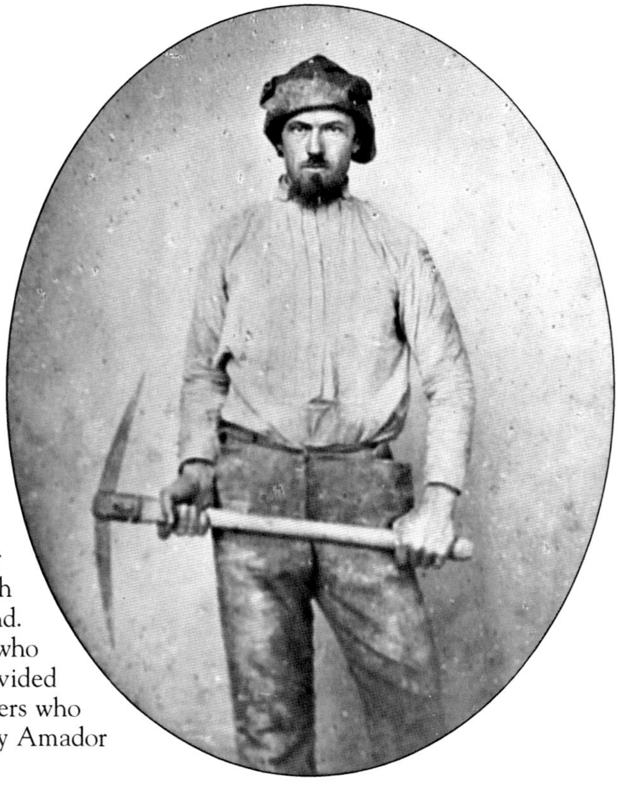

Traveling back towards Sutter Creek and crossing the Golden Chain highway to the east, one would have traveled 14 or so miles to the mining community of Volcano. A young Amador miner is captured in this classic portrait, with the tool of his trade—a pick—in hand. He, along with the thousands of men who flocked to Volcano, would have provided brewers with a steady flow of customers who had a ready source of gold. (Courtesy Amador County Archives.)

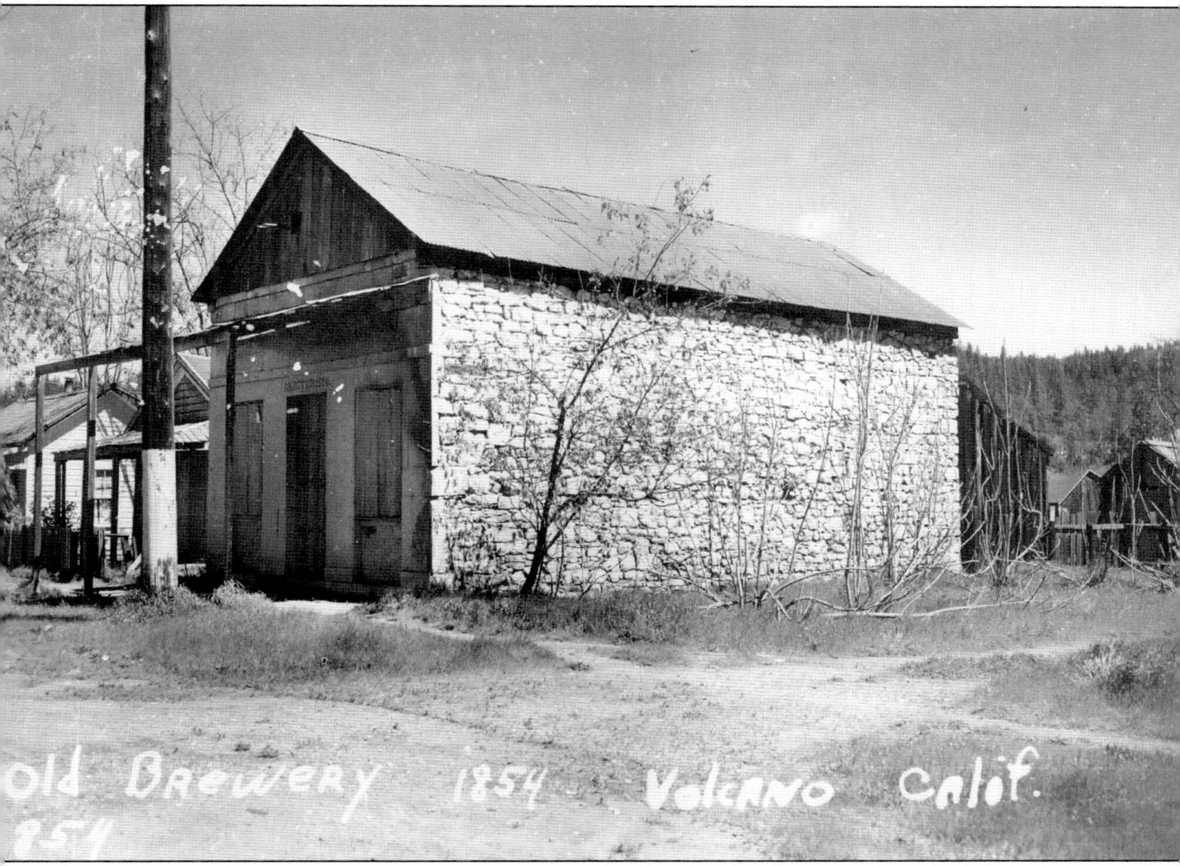

Contrary to what one might think today, the town of Volcano was once home to nearly 20,000 men, women, and children—and after the Gold Rush, almost no vegetation. The population was soon large enough to house at least one substantial brewery, if not more, though tracking the history of the breweries in Volcano is almost as elusive as the search for gold. This image shows a view of the Volcano Brewery around the 1940s. The stonework is stunning, with walls close to two feet thick and a full basement that would have provided cool summer storage. Other than a sealer, little repair has been needed on the stonework over time. (Courtesy Amador County Archives.)

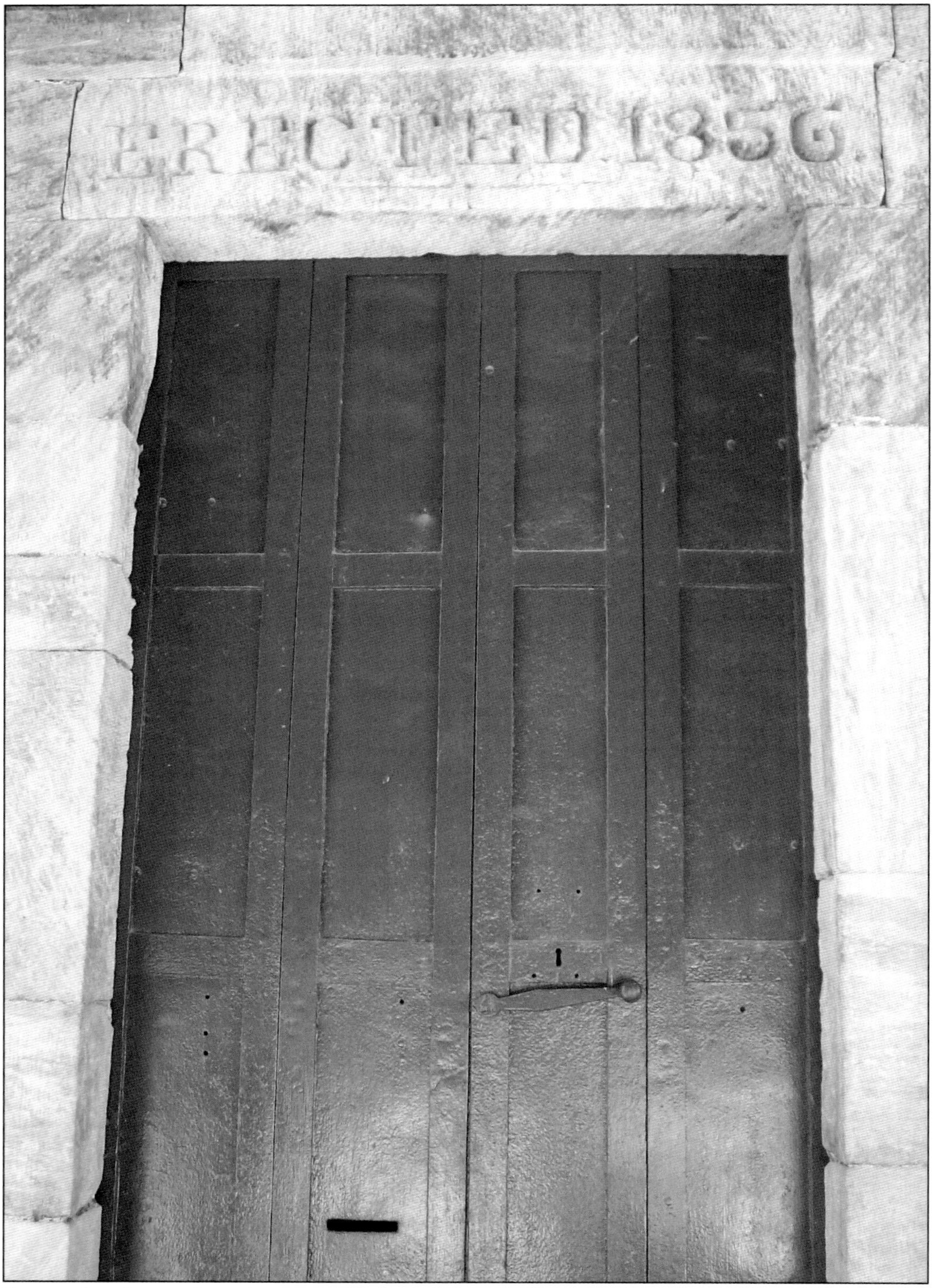

Depicted in this modern photograph is the lintel above the main entrance to the Volcano Brewery; "erected 1856" is carved into the beautiful marble facade. The brewery operated from at least 1856 into the 1870s. The story that Volcano was home to several breweries is part of the local lore, and there has been speculation that the Upper Flat Brewery, the Bavarian, the Seible, and the Volcano breweries are all actually one and the same. (Courtesy authors' collection.)

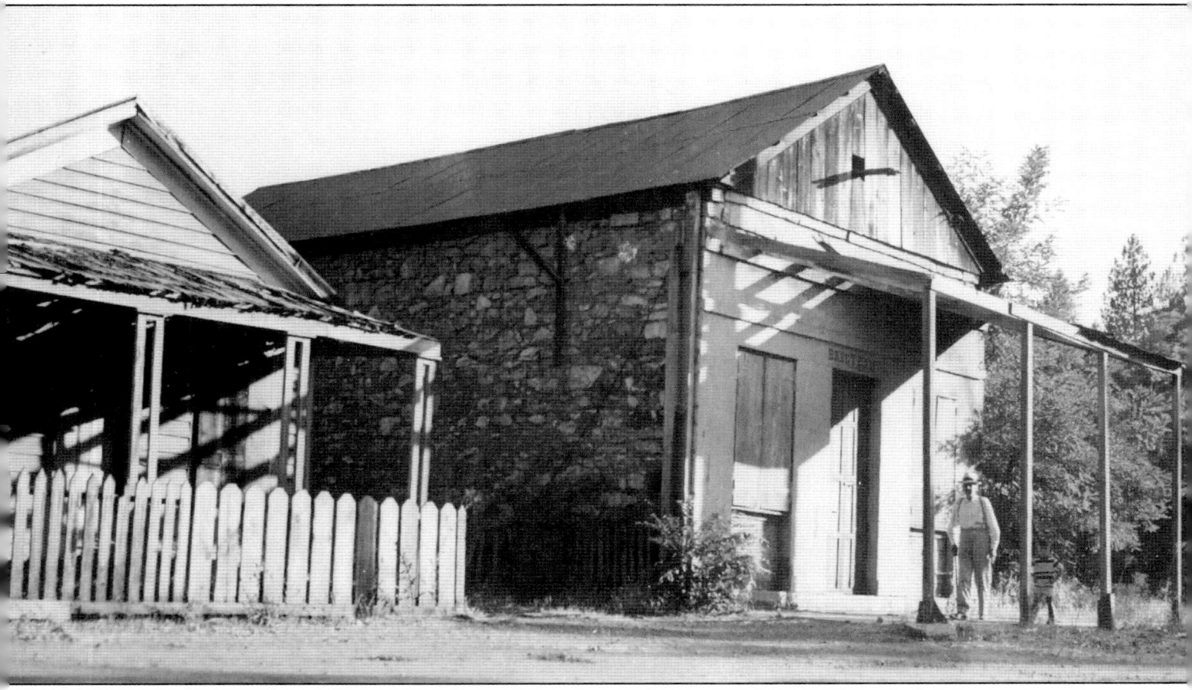

This image shows the Volcano Brewery in a state of disrepair, shuttered with heavy iron fire doors. Next door to the brewery was a wood framed house that is no longer standing. When this photograph was taken in the 1940s, the brewery was nearly 90 years old and its history is convoluted. The Upper Flat Brewery was operated by Jacob Griesback in 1856. During this same year, John Ritter, and again Julius Obil, were listed under Volcano Brewery (or Bavarian Brewery). Again, in the 1860s and 1870s, Griesback is listed as the proprietor of the Volcano Brewery. John Seible is listed as proprietor in 1871 of a "brewery" and his name remains associated with the brewery pictured here. (Courtesy Amador County Archives.)

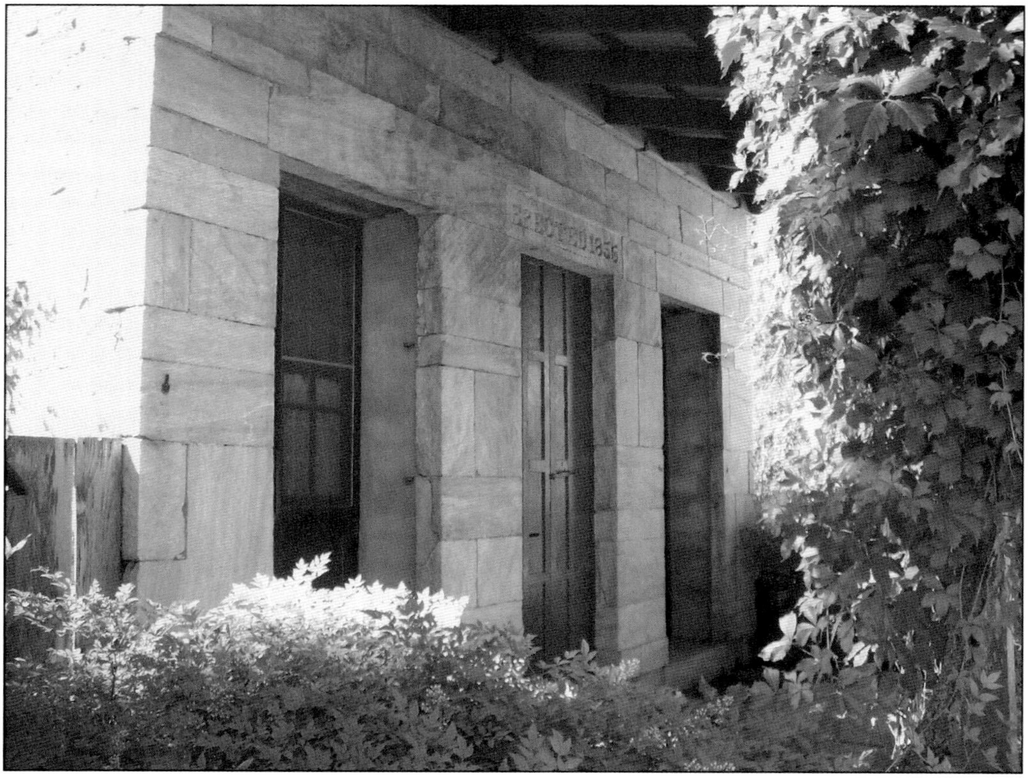

The beautiful marble work that completes the front facade of the building is fitted together tightly, like a big stone puzzle. The heavy iron fire doors and shutters were commonly found on stone buildings in Gold Rush towns, many of which had the bad habit of burning down several times before the 1880s. The combination of stone, brick, and even adobe walls with iron doors and tin roofs helped slow fires substantially. (Courtesy authors' collection.)

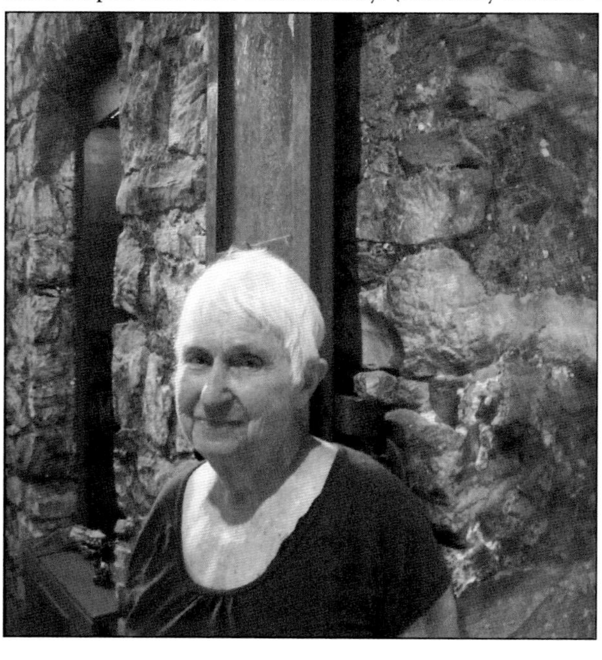

By the 1930s, the stone brewery building was all but abandoned, and the population of Volcano had dropped to a few hundred from its Gold Rush heyday. In 1965, Ruth Gottstein (pictured here) and her husband, Howard, fell in love with the town and the building. They began an extensive remodeling project that spanned 17 years and saved the brewery, while keeping the historical flavor of the building intact. Today, the publishing house Volcano Press, whose focus is on domestic violence and women's health, operates out of the brewery. The old stone building forms the core of the home of its publisher emeritus, Ruth Gottstein. (Courtesy Ruth Gottstein.)

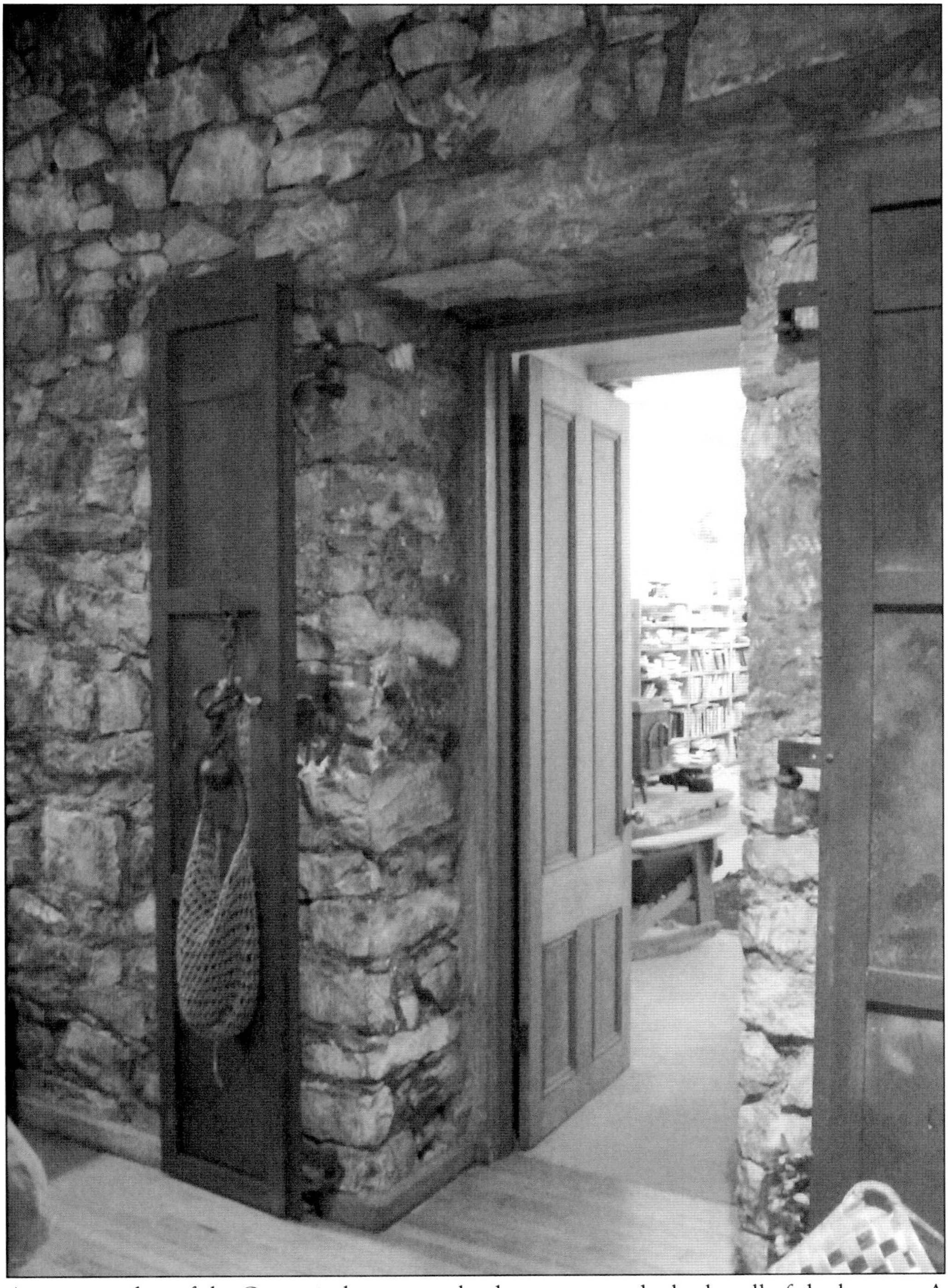

An interior shot of the Gottstein home reveals what was once the back wall of the brewery. A peek into the actual interior can be seen past the two-foot-thick walls. A full basement runs under the upper story. The remodeling was completed by Ruth's son Dan Gottstein. (Courtesy Ruth Gottstein.)

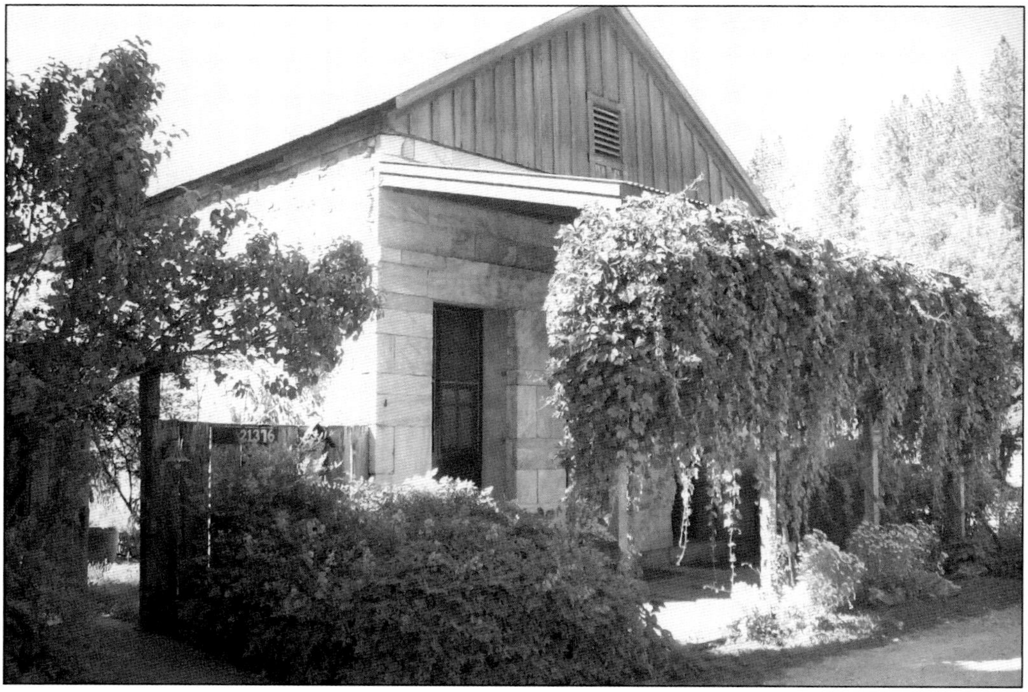

Seen here is a contemporary view of the Volcano Brewery, draped in its summertime vegetation. The Gottstein family has been very careful to preserve the historical fabric of the building, and one can still imagine John Doble walking up to the front door and stepping inside for a pint. (Courtesy authors' collection.)

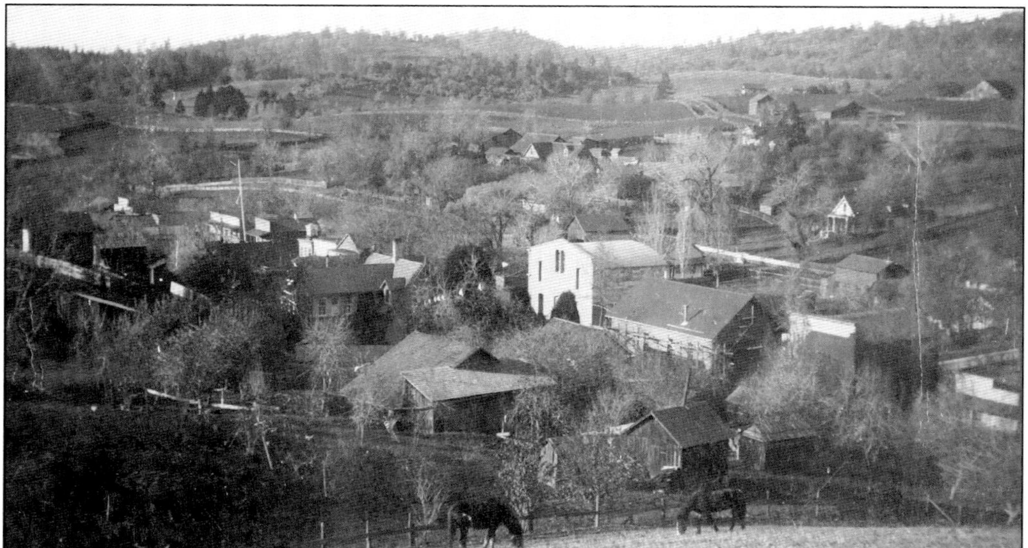

Compared to the history of Volcano's breweries, the history of the brewery in Fiddletown is straightforward. In 1866, the probate file of Margaret Mahoney, a prominent local merchant, lists: "Thielen & Muller, beer, barley," indicating the brewery was open relatively early. In 1871, Nicklas Thielen and Conrad Muller had a house and lot on Main Street known as the Fiddletown Brewery. In this post-1870 overview of Fiddletown, the brewery stood to the left of the prominent Schallhorn Building. (Courtesy Amador County archives.)

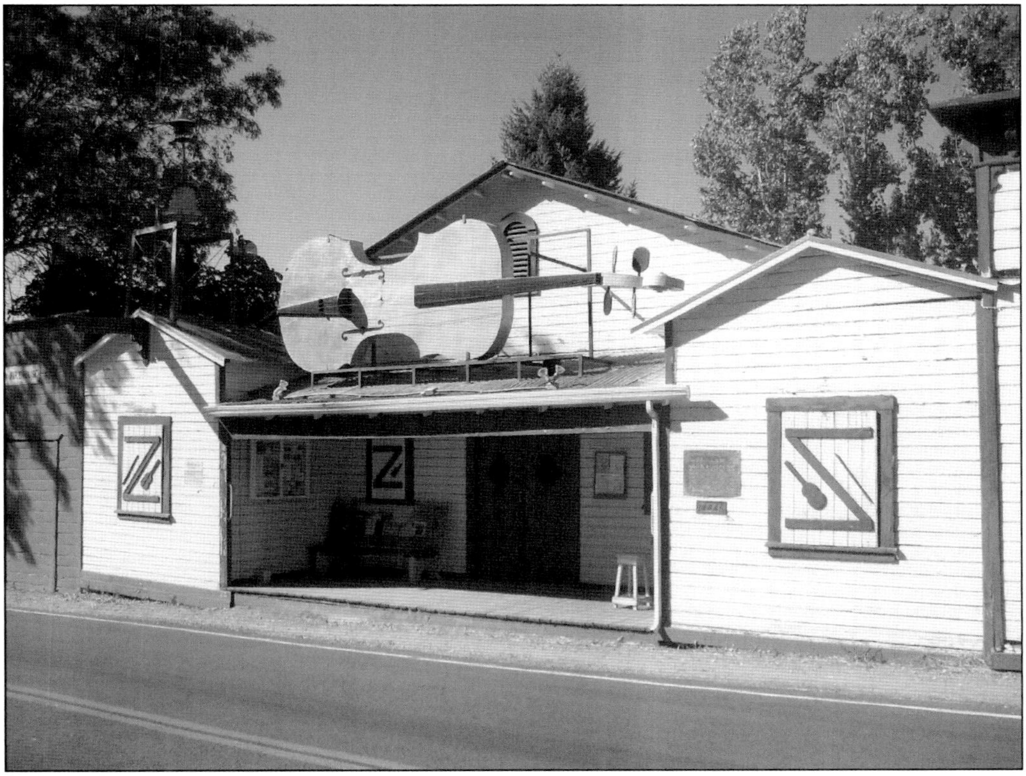

Fiddletown was named for the fiddling that residents enjoyed during its earliest Gold Rush camp days. In 1878, the town's name was changed to Oleta in order to give itself a better image, but the name was changed back in 1932. While this photograph may look like it was taken in the 1940s, the photograph is contemporary; it is a town that celebrates its unique heritage. (Courtesy authors' collection.)

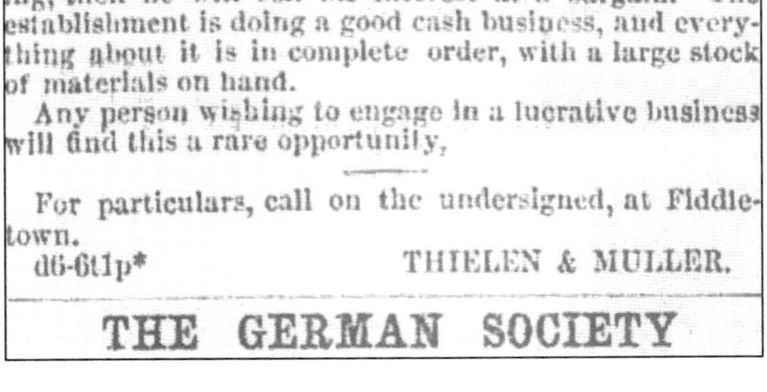

READ THIS!

ONE OF THE UNDERSIGNED being compelled to go East on urgent business, one-half the FIDDLETOWN BREWERY will be rented for one year or more. If he does not succeed in renting, then he will sell his interest at a bargain. The establishment is doing a good cash business, and everything about it is in complete order, with a large stock of materials on hand.

Any person wishing to engage in a lucrative business will find this a rare opportunity.

For particulars, call on the undersigned, at Fiddletown.

d6-6t1p* THIELEN & MULLER.

THE GERMAN SOCIETY

"Urgent business" compelled the proprietors of the Fiddletown Brewery to place an advertisement for investments in half of the ownership for a year or more in the *Sacramento Daily Union*, December 13, 1870. The advertisement was a success, and by 1871, Henry Schroeder was a partner brewer. He continued to operate the brewery into the 1890s. Little is known about the types of beers the Fiddletown Brewery crafted; today Fiddletown is more famous for its wines. (Courtesy Amador County Archives.)

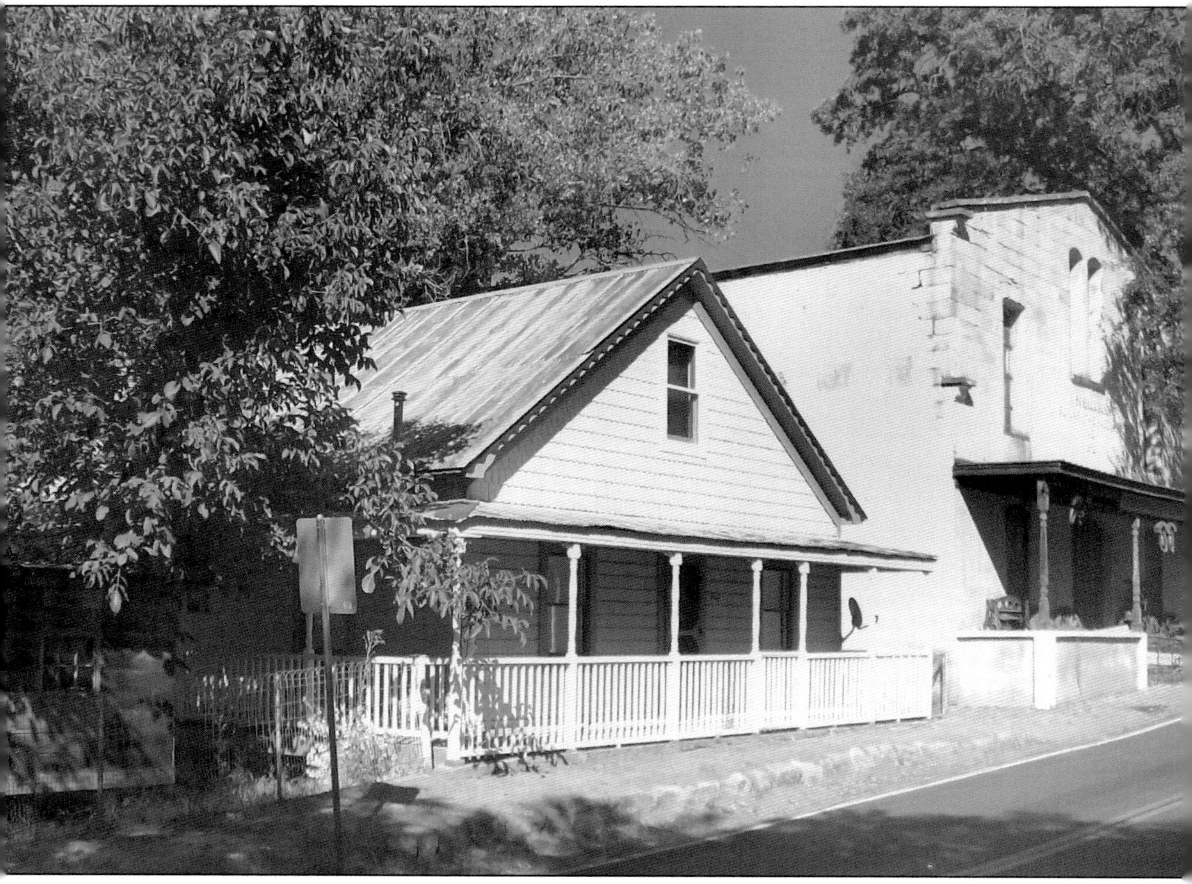

In the 1920s or 1930s, the wooden house on the left was built on the stone foundation of the Fiddletown Brewery. The structure next to the brewery is the prominent Schallhorn's Blacksmith & Wagon Works. Its rhyolite stone block construction is very similar to the lower story of the Fiddletown Brewery, seen in the detail of the basement on the following page. (Courtesy authors' collection.)

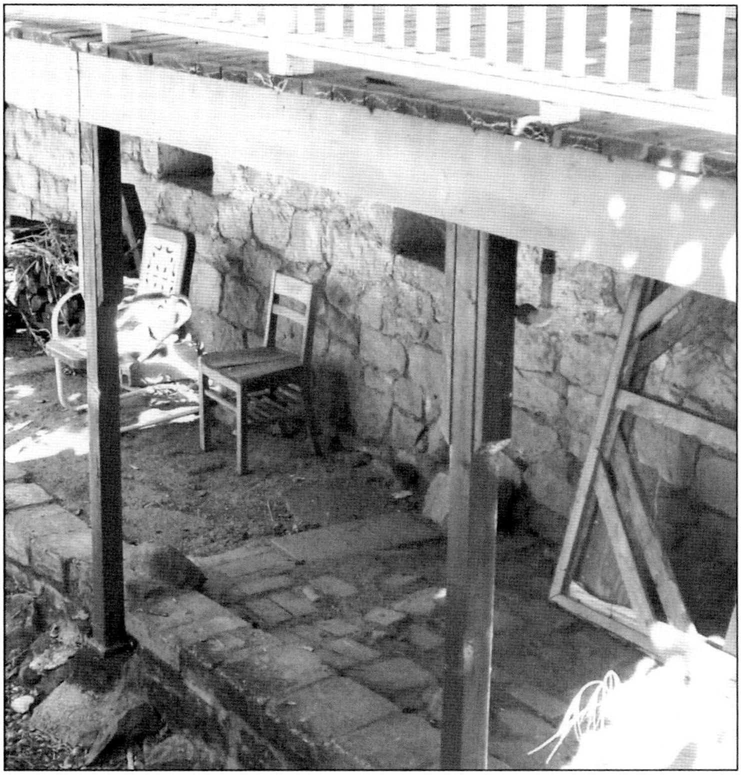

Two views of the beautifully crafted rhyolite basement of the Fiddletown Brewery show the multiple vents that were important for brewing cellars. When Conrad Muller died in 1874, probate records show 525 gallons of beer on hand, as well as brewery equipment, including kegs, copper skimmers, tubs, bungs, corks, and buckets. The property and adjoining lot contained the brewery building, a small office, and a malt mill. The brewery's barley house was located up American Flat Road. (Courtesy authors' collection.)

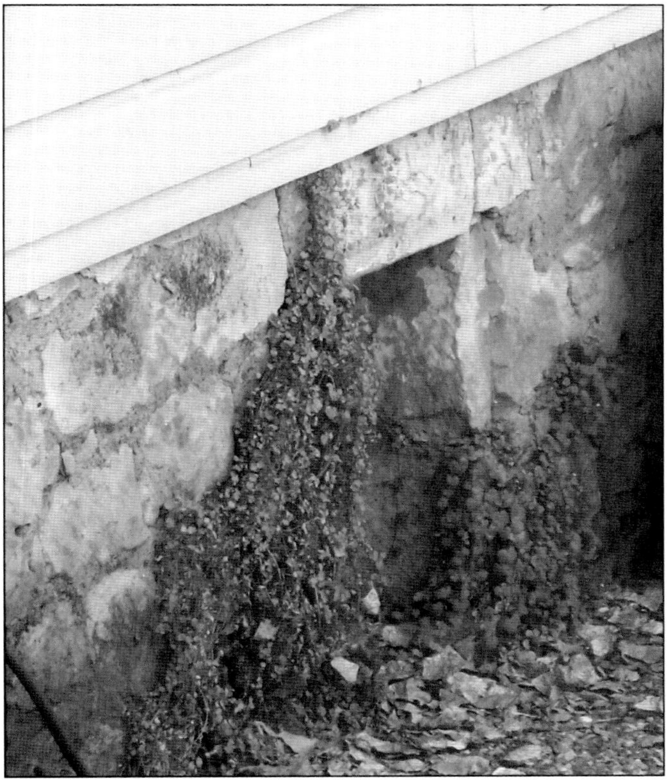

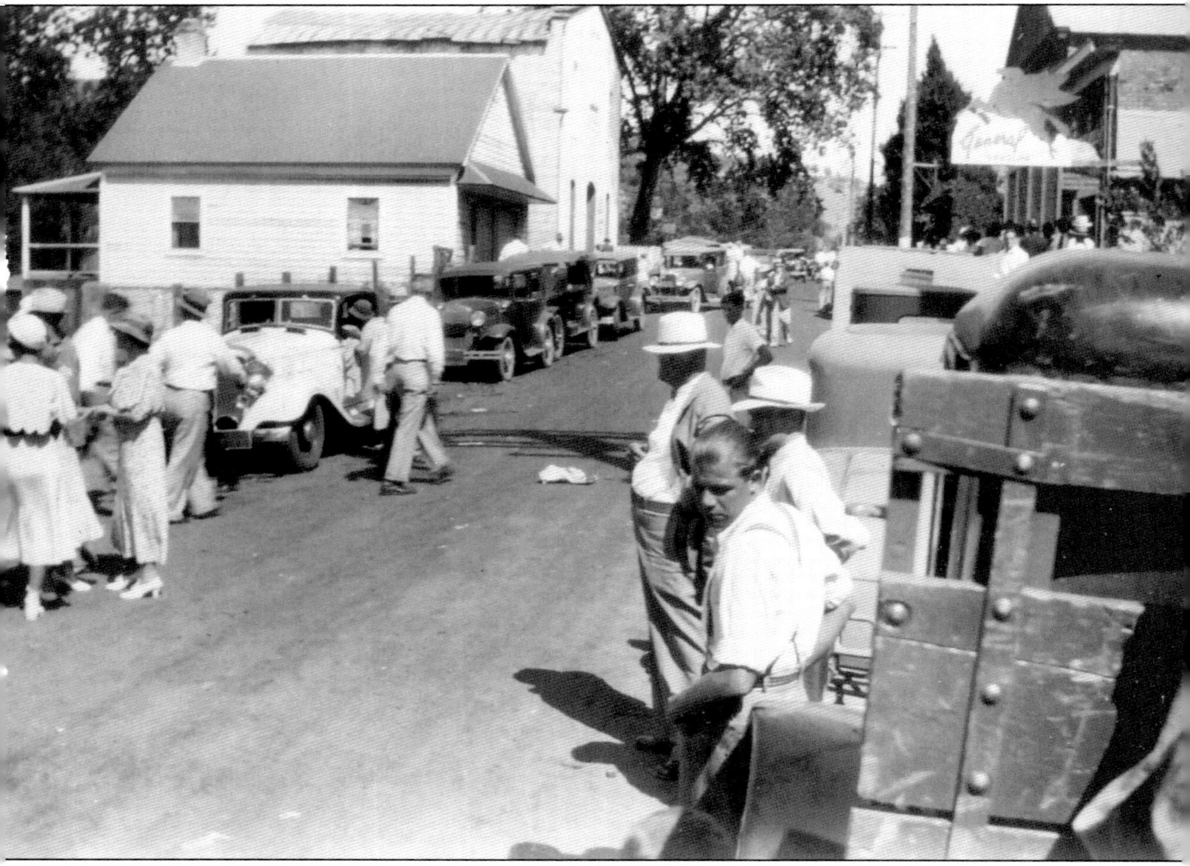

Prohibition had just ended when this image of Fiddletown was taken, but by then its brewery had been closed along with almost all in Amador County. The relatively new home, constructed on top of the brewery's original rhyolite foundation, can be seen standing next to the Schallhorn Building. (Courtesy Paula and Gary Wooten.)

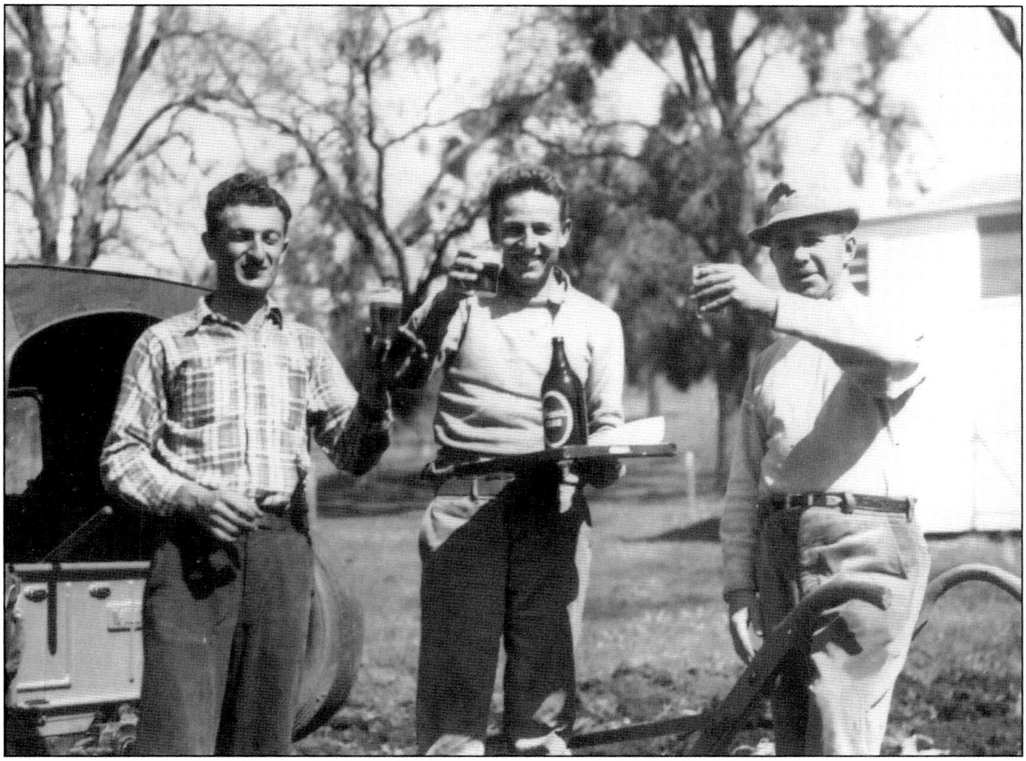

Taking a break from working in the vineyards, these three men are drinking Bohemian Club Beer, which was bottled by Southern Brewing, Los Angeles. One might question why they were not drinking a local lager. To their credit, there were no operating breweries left in Amador County by the time this photograph was taken in the 1950s. Pictured here holding up a pint are Armenio D'Agostini (left), Altero D'Agostini (center), and Mr. Green, a Fiddletown rancher. (Courtesy Mary Lou D'Agostini.)

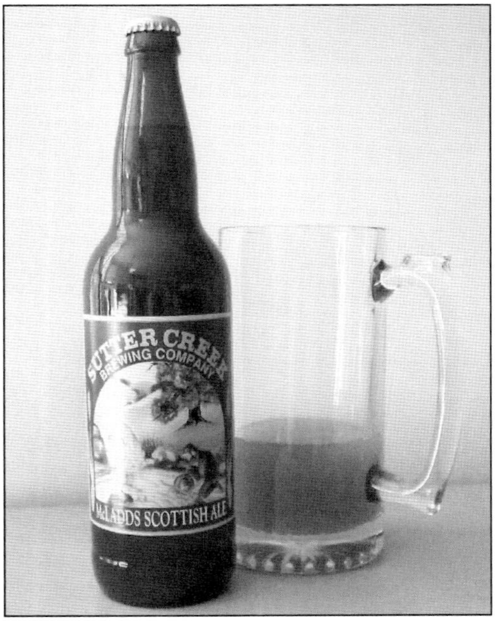

Commercial brewing in Amador County has proven to be as elusive today as it was a century ago, with local breweries lasting only a few short years, in spite of the quality of the beer. The Sutter Creek Brewing Company was opened in the 1990s. The brewery, located on Church Street, operated successfully for a number of years, producing delicious, locally named labels, such as McLadds Scottish Ale (pictured here), Powder House Ale, and Knight Foundry Brown Ale. Like most of Amador County's small breweries, it exists today only as part of the history of the community. The town and the county await the opening of the next saga of brewing history, perhaps a return to California's own steam beer roots in the same community where it was produced more than a century earlier. (Courtesy Janette Molin.)

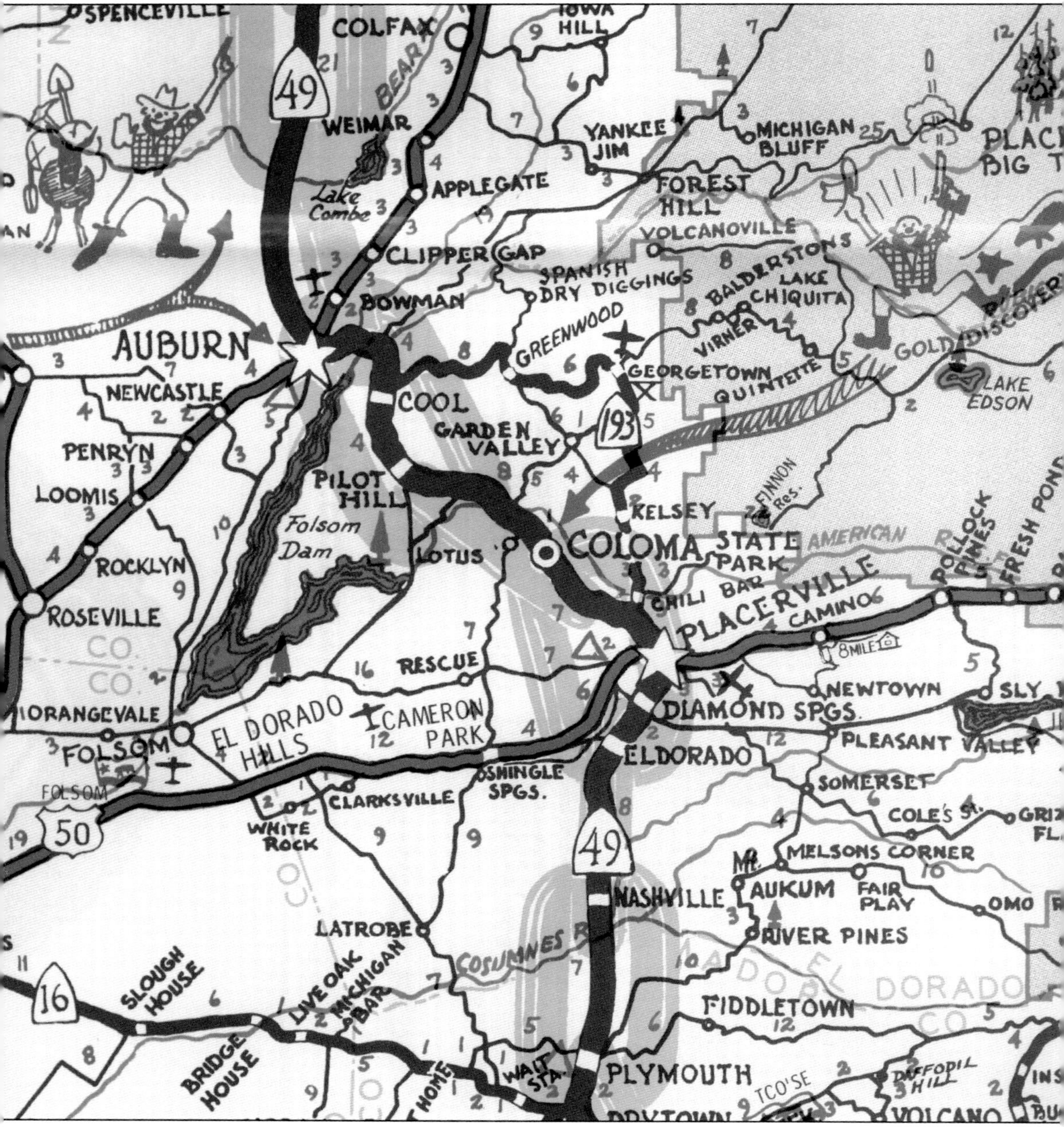

The Golden Chain Highway passes over the Cosumnes River, dropping off travelers in Yeomet and Nashville. Winding through the steep hills, one arrives in El Dorado, once home to John Thiesen's Mud Springs Brewery. Following the road to Placerville, there were a number of breweries, including the Mountain and California breweries, neither of which survived Prohibition. The road continued north towards Coloma, the site where gold was discovered and which housed Brewery Lane. (Courtesy Golden Chain Council.)

Four

El Dorado County
Gold Discovery County

"When we drink, we get drunk. When we get drunk, we fall asleep. When we fall asleep, we commit no sin. When we commit no sin, we go to Heaven. So, let's all get drunk and go to heaven."

—Irish proverb, author unknown

El Dorado County is truly the heart of the Gold Country, and it was here, in 1848, that John Marshall found gold in the tailrace of John Sutter's sawmill on the South Fork of the American River. This discovery set off the famous California Gold Rush, and soon thousands of Argonauts were roaming the hills of this region. It was not long before small communities began to spring up, with names like Mud Springs, Hangtown, Greenwood, and Georgetown. By the 1850s, each of these had sprouted breweries.

As these towns became more established, they became more settled and more "civilized;" Mud Springs became El Dorado, and Hangtown became Placerville. The breweries expanded, becoming integral parts of their surrounding communities. Several of these breweries lasted until Prohibition, when all were closed.

Like most breweries in California, these were operated by German immigrants. Placerville had a prolific brewing industry. In that community, the California Brewery was run by Bavarian Jacob Zeisz and his family for at least two decades. The Mountain Brewery was opened in Placerville in 1853 by John Dangeleisen, who sold it to William Krahner a few years later. In turn, Krahner sold it to Frederick Giebenhain, yet another German immigrant. The Mountain Brewery remained in operation under the same family until Prohibition. Then there was John Mulbach, the merry German brewer of Greenwood, of whom it was said was "jovial, kindly to a fault and no one ever went hungry from his door if [he] had a bit of meat and drink in the house."

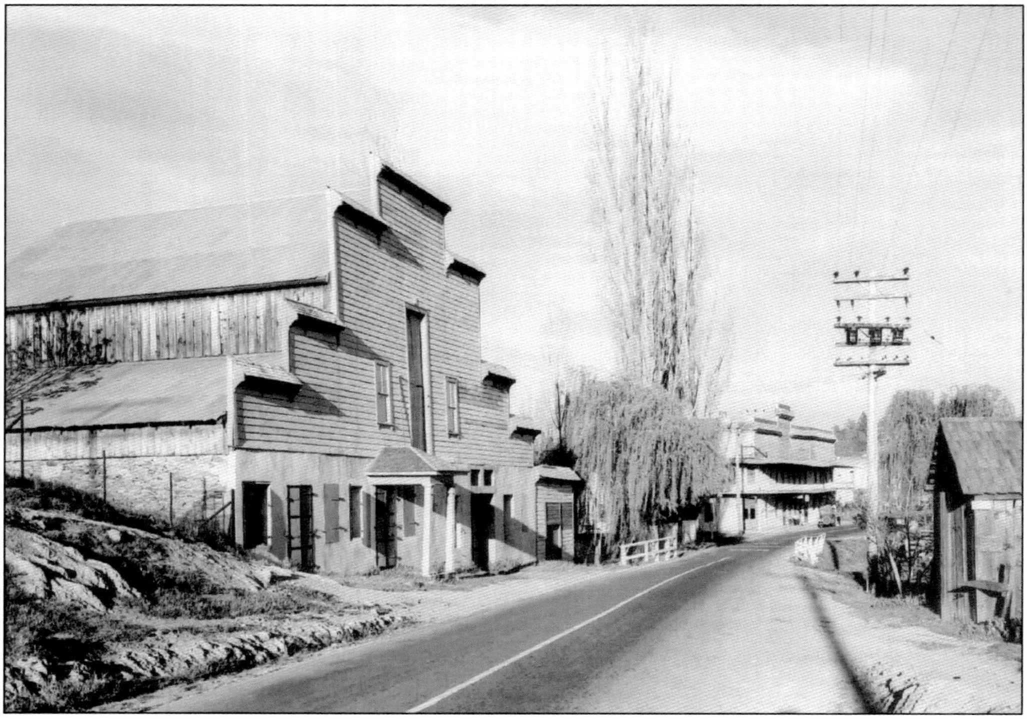

El Dorado County is currently home to more Gold Country breweries than any other county discussed in this volume. At the time of this publication, there are operating breweries located in Placerville, El Camino, and Goldhill. A portion of El Dorado's downtown core is seen in this 1934 image. Originally founded in 1849, the town had the idyllic name of Mud Springs. An 1862 advertisement in Heckendorn and Wilson's directory for the Mud Springs Brewery is seen below, where proprietor John Thiesen would deliver "free to all parts of the County." (Both, courtesy authors' collection.)

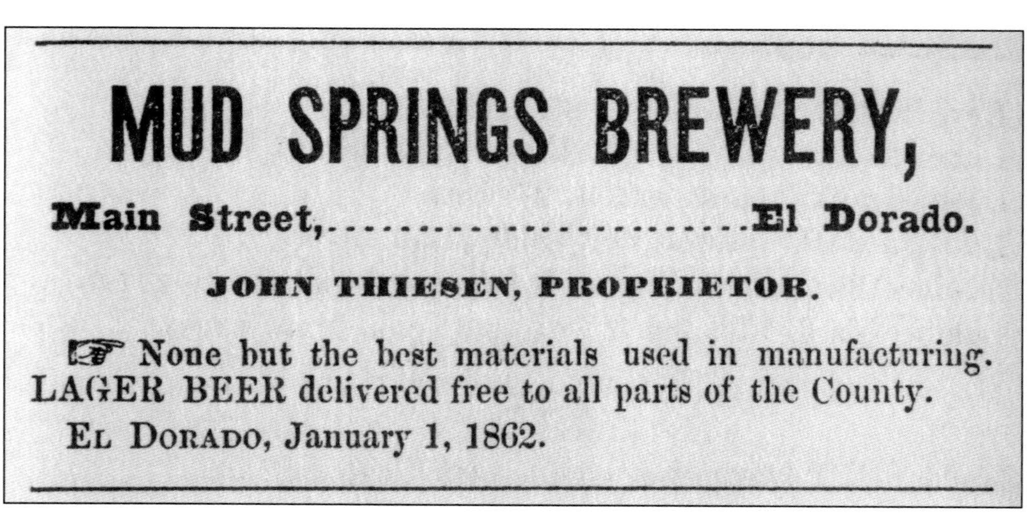

MUD SPRINGS BREWERY,

Main Street,........................El Dorado.

JOHN THIESEN, PROPRIETOR.

☞ None but the best materials used in manufacturing. LAGER BEER delivered free to all parts of the County.

EL DORADO, January 1, 1862.

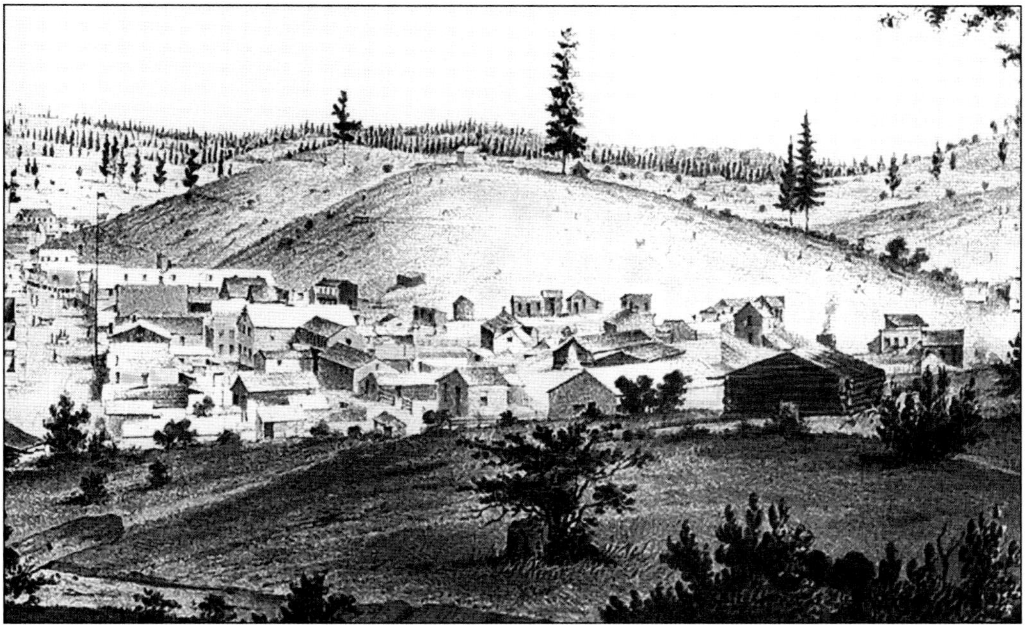

This image shows an early overview of Placerville, when many of the buildings were still log structures, as seen in the foreground on the right. The Mountain Brewery was established by John Dangeleisen and H. Becker in Placerville around 1853. In that year, the brewery was sold to William Krahner. Originally housed in a log cabin, the image below shows the later wood-framed structure as it appeared after 1857. (Courtesy El Dorado County Historical Museum.)

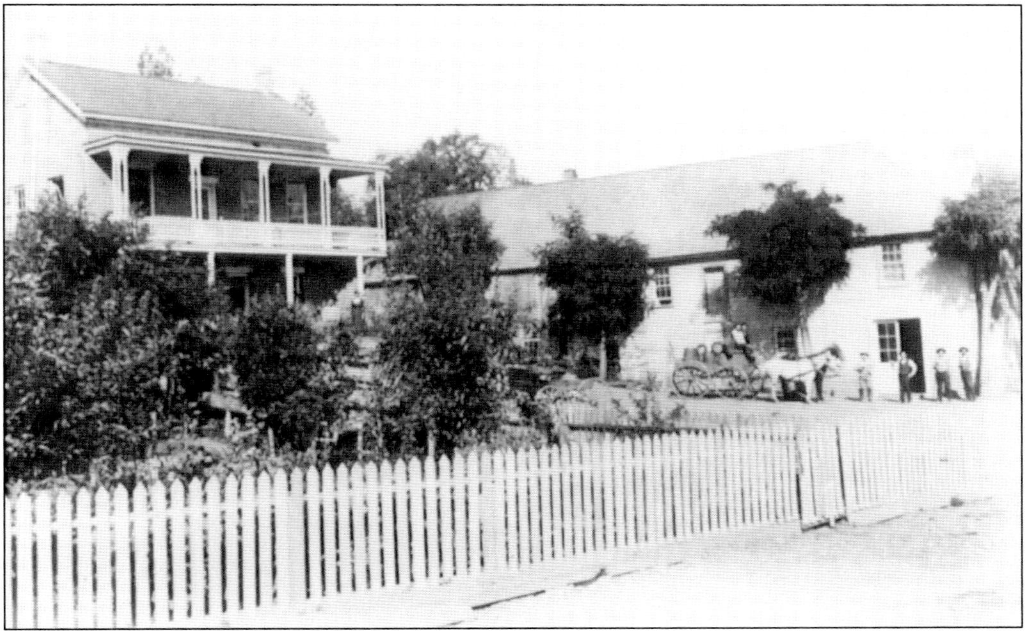

In 1857, William Krahner sold the Mountain Brewery, seen on the right, to Frederick Giebenhain. The Giebenhains worked hard to expand and improve the brewery to include a saloon, hydropower, and electricity. The Mountain Brewery remained in the same family for the next 62 years. It was ultimately closed by Prohibition in 1919. Note the wagon loaded with kegs of beer in front of the brewery. (Courtesy El Dorado County Historical Museum.)

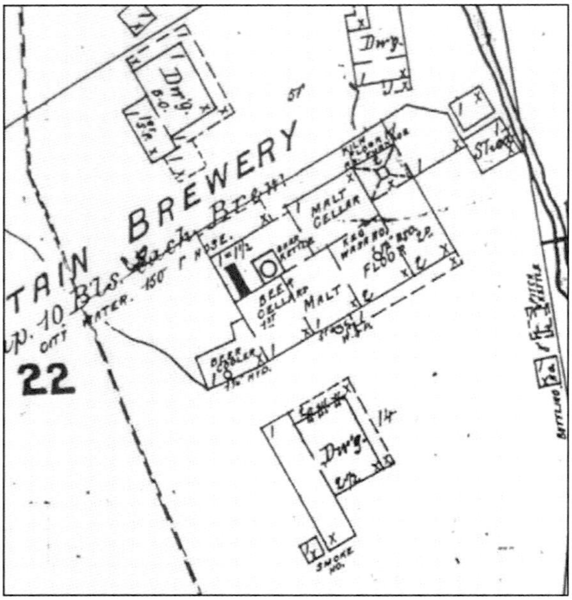

This 1890 Sanborn map shows the close geographical relationship of the Mountain Brewery and the Fausel House. It also shows the general layout of the brewery. The malt floor was located on the top story, with a kiln below to dry the malt. Not apparent on the map is the hillside into which the back of the brewery was built, which situated the second story at ground level at the rear of the building. This allowed the unloading of barley and hops onto the second story, where the brew kettle and malt floor were located. Once the barley was malted, it could be removed directly to the brew kettle on the same floor. Once brewed, the beer was removed to the beer cellar in the basement. In the brew cellar the beer was fermented and kegged.

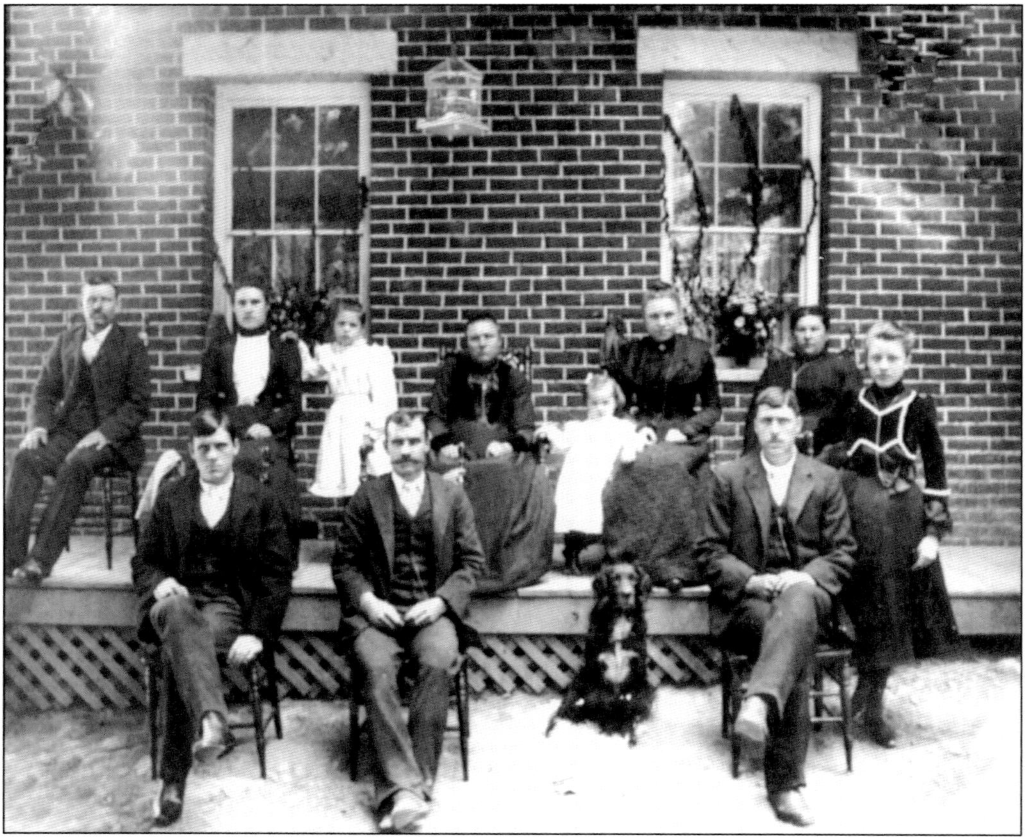

Mary Foster Giebenhain is seen in the center of this c. 1885–1895 portrait, taken on the porch of her home (see Page 79). She is surrounded by her family; her husband had died in 1875. Born in Hesse-Cassel, Germany, Mary married Frederick Giebenhain in 1857. Mary died in 1913, preceded in death by four of her five sons. (Courtesy El Dorado County Historical Museum.)

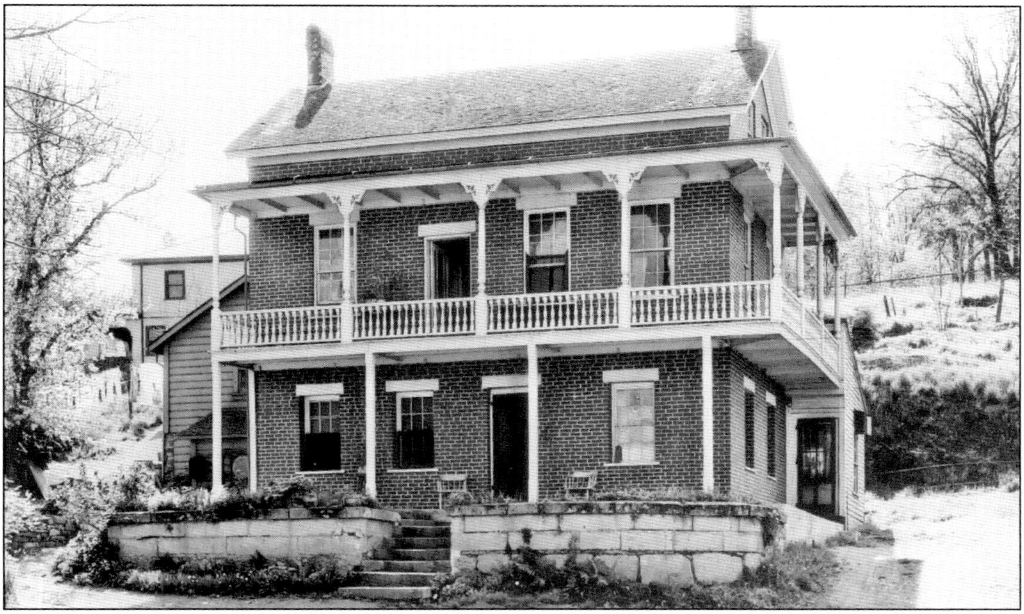

After purchasing the Mountain Brewery, Frederick Giebenhain quickly built a well-appointed brick home adjacent to the brewery. Locally known as the Fausel House, this two-story brick structure still stands on Pacific Street. In 2007, the Fausel House was carefully lifted and repositioned 40 feet away from its original location, allowing for development of the surrounding property. This photograph of the Fausel House dates to 1934, after Prohibition had closed the brewing facility and turned the family to manufacturing sodas. (Courtesy authors' collection.)

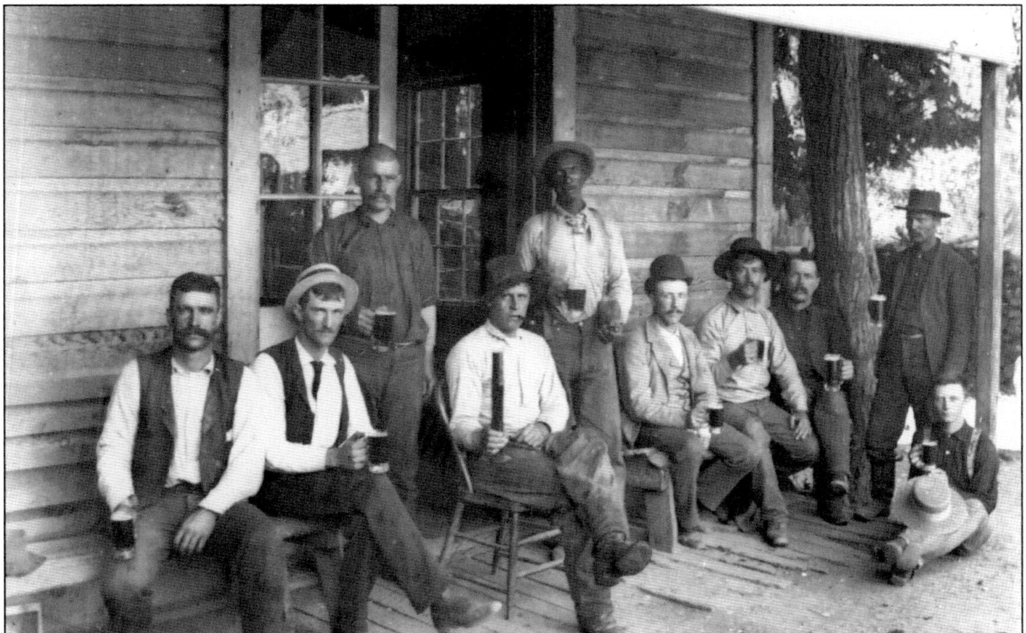

This image shows members of the Giebenhain family and employees of the Mountain Brewery sitting on the porch of the brewery enjoying the fruits of their labor. The gentleman in the middle is holding a tubular beaker, which was used with a hydrometer to measure the alcohol content of the beer as it was fermenting. (Courtesy El Dorado County Historical Museum.)

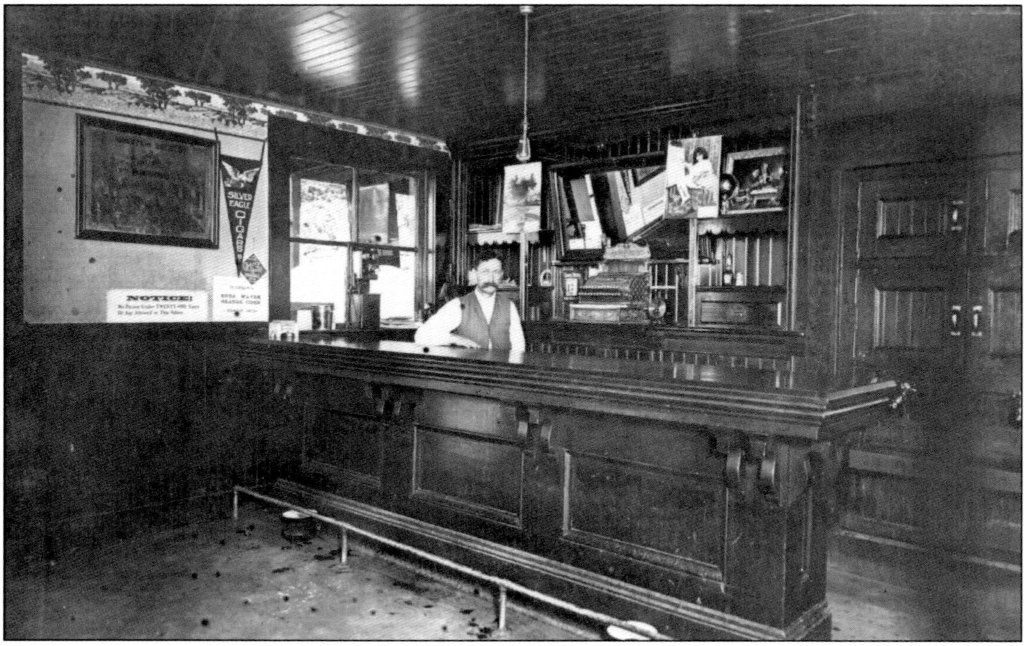

Like many breweries of the period, the Mountain Brewery housed its own saloon to dispense its products. To the right can be seen the beer taps, a Mountain Brewery tapestry on the wall to the left, and spittoons and a boot rail on the floor before the bar. (Courtesy El Dorado Historical County Museum.)

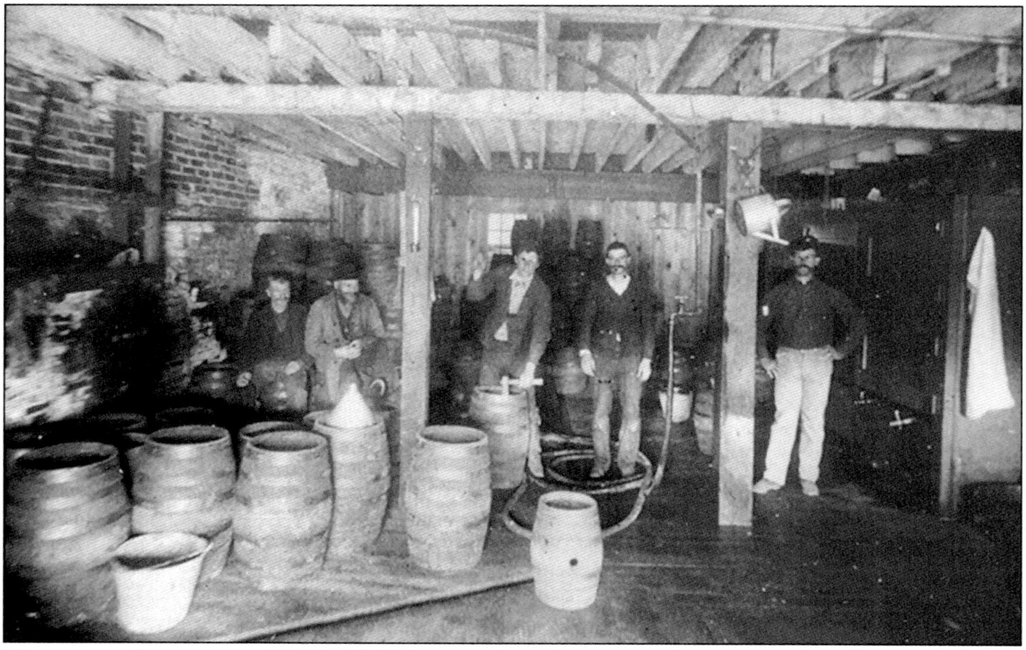

This image shows a rare view of the inside of a working 19th-century brewery. Photography was still a new technology and not widely accessible, and it was uncommon to photograph everyday work scenes. The photograph shows men at the Mountain Brewery kegging beer in the beer cellar. Note the man in the center with the mallet and wooden bung. The beer coolers are to the right. (Courtesy El Dorado County Historical Museum.)

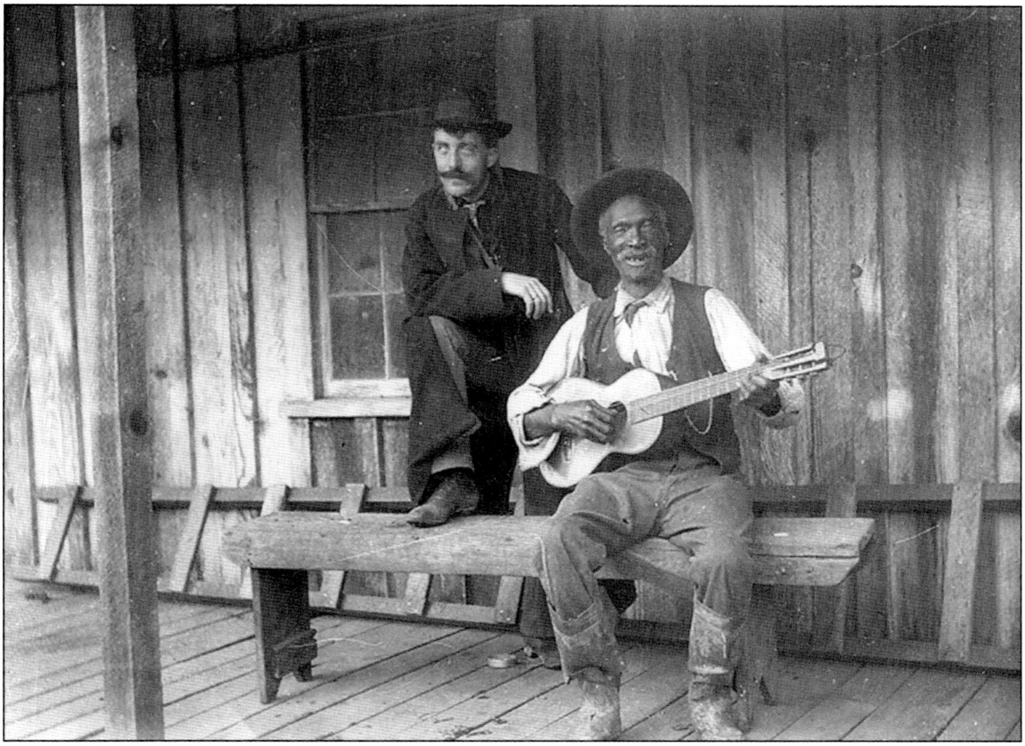

Seen here are Oscar Regg and Francis Marion Ray on the porch of Placerville's Mountain Brewery. While many breweries in the Gold Country took photographs on the front porch, often staged, few images of the working interiors of these breweries are known to exist. (Courtesy El Dorado County Historical Museum.)

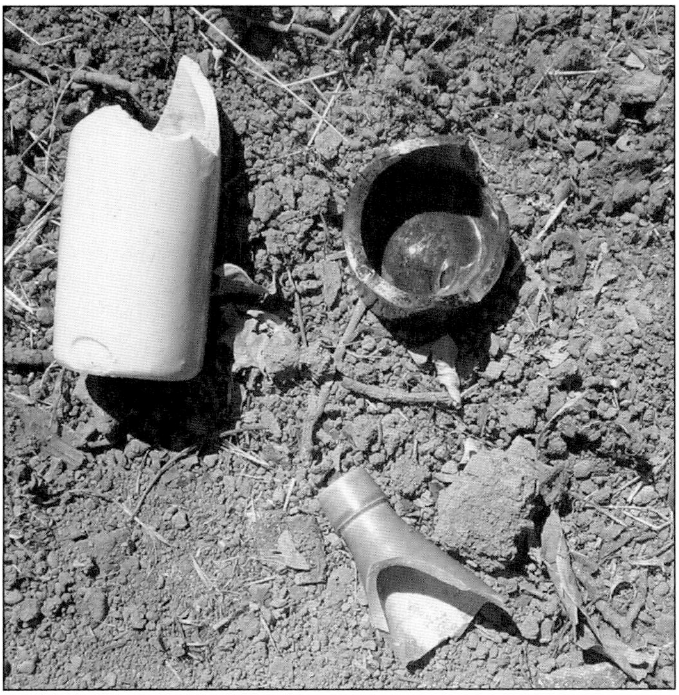

In preparation for the move of the Fausel House in 2007, archaeologists excavated the brewery foundations and area around the home. One of the earliest residential buildings in Placerville, artifacts included items associated with both the Giebenhain family's daily lives as well as the brewery. The remains of a stoneware ale bottle and the base of a dark brown glass beer bottle were just a few of the artifacts uncovered. (Courtesy authors' collection.)

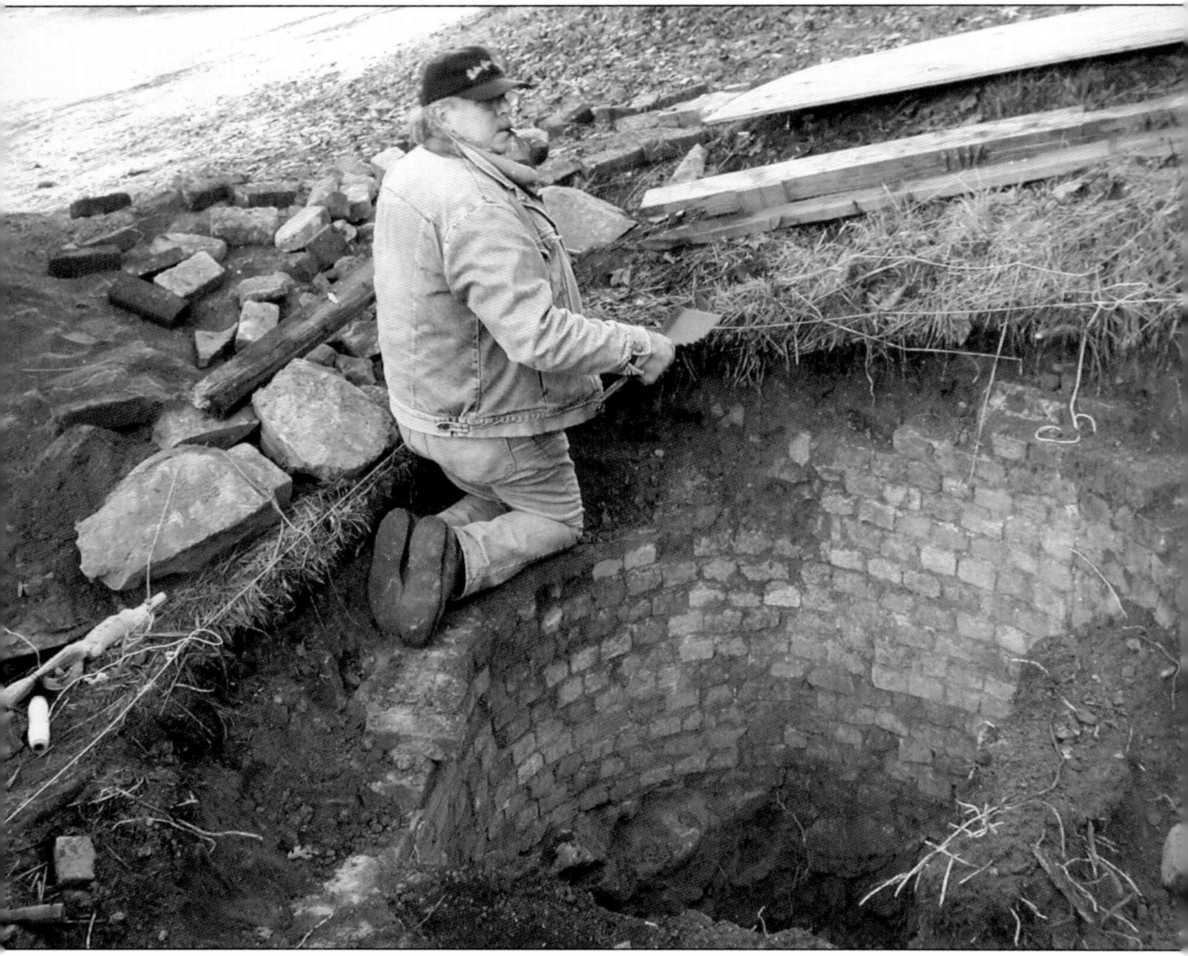

The Mountain Brewery and Fausel House were the subjects of archaeological investigation between 2004 and 2008. Identified during this process were a number of features associated with the Mountain Brewery, including the beer cellar, furnace for the brew kettle, mount for the water turbine, and well. The photograph above shows archaeologist Brad Deveraux excavating the well at the brewery. Also identified was a privy pit (outhouse) associated with the Giebenhain family home. Analysis of these artifacts and surrounding soil from the family's privy revealed the family consumed a traditional German diet, augmented by such exotics as bananas, while suffering from painful parasites, including roundworm. (Courtesy authors' collection.)

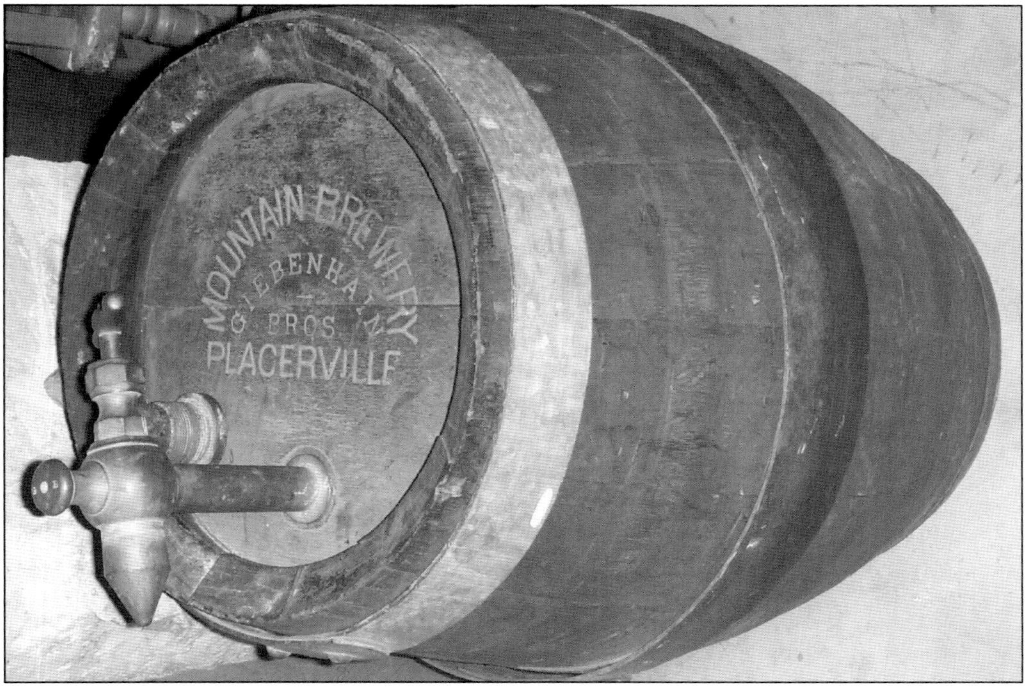

When the Mountain Brewery was closed, the family retained several of the furnishings, many of which remain in the private collections of descendants of the family. One of the few items from the brewery available to public view is this beer keg, which is on display at the El Dorado County Historical Museum. (Courtesy authors' collection.)

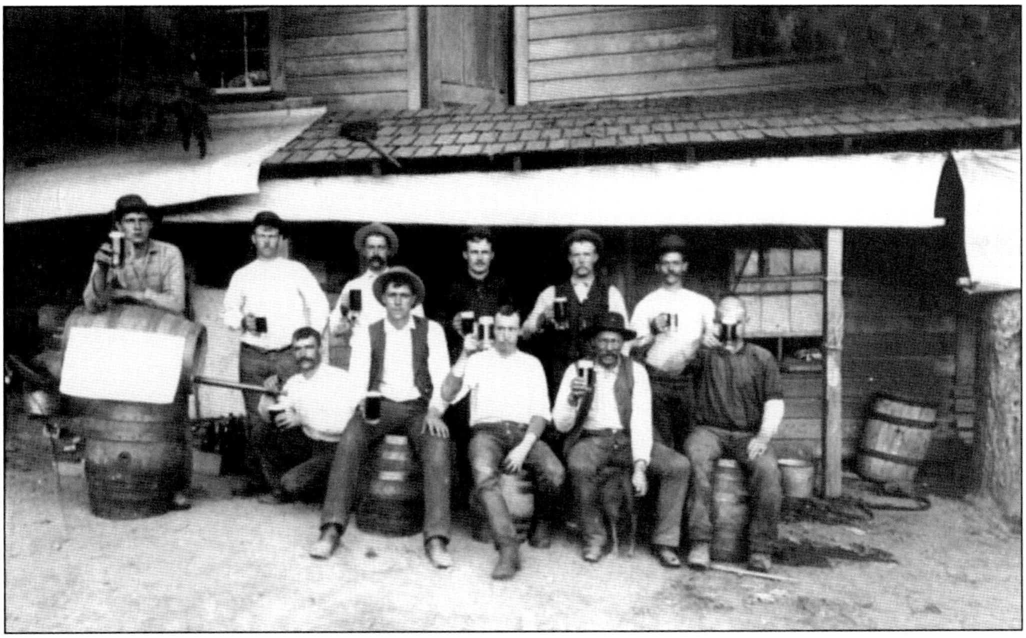

Unidentified employees of the Mountain Brewery toast the photographer around 1890–1900. The front porch of the brewery was a popular place for photographs, and in spite of the relatively abundant photographs such as this one, few photographs exist of the actual process of making beer. (Courtesy El Dorado County Historical Museum.)

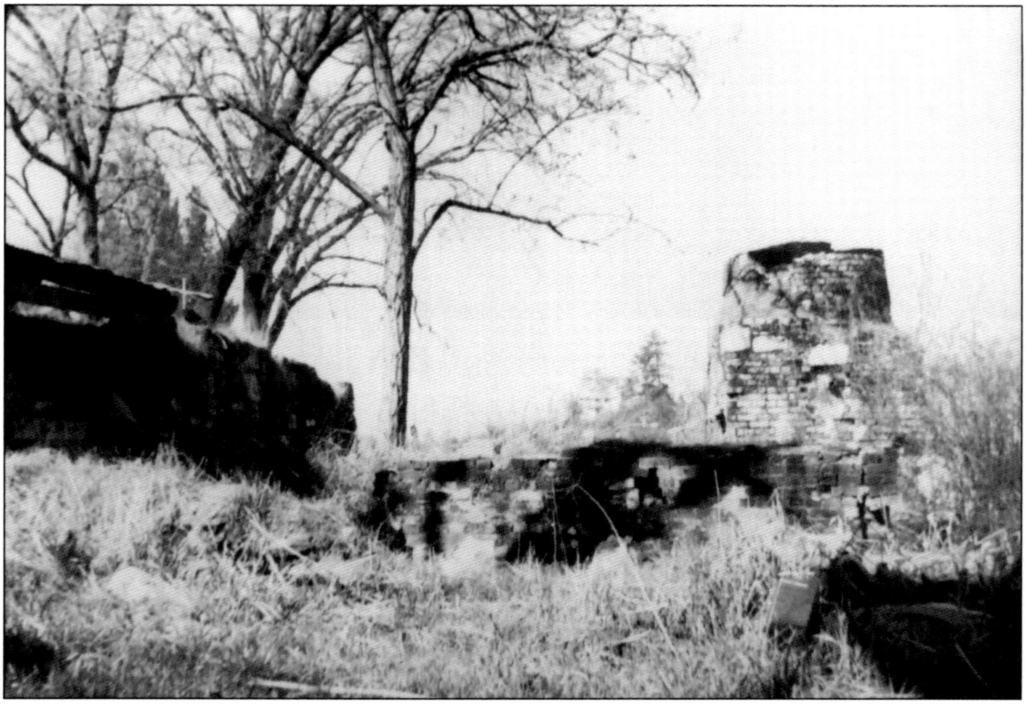

The ruins of the Giebenhain family's brewery are seen in this photograph, where only the rock walls and concrete cellar floor remain. While one of the early successful breweries, the Giebenhains were unable to survive Prohibition. (Courtesy El Dorado County Historical Museum.)

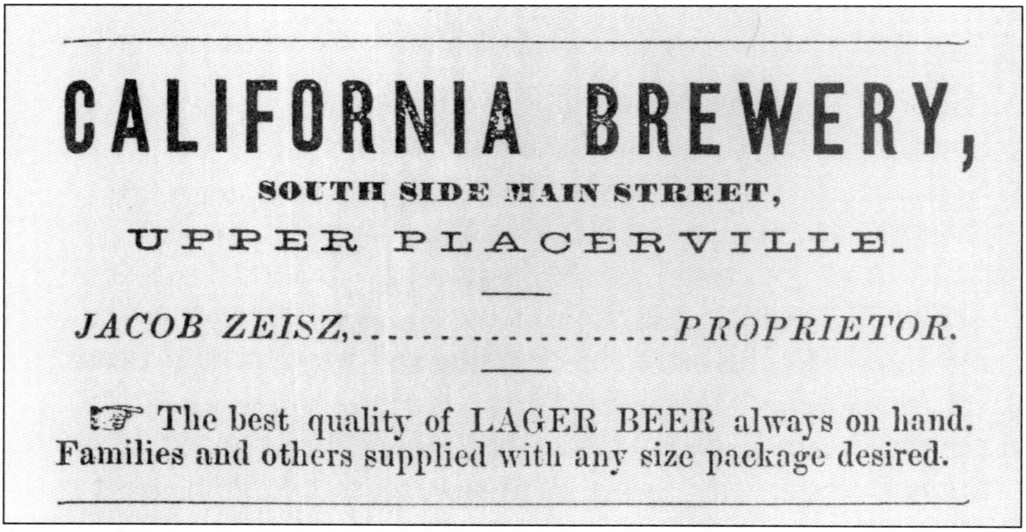

Another of Placerville's breweries, the California Brewery, was located on Main Street, as noted in this 1862 Heckendorn and Wilson's *Miners and Business Men's Directory* advertisement. Jacob Zeisz began construction of this brewery in 1859. The brewery's primary building was constructed of limestone blocks from Smith Flat and housed a saloon and beer cellar. Most of the brewery was housed in a wooden structure to the left, which produced seven barrels per brew.

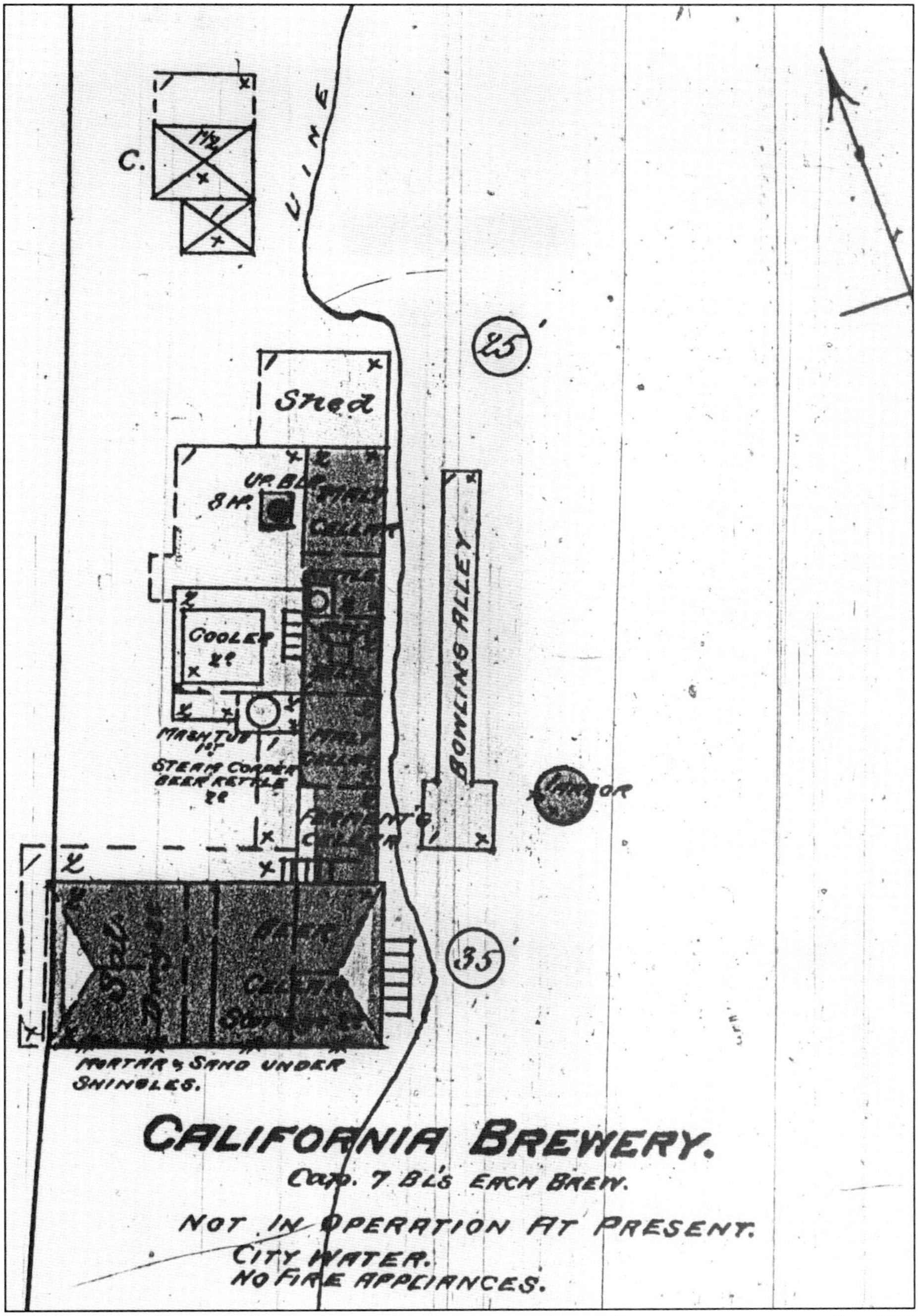

This Sanborn map provides the general layout of the California Brewery as it appeared in1891. It is atypical of most breweries of the period in that it was laid out horizontally, rather than vertically. It demonstrates an unorthodox configuration, with two malt cellars, a centrally located brew kettle and mash tub, with the fermentation cellar and storage room on the far left. Such a layout would have required substantial labor in moving malt, wort, and beer around the brewery by hand. The brewery also housed a saloon and a bowling alley. Bowling, a derivative of a medieval German game, was common at saloons serving German clientele. The map indicates the brewery was not in operation at the time.

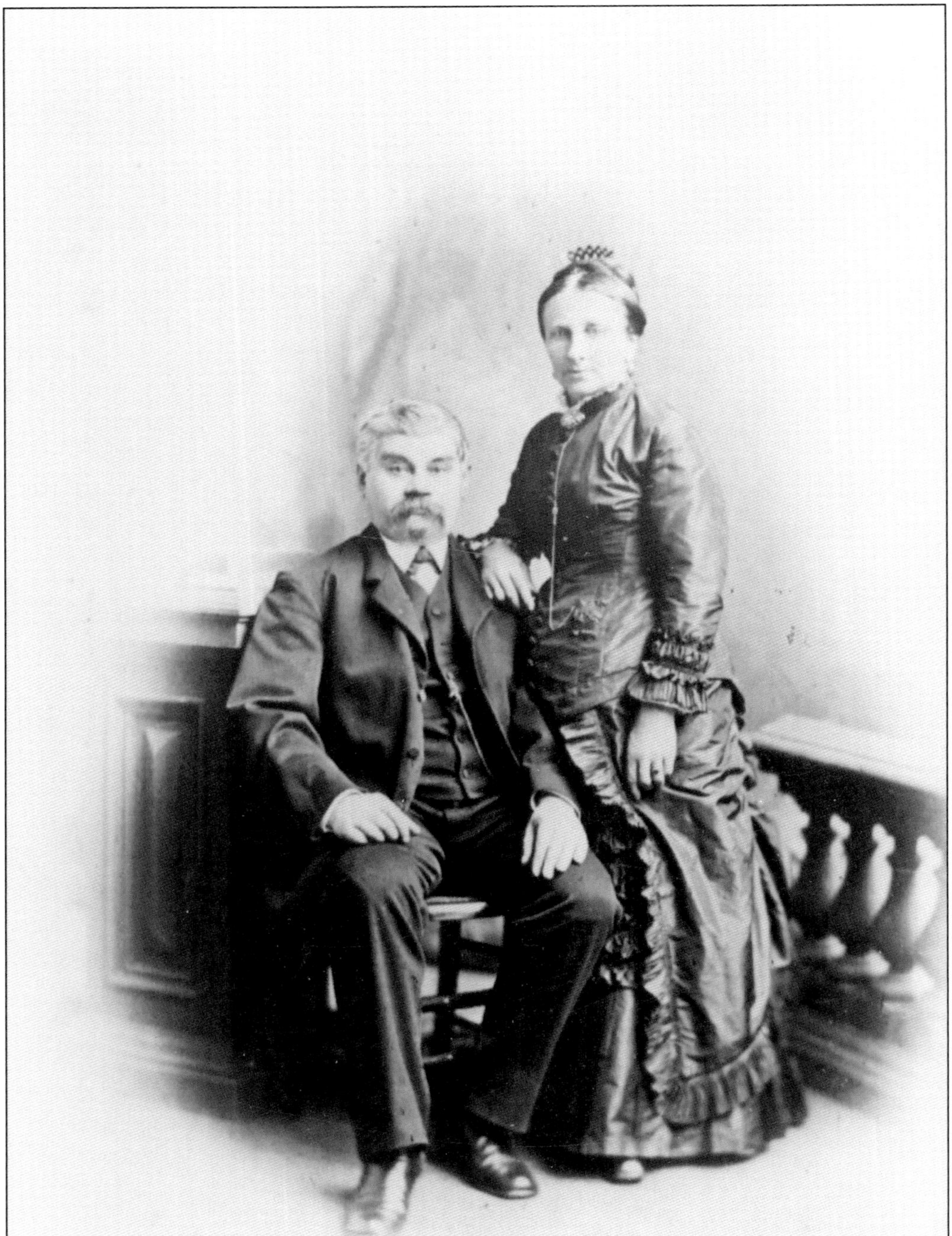

This image shows Jacob Zeisz and his wife, Dorothea. Either his life in California did not appeal to Jacob, or stronger ties pulled him home. Regardless of the reason, Jacob left his wife and family in 1884 to go back to Bavaria. He never returned. (Courtesy El Dorado County Historical Museum.)

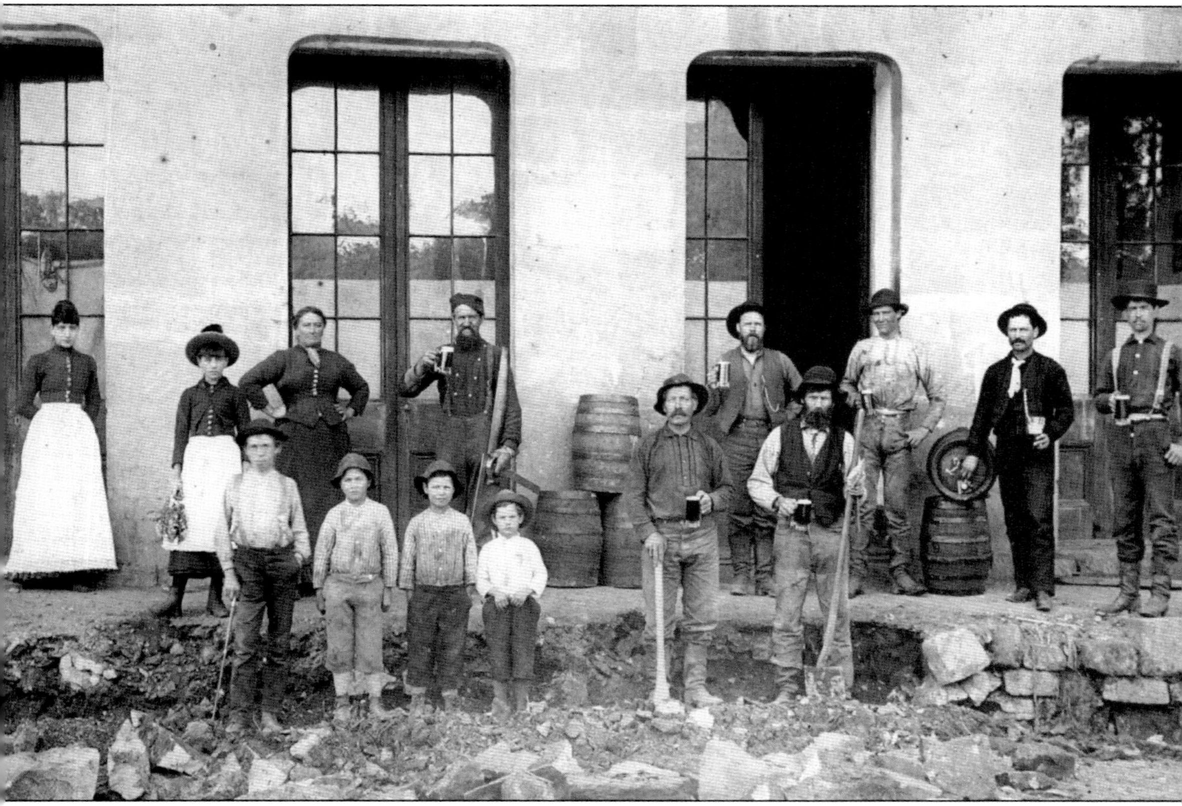

As evidenced by the rubble and workmen with hammers in hand, this view of the California Brewery apparently shows a remodel of the porch in progress. Shown on the porch are several of the Zeisz children. To the left are Eugenia and Dorothea, second from the right is George, and the youngest, Frank, is in the front row. (Courtesy El Dorado County Historical Museum.)

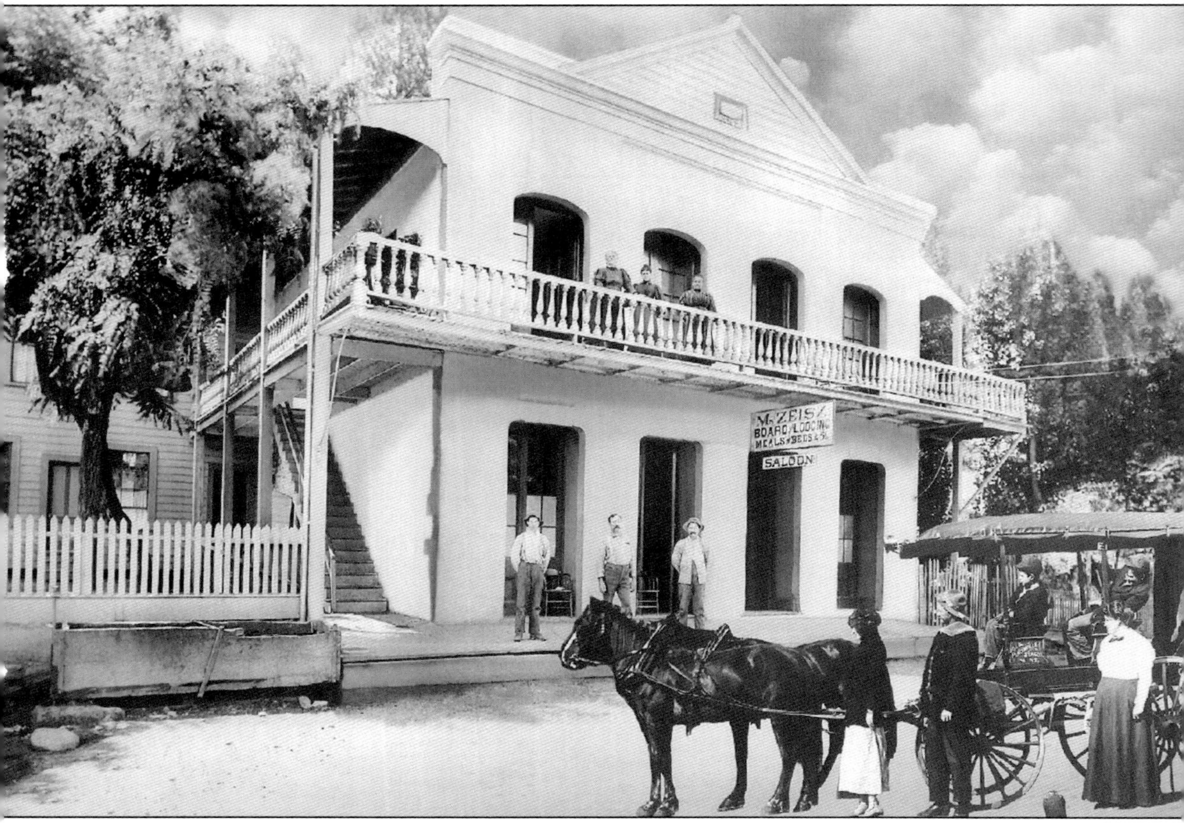

In 1884, Jacob Zeisz returned to Bavaria, leaving his wife, Dorothea, and their 10 children to run the California Brewery. To help support her family, Dorothea opened up part of the brewery as a boardinghouse. This image above shows the brewery during this period; the sign over the door notes: "Mrs. Zeisz Boarding and Lodging Meals and Beds." Close examination reveals that the customers and wagon have been pasted into the image. (Courtesy El Dorado County Historical Museum.)

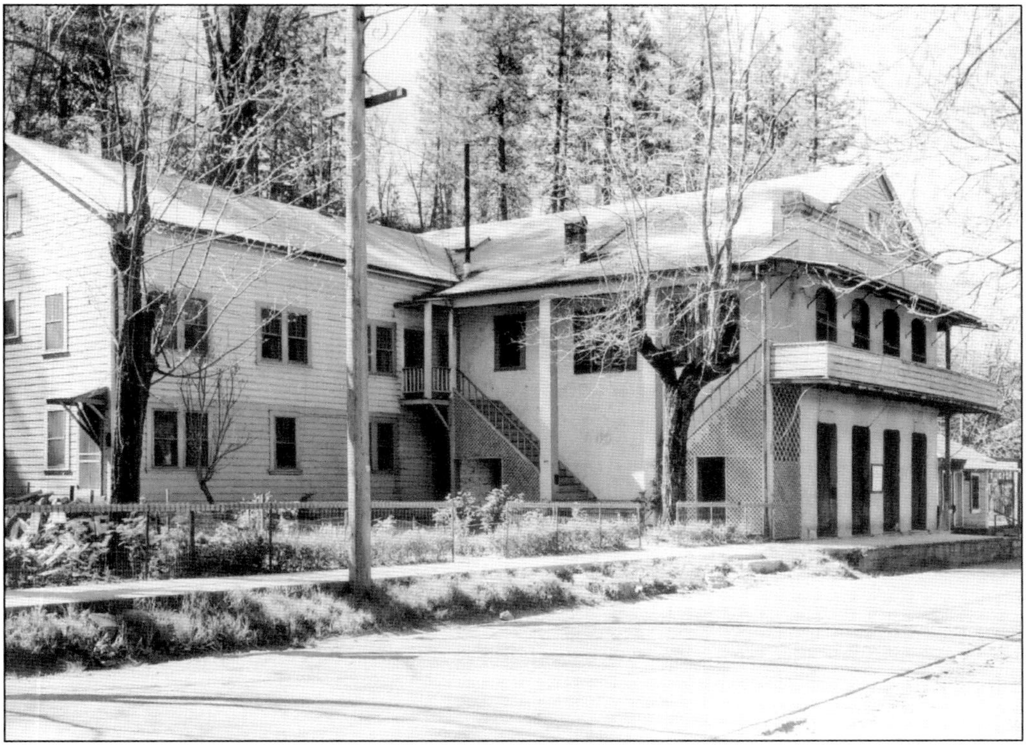

Above is the Zeisz's brewery as it was in 1934. While the building survived Prohibition, the brewery operations did not. The image below shows one of the last vestiges of the California Brewery. It is the same sign seen on the building in 1884 (Page 88). It is now housed at the El Dorado County Historical Museum. (Both, courtesy authors' collection.)

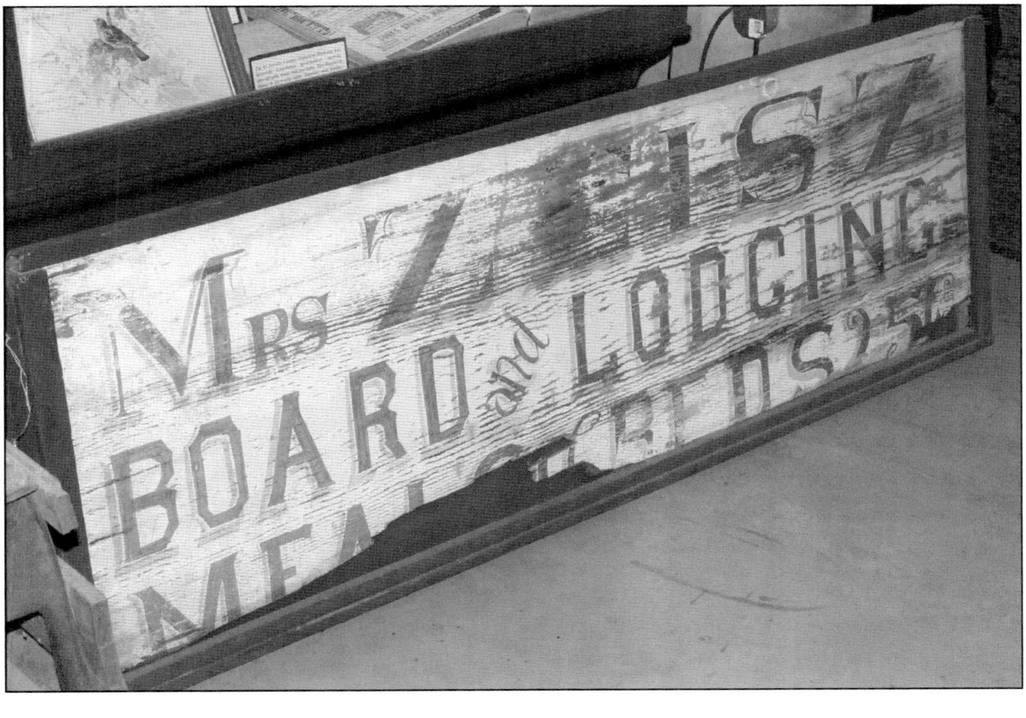

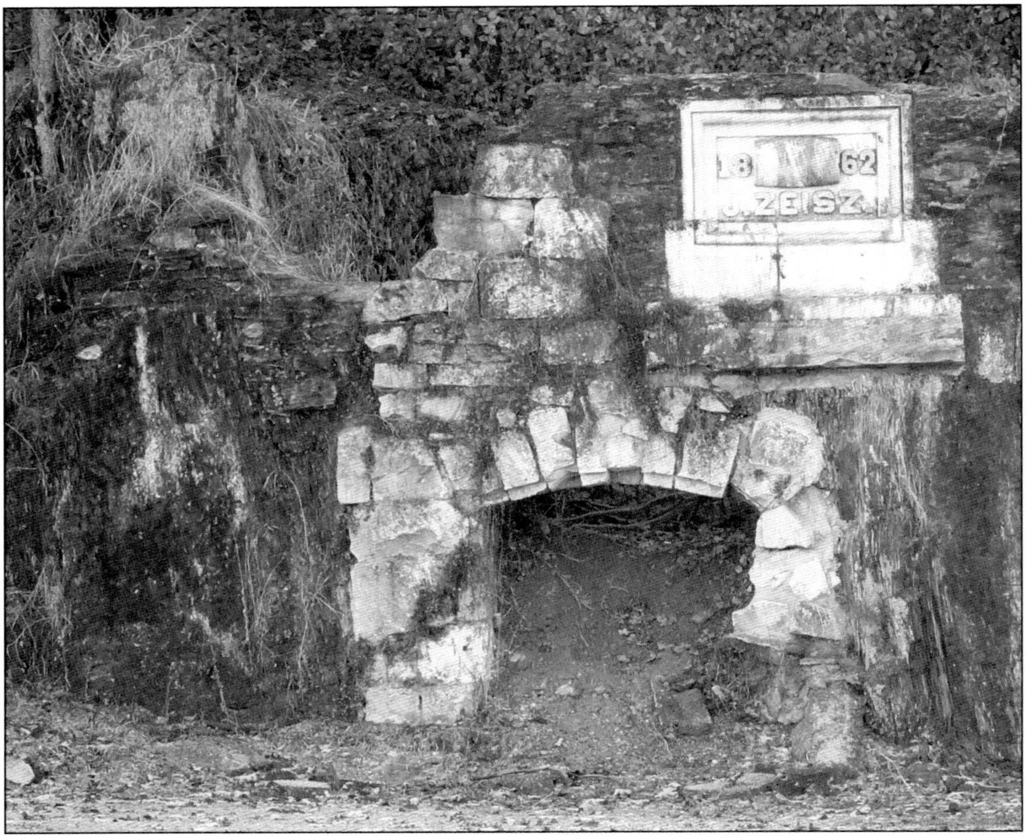

Today, all that remains at the site of the California Brewery is an overgrown and rather mysterious archaeological site, with crumbling walls, arches, and stairs that lead nowhere. The marble plaque can be found on Main Street in Placerville. The site of this once-proud brewery is now a parking lot. (Courtesy authors' collection.)

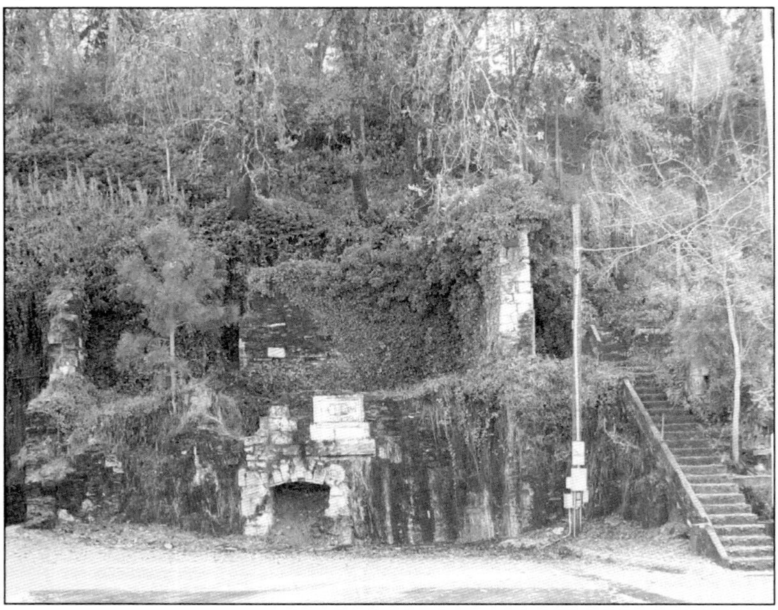

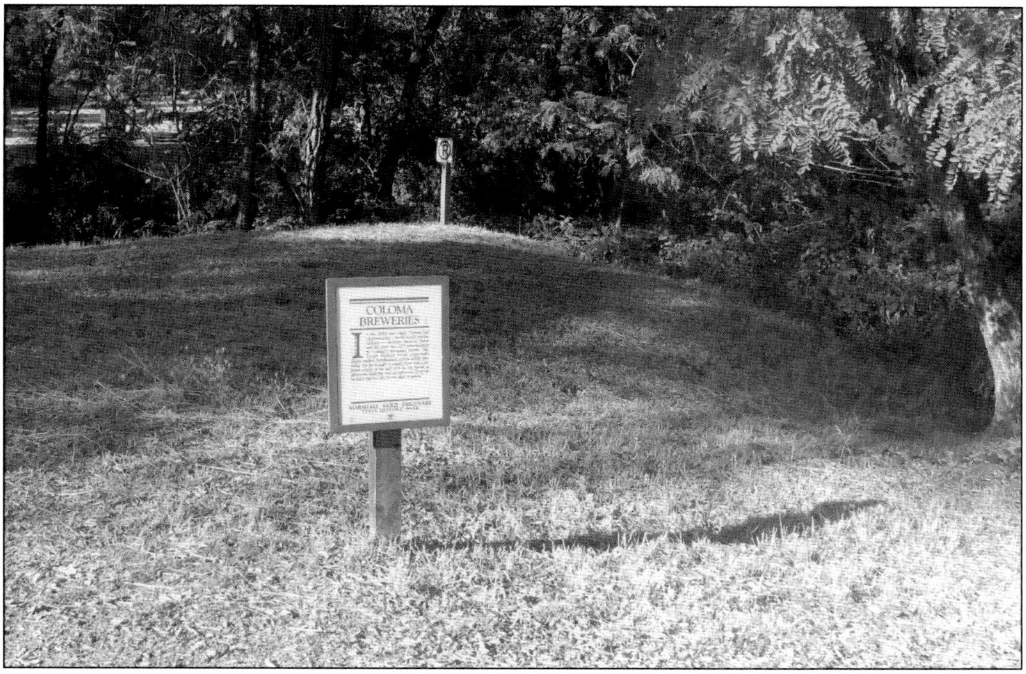

This plaque marks the location of the Coloma Brewery, established early in Coloma's history. The sign reads: "In the 1850s and 1860s Coloma had two breweries, the El Dorado and the Coloma, between Brewery Street and the river." An 1853 advertisement in Coloma's newspaper stated: "Mr. Joseph Wellman would respectfully inform traders, hotelkeepers and the public generally, that he is ready to supply them a superior article of ale and cider by the barrel or otherwise, from his own manufactory. Draft ale on hand for sale, by the glass or gallon." (Photograph by S. Whittle, courtesy HMdb.org.)

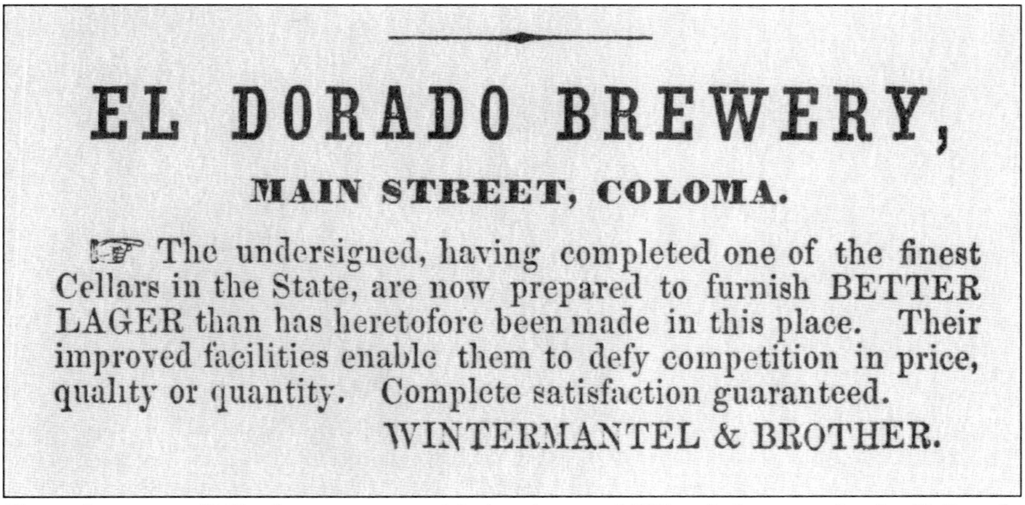

Shown here is an 1862 advertisement in Heckendorn and Wilson's directory for the El Dorado Brewery, operated by Wintermantel & Brother. This brewery was also located on Brewery Street and was the direct competition with the Coloma Brewery. By the time the 1880 McKenny business directory was printed, no brewers or breweries were listed in Coloma. In contrast to brewing, the town had a strong emphasis on winemaking, with 10 individuals of what was a relatively small population listed as operating a winery or vineyards, or winemaking.

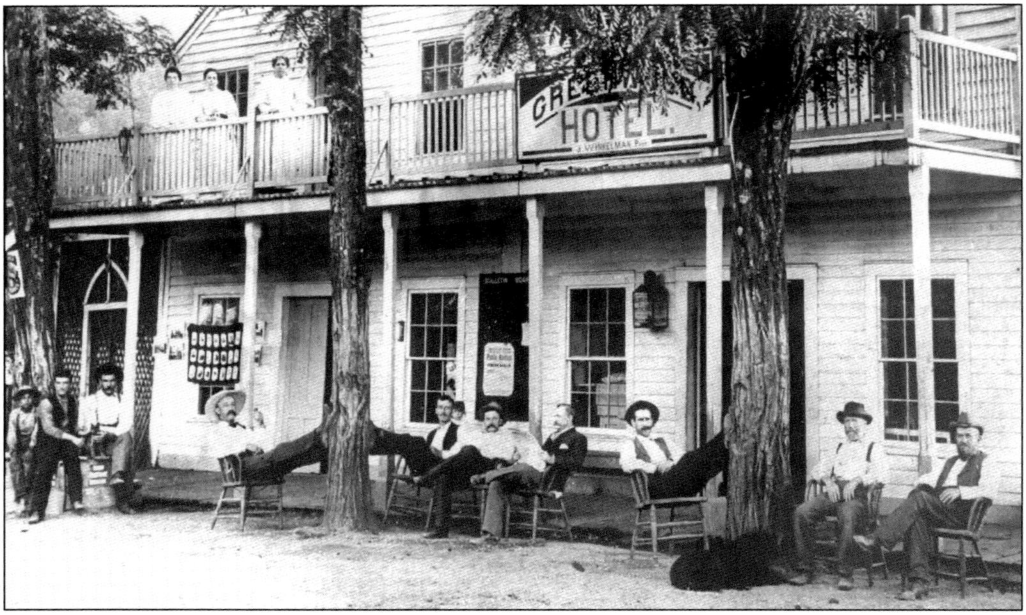

In the 1850s, Jacob Winkelman opened a brewery in the booming community of Greenwood. In 1856, he built a hotel adjacent to his brewery; it became known as "The Brewery Hotel" (shown above). Around 1861, the brewery was either moved to Placerville or sold to another local party, and from then the hotel was known as "Winkelman's Hotel." Jacob died in 1879, and his son, Jacob Jr., took over the business. The building was finally torn down in the early 1930s. (Courtesy El Dorado County Historical Museum.)

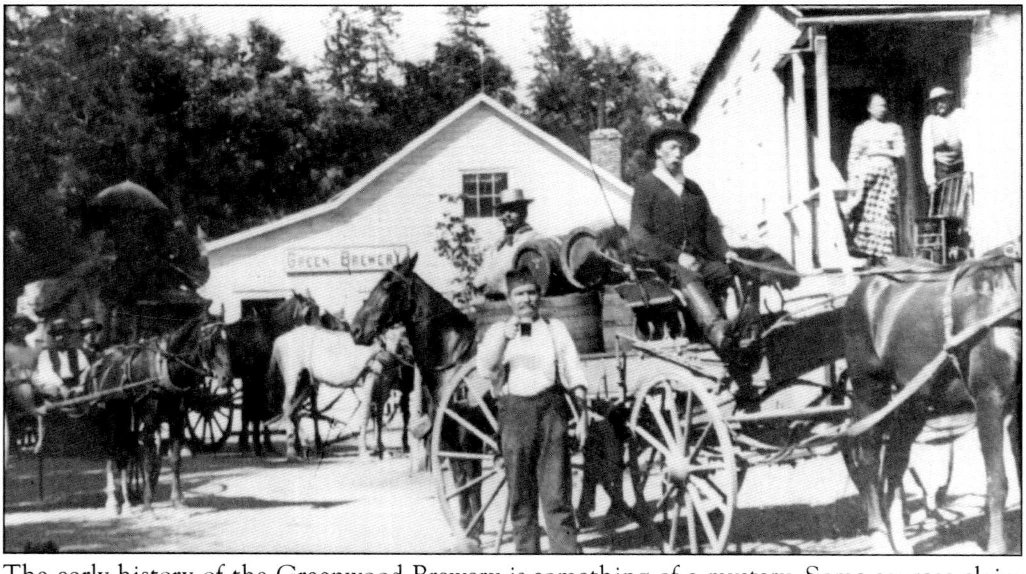

The early history of the Greenwood Brewery is something of a mystery. Some sources claim its beginnings were in the old Winkelman Brewery. Other sources claim it was started by A.J. Schwab and Herman Haiz. In 1885, Schwab sold his share in the brewery to Haiz, who in turn sold the brewery to its brewer, John Mulbach. Originally from Baden, Germany, Mulbach arrived in Greenwood about 1872. Under Mulbach's management, the brewery became quite popular, as he greeted passersby to "Come in and have a snootful," receiving a schooner of beer for a nickel. (Courtesy El Dorado County Historical Museum.)

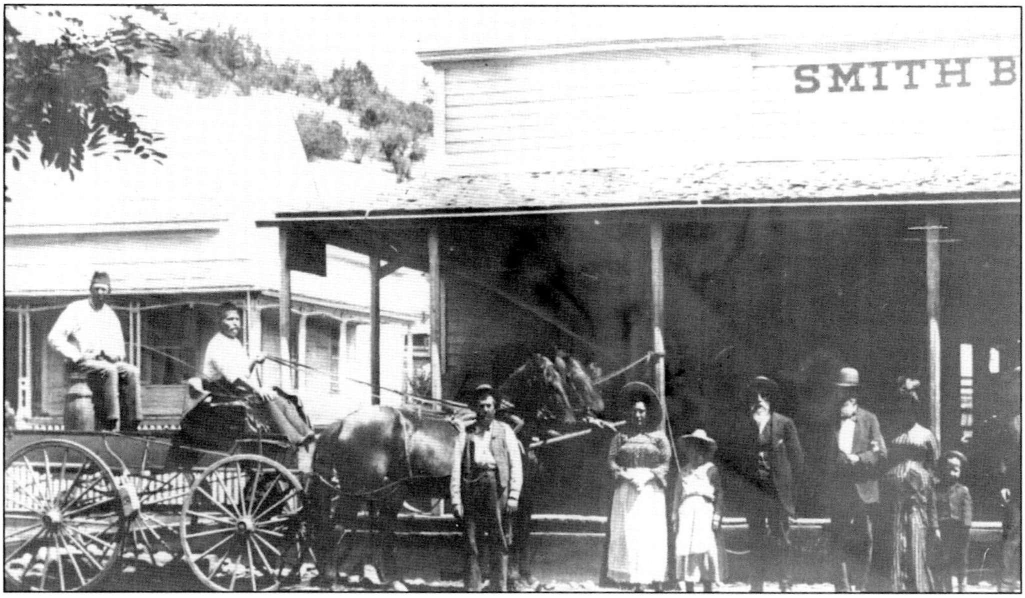

This image shows the Greenwood Brewery delivery wagon in front of the Thomas Smith home and Smith Brothers Store in Greenwood. From left to right are Thomas Stephenson, John Mulbach (at the reins of his wagon), John Smith, Mrs. Smith, Myrtle Smith, F.R.J. Dixon, Mr. Watson, Mrs. S.J. Kaiser, Dave Shepherd, and P.G. Miller (barely visible). As the Greenwood Brewery grew in popularity, Mulbach used his trusty wagon to deliver beer further afield to Georgetown, Garden Valley, and Kelsy. (Courtesy El Dorado County Historical Museum.)

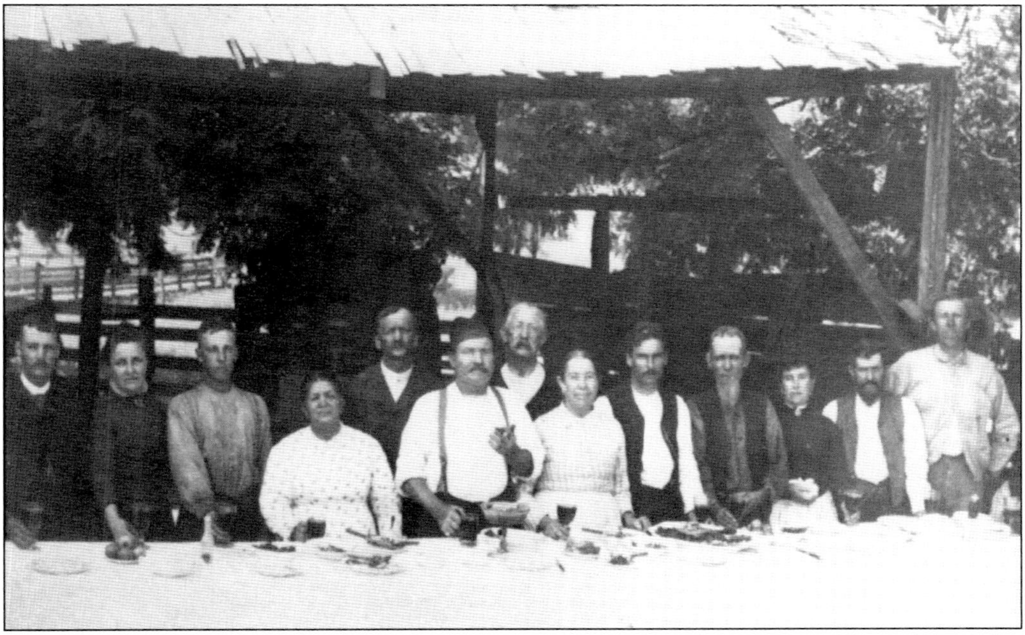

John Mulbach was apparently a very jovial fellow, throwing his wife, Nancy, and himself birthday parties two or three times a year. At the party are, from left to right, Fred Dixon, Florence Nagler, Jack Dixon, Mrs. Canfield (Nancy Mulbach's sister), Mr. Miller, John Mulbach, Mr. Belty, Nancy Mulbach, Henry Deleat, L. Leetts, Mrs. John Smith, John Smith, and Tom Stevenson. (Courtesy El Dorado County Historical Museum.)

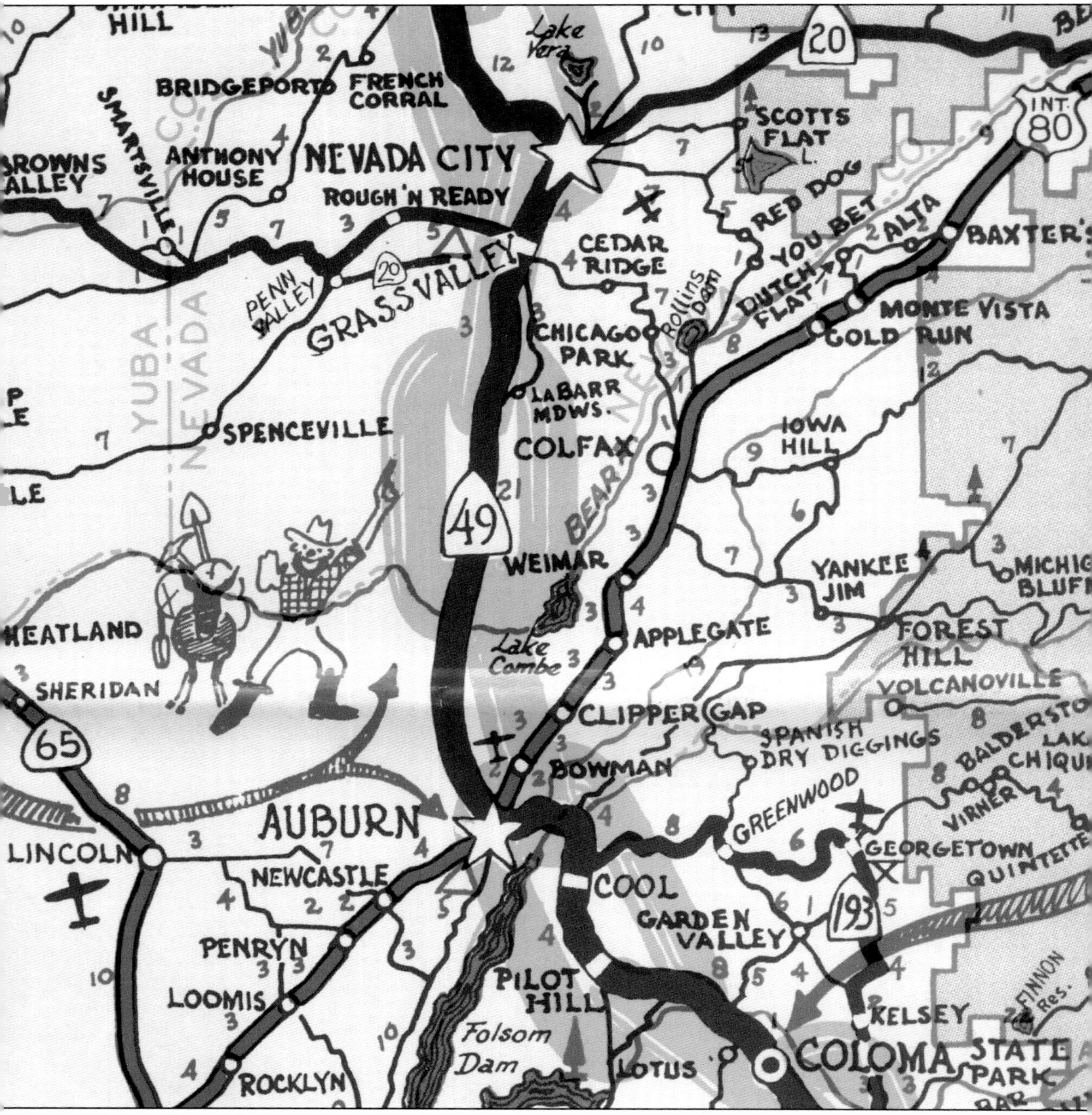

From El Dorado County, one passes into Placer County, coming first to the county seat of Auburn, just north of the North Fork of the American River. Here, one would have found the aptly named Auburn Brewery and a family tragedy surrounding it. (Courtesy Golden Chain Council.)

Five

Placer County
Continent within a County

"Beer in small quantities said to make one fat; in large quantities it is known to make one lean."

—*Placer Herald*, June 2, 1898

Placer County found its feet in the earliest days of the Gold Rush, and Auburn, the largest community in the county, was established in 1849. The first residents were two "Chilenos" panning in Rich Ravine. Others quickly arrived, and Auburn exploded into a full-fledged town. Other communities with names like Michigan Bluff, Deadwood, Yankee Jims, and Dutch Flat followed, and along with them came breweries. Gold mining was to remain important for years, but an equally important industry was soon heralded: transportation.

The region had long been an important transportation corridor, but Placer County's role grew when the transcontinental railroad was started in 1861. It did not take long for the Central Pacific Railroad to go from Sacramento to Auburn, forever altering the face of the community. With the completion of the railroad, Placer County was a hub tied into the nation's transportation system and economy. In the 20th century, the county's importance was only enhanced with the construction of the modern highway system. This included one of the largest and longest roads in the country, Interstate 80, connecting the region to shipping ports in San Francisco Bay and industrial centers in the east.

At the time of writing, the price of gold is at an all time high, driving renewed interest in the area's untapped mineral resources, and possible renewal in the county's mining operations. Today, Placer County is home to at least one regional brewery, providing locals with that familiar refreshing elixir.

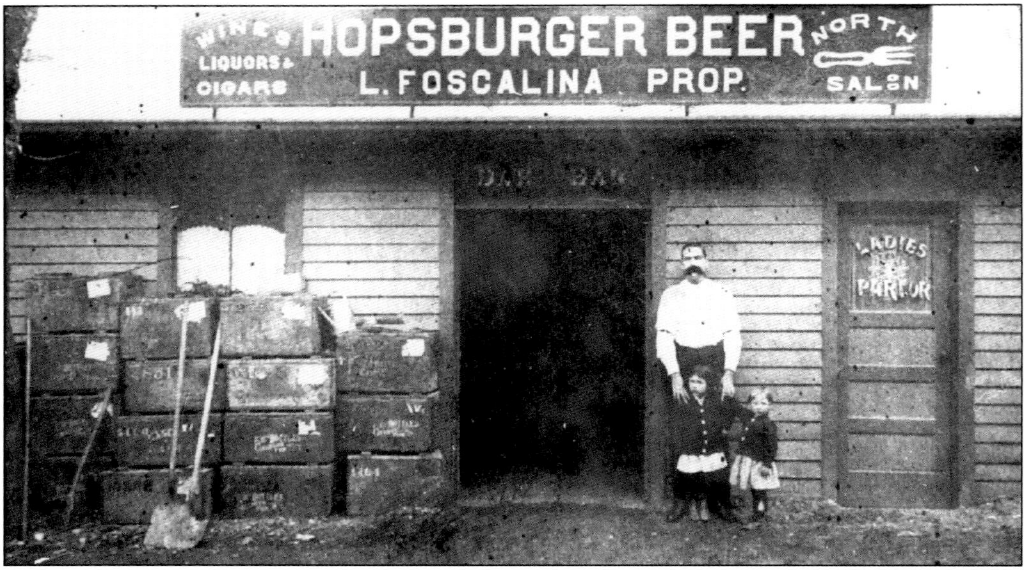

Like many breweries of the period, Auburn's Hopsberger Brewery had its own saloon attached to the business. This relatively early image provides a plethora of minute details regarding breweries and saloons of this period, including the notice of a separate entrance and parlor for ladies. It was considered uncouth for "proper" women to associate with men in saloons. Following a European tradition, some saloons provided a separate entrance and saloon for women, usually devoid of gambling and other vices. The clever North Fork Saloon moniker referred to its location near the North Fork of the American River. (Courtesy Placer County Museums.)

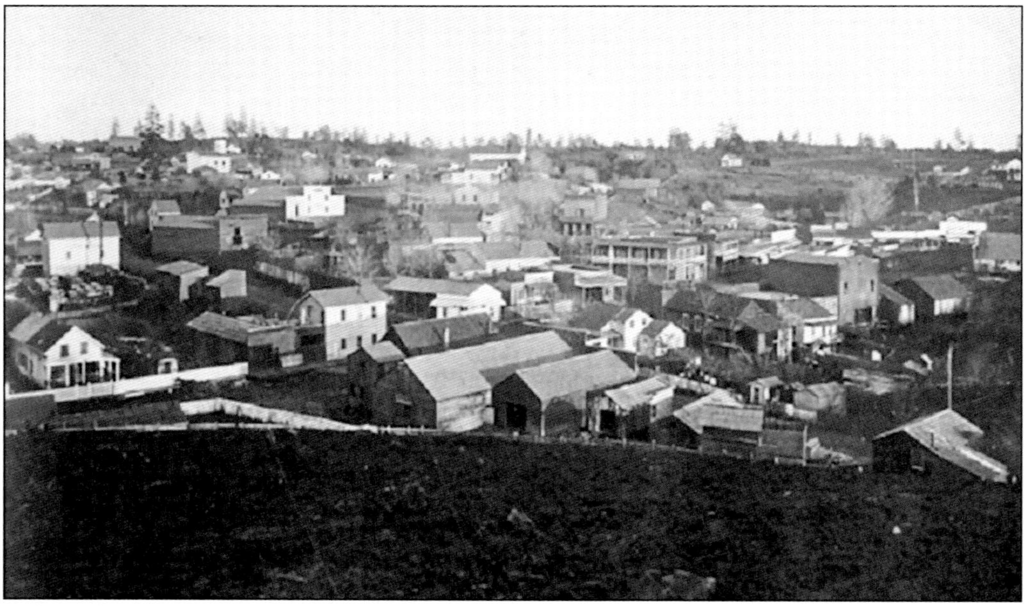

Auburn, like many early placer mining communities in the Motherlode, was a devastated landscape in terms of modern standards. Trees were cut down to fuel everything from cookstoves to large boilers. What was not cut and burned was washed down the rivers in the process of placer mining. In a barren landscape such as this, one might spend his whole day's earnings washing the dirt down with a cold beer. Brewers could make a good living selling their libations. (Courtesy Placer County Museums.)

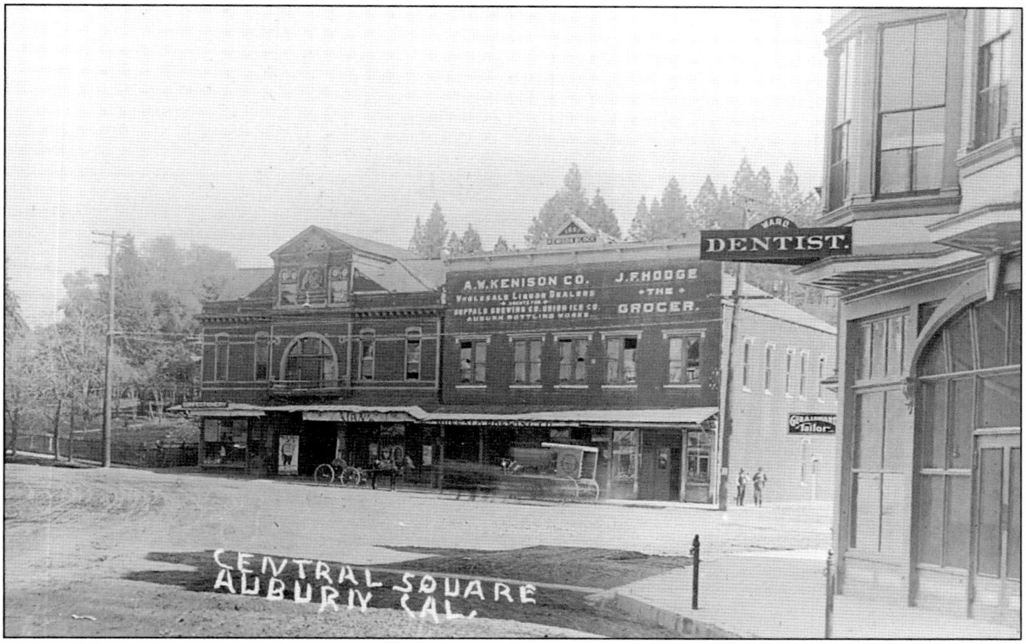

Central Square in Auburn was the heart of the business district. To the center right of this image is A.W. Kensison's establishment, which provided Buffalo Beer, bottled sodas, and ice. Another view of this center can be seen later in the chapter. (Courtesy Placer County Museums.)

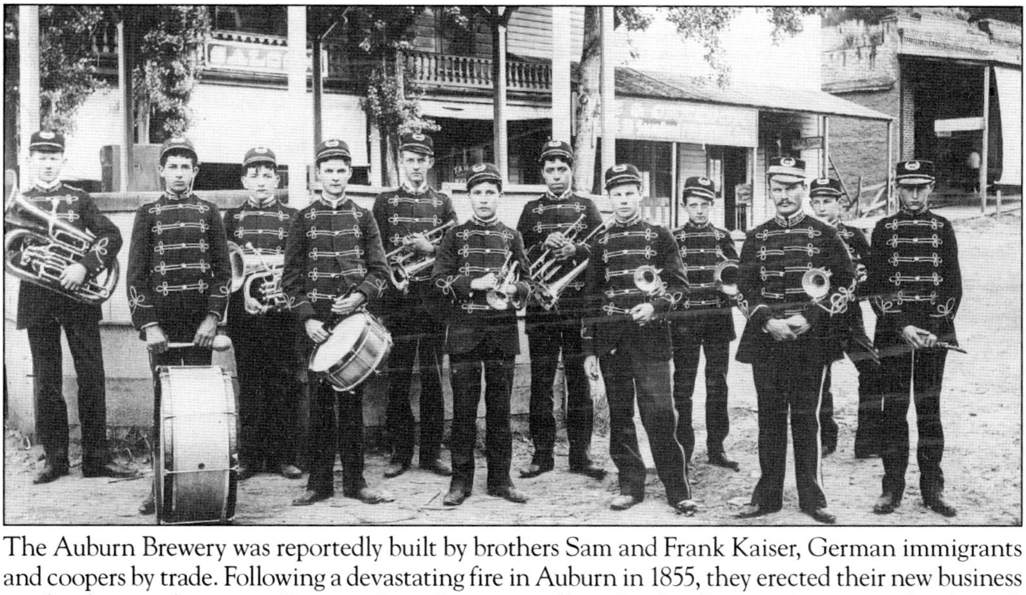

The Auburn Brewery was reportedly built by brothers Sam and Frank Kaiser, German immigrants and coopers by trade. Following a devastating fire in Auburn in 1855, they erected their new business at what became known as "Brewery Lane," a name still used today. Brewery Lane was also the red-light district. As coopers, they made their own kegs, and when filled, they supposedly rolled them down the hill to the front doors of the patrons in "Lower Town." The Kaisers eventually sold the brewery. Samuel moved to Placerville, while Frank stayed on in Auburn, as an integral part of the German community there. In the 1895 image above are two of Frank Kaiser's children, along with their bandmates. Shown from left to right are (first row) Fred Kaiser, Alec Monroe, Charles Rice, Bill Johnson, Harry Branch, and Reuben Jesky; (second row) George Johnson, Ed Lozano, Amiel Mundt, Herman Kaiser, Vic Johnson, and Ed Forester. (Courtesy Placer County Museums.)

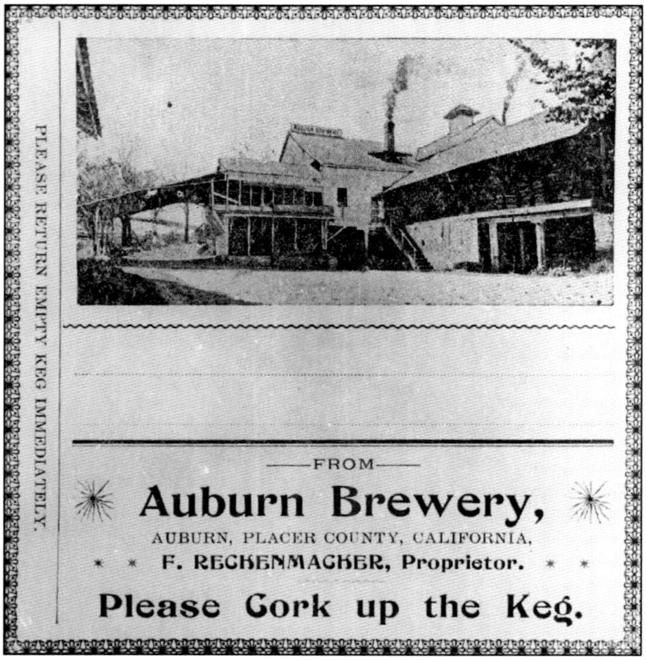

Following the Kaisers' sale of the Auburn Brewery, the chain of ownership is less than clear. In 1868, the brewery was purchased by Frank Lux. About this time, the brewery began bottling beer, rather than just selling it in kegs. It was later owned by Julius Weber and Jake Roll. Weber then ran the brewery for several years as a sole proprietor. This image shows an original keg label for the Auburn Brewery after 1895, when Ferdinand Rechenmacher was the proprietor. The label pictures the brewery at its prime. Kegs were marked with the brewery's name so they could be returned and refilled. (Courtesy Placer County Museums.)

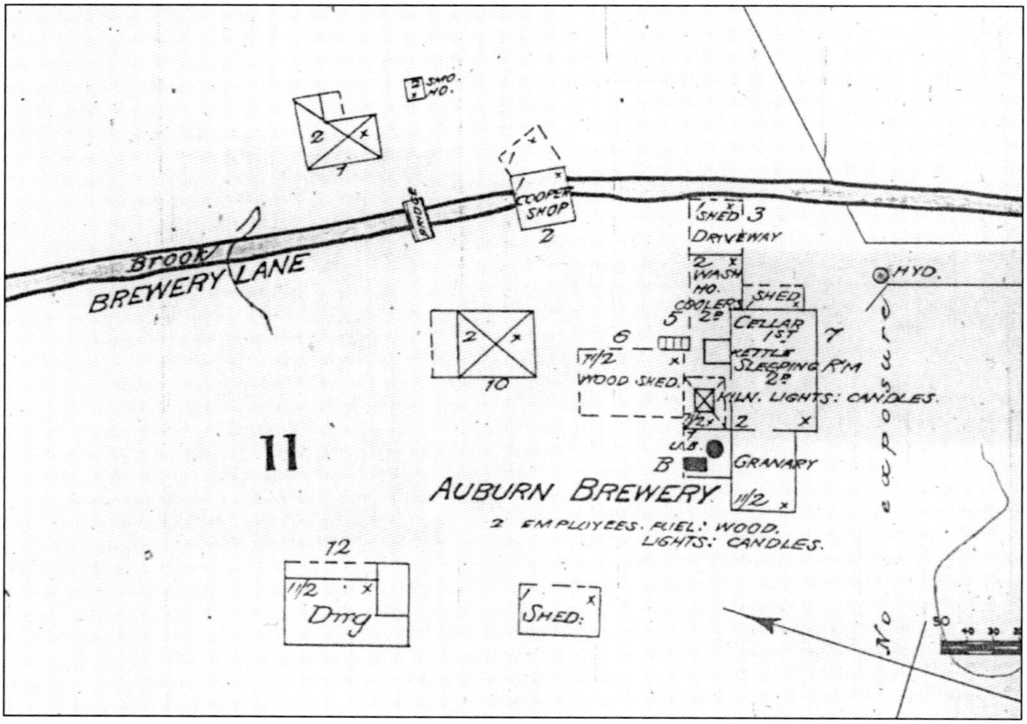

This Sanborn map shows how the Auburn Brewery was configured in 1891. It notes a malt kiln, brew kettle, wash house, granary, and cellar. Cordwood was used for the brew kettle and kiln. The fourth floor of this large brick and wood structure was for drying the malt sprouted in the basement. The brew kettle was set on a brick stove outside, under a covered porch. Although this brewery did not have a saloon, it reportedly had a stein room, where one could get a mug of beer. Water for brewing was drawn from a natural spring on site and the town reservoir.

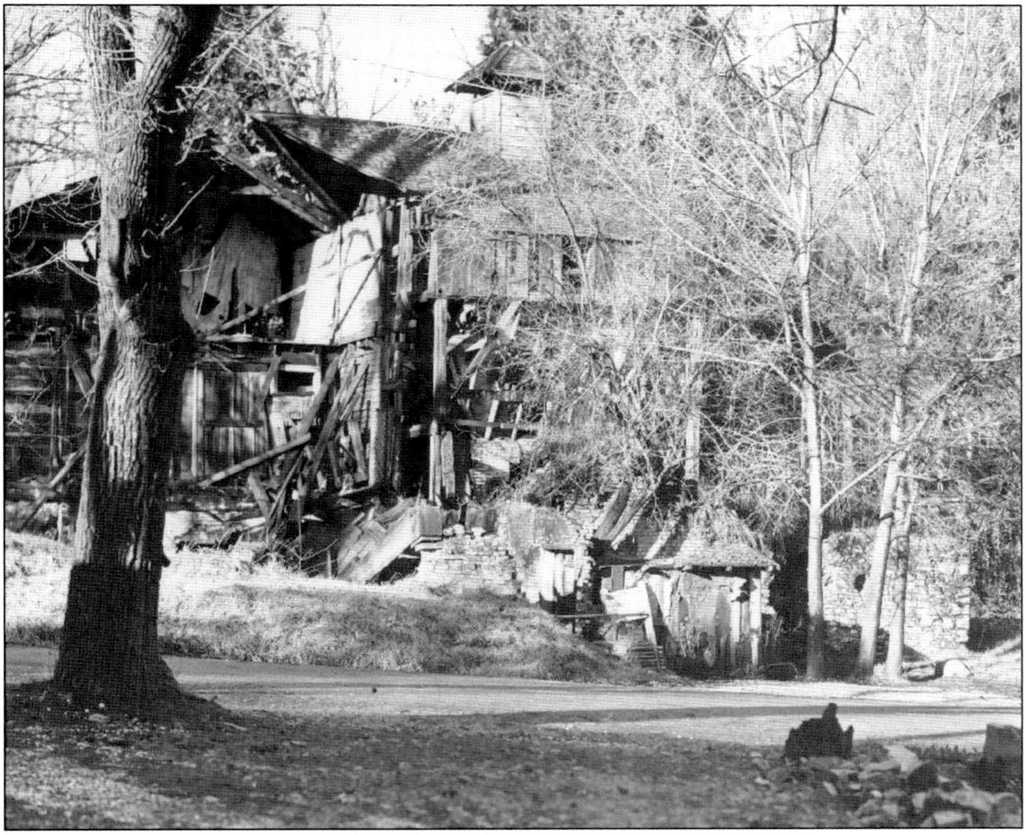

Ferdinand Rechenmacher and his family lived adjacent to the Auburn Brewery for 15 years. He won two world prizes for his steam beer. A detailed description of the brewery was given by his daughter Lillian Rechenmacher, who recalled swimming in the copper vats. Ferdinand closed the Auburn Brewery in 1908. From there he moved to Truckee, where he operated the Truckee Brewery until his death in 1910. These two photographs show the ruins of the Auburn Brewery around 1959. (Both, courtesy Placer County Museums.)

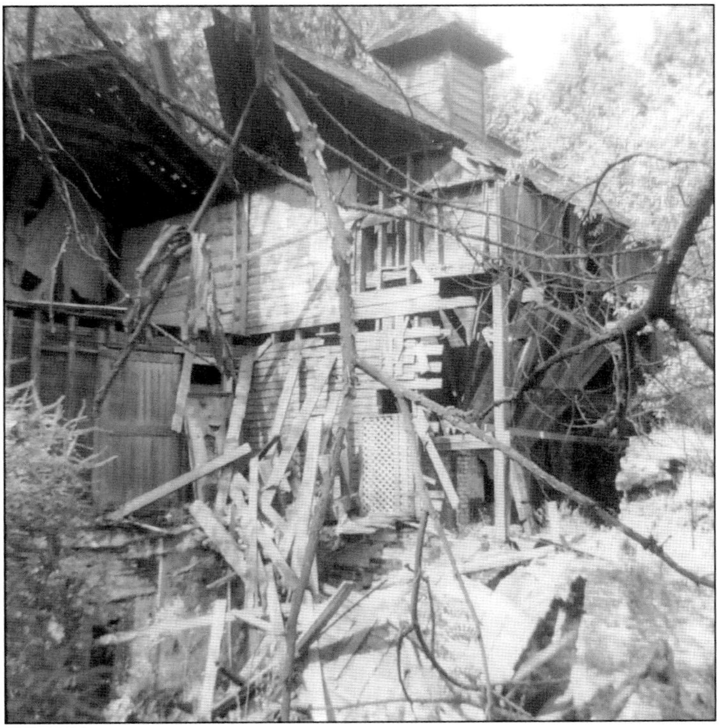

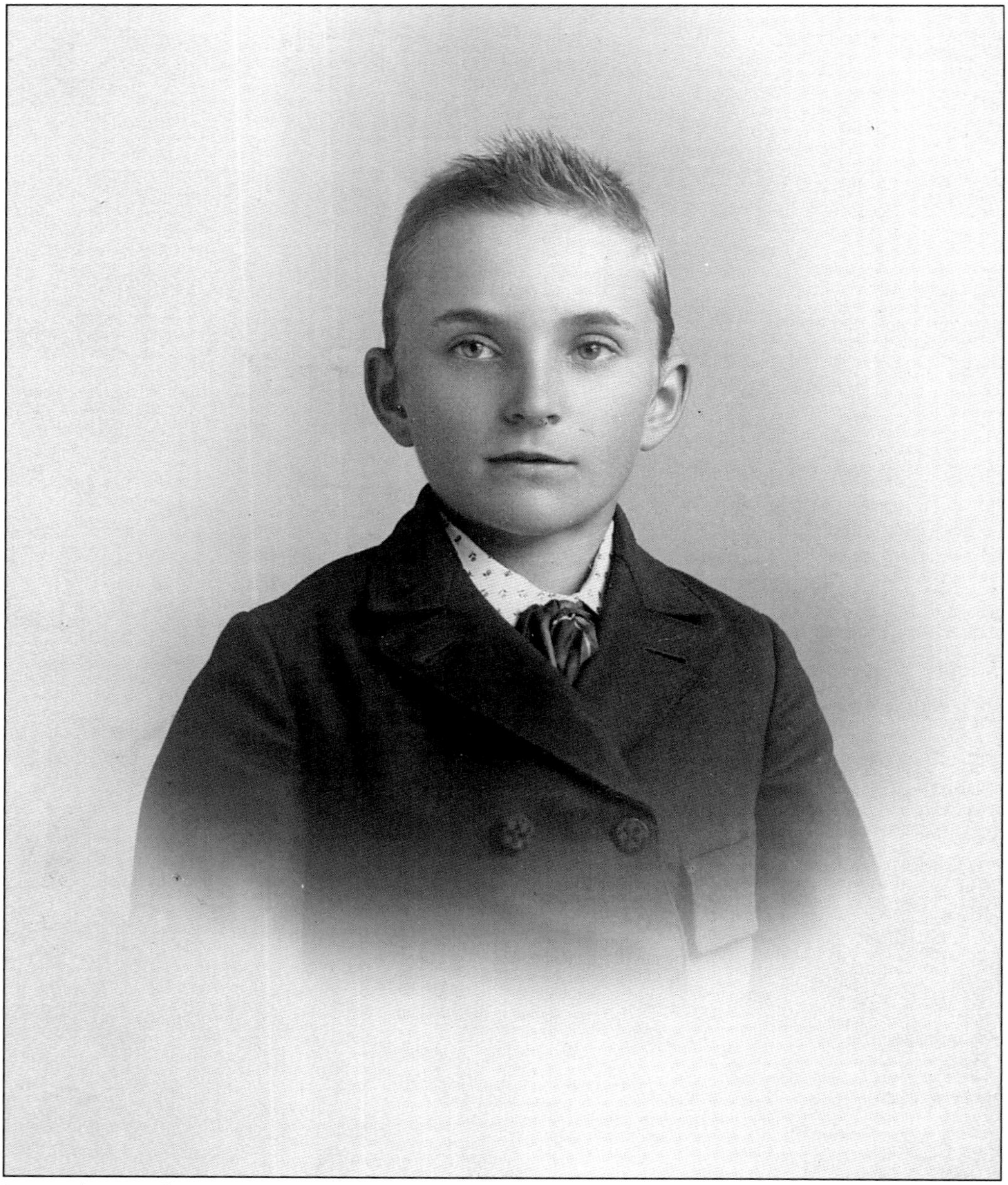

In a sad turn of events, the Weber family came to a tragic end. A few years after the sale of the brewery to Ferdinand Rechenmacher, Julius Weber's son, Adolph, went on a violent rampage. He robbed the Placer County Bank at gunpoint, having boldly—or stupidly—walked down the street with his robbery mask on. He got away with $6,335. His father learned the crime had been perpetrated by his son, resulting in a high-spirited verbal altercation. That evening, Adolph shot his father while Julius was bathing, shooting his mother as she telephoned for help. He then shot his sister and beat his mentally handicapped younger brother unconscious, setting the house on fire to cover up his crime. The undated image above shows the culprit, Adolph Weber, as a boy. He was only 19 when he committed the crimes. (Courtesy Placer County Museums.)

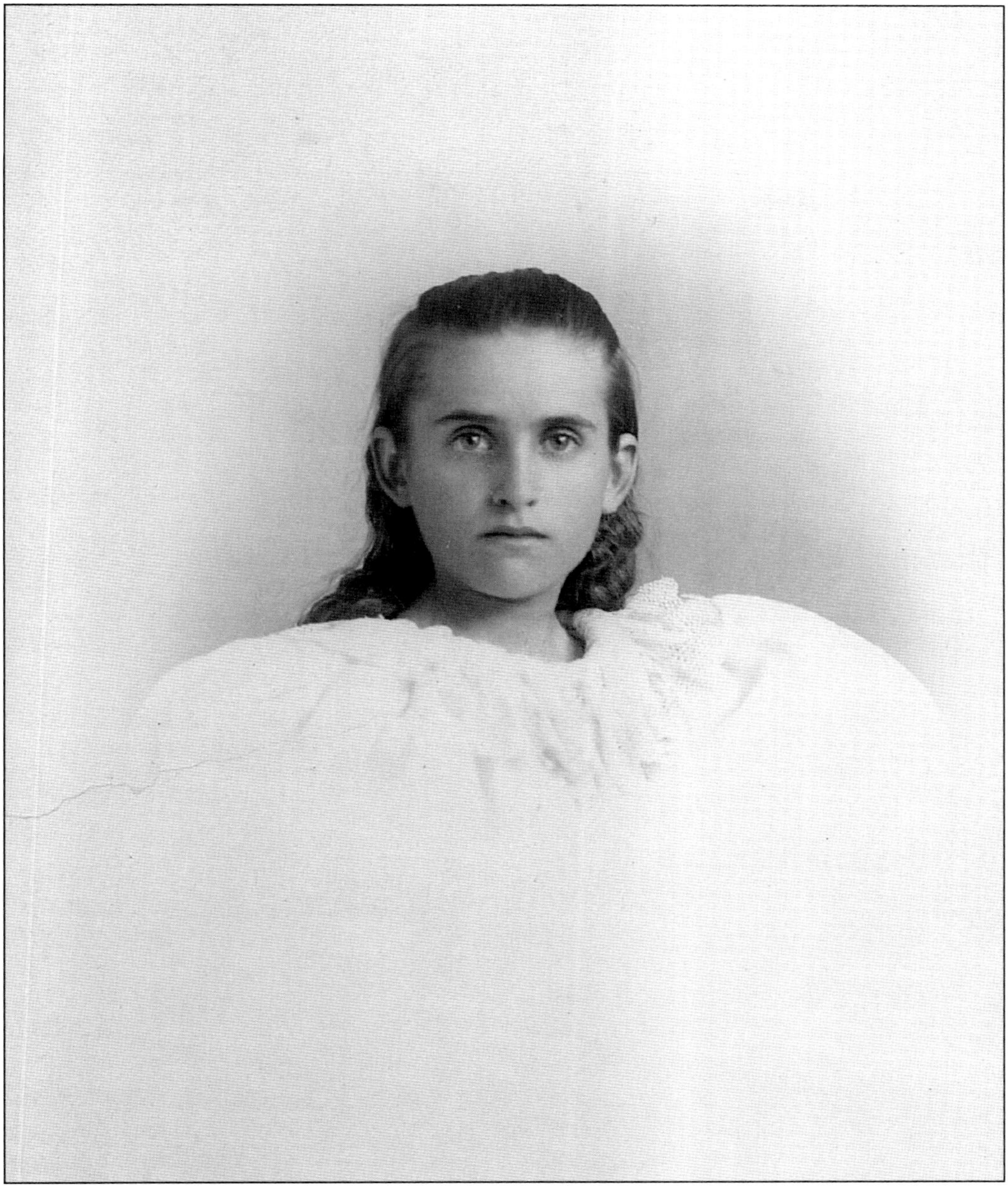

This image is of Bertha Weber, who was murdered by her brother, Adolph. He shot her while she was practicing piano. In an attempt to conceal his crimes, Adolph set the home on fire. Things did not go as planned, and the bodies of his family were discovered. Nonplussed, he invited a group of folks out for ice cream while his home still smoldered. The day's events were witnessed by the Rechenmacher family, neighbors and family friends of the Webers. After a lengthy trial, Adolph was found guilty and hanged. (Courtesy Placer County Museums.)

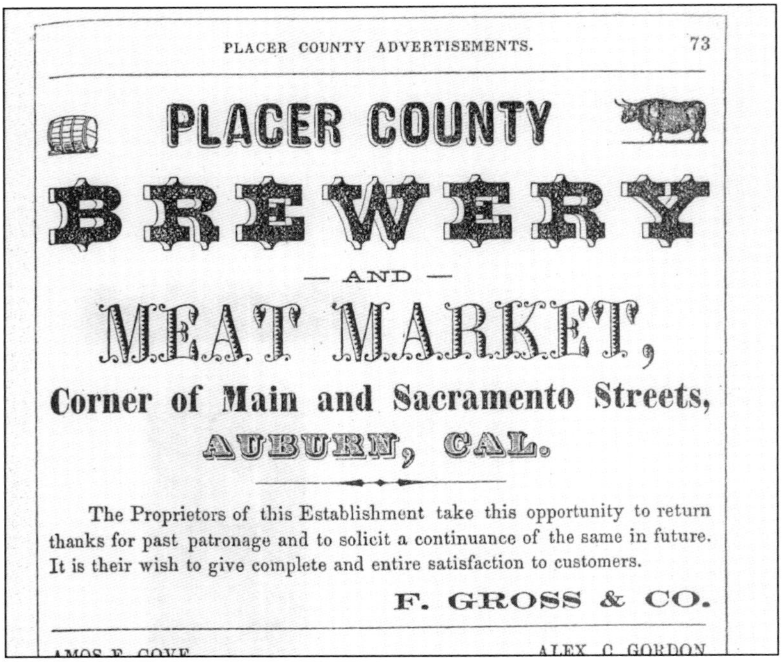

PLACER COUNTY ADVERTISEMENTS. 73

PLACER COUNTY

BREWERY

— AND —

MEAT MARKET,

Corner of Main and Sacramento Streets,

AUBURN, CAL.

The Proprietors of this Establishment take this opportunity to return thanks for past patronage and to solicit a continuance of the same in future. It is their wish to give complete and entire satisfaction to customers.

F. GROSS & CO.

Some sources indicate that Fred Gross was owner of the Auburn Brewery from 1874 to 1880. However, this advertisement from an 1861 business directory indicates he may have had another brewery as well. (Courtesy Placer County Museums.)

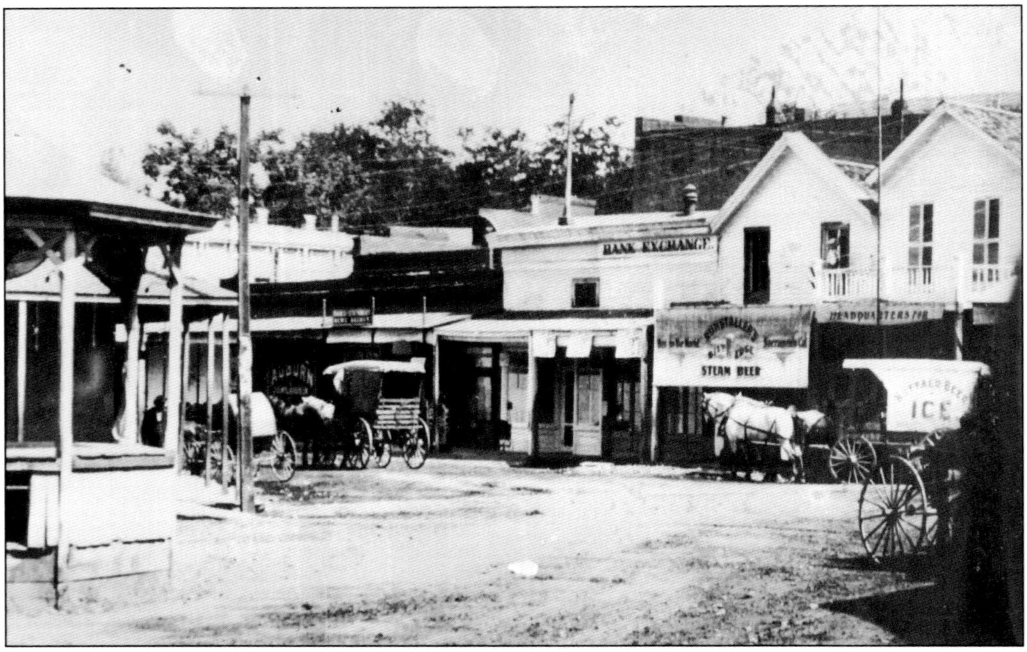

This image along Auburn's Main Street in the 1890s shows a saloon advertising Ruhstaller's "Gilt Edge" steam beer. In front of the bar is the competition, where a two-horse team stands with a Buffalo Beer delivery wagon. Ruhstaller's and Buffalo Brewing Co., regional breweries from Sacramento, both produced steam beer. (Courtesy Placer County Museums.)

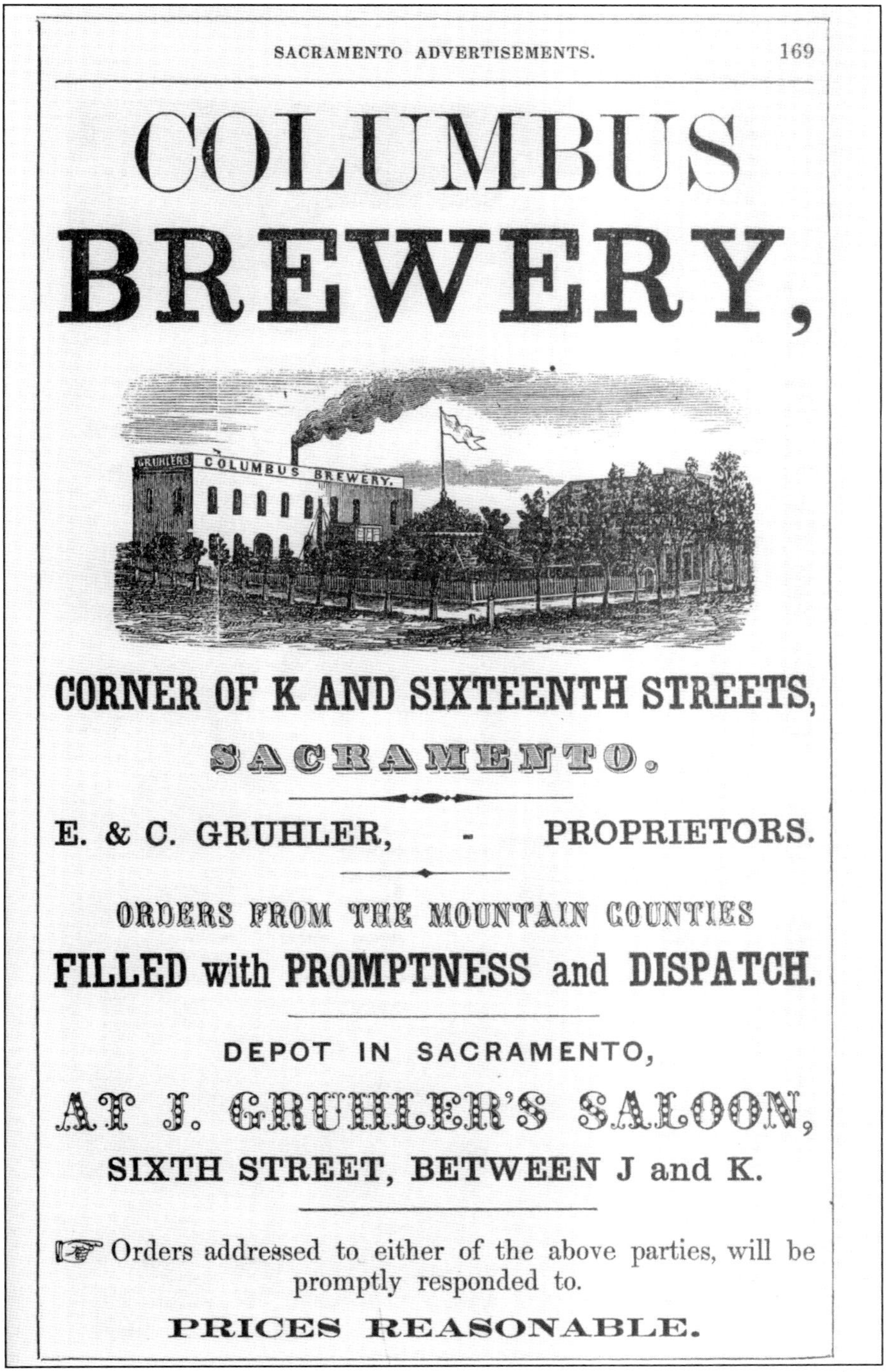

SACRAMENTO ADVERTISEMENTS. 169

COLUMBUS

BREWERY,

CORNER OF K AND SIXTEENTH STREETS,

SACRAMENTO.

E. & C. GRUHLER, - PROPRIETORS.

ORDERS FROM THE MOUNTAIN COUNTIES

FILLED with PROMPTNESS and DISPATCH.

DEPOT IN SACRAMENTO,

AT J. GRUHLER'S SALOON,

SIXTH STREET, BETWEEN J and K.

☞ Orders addressed to either of the above parties, will be promptly responded to.

PRICES REASONABLE.

With Auburn a transportation hub, larger regional breweries in Sacramento, Stockton, and San Francisco could compete more easily with local breweries. The Columbus Brewery based in Sacramento advertised "reasonable prices" with a promise that "orders from the Mountain Counties filled with promptness and dispatch." The Columbus Brewery was owned by Elias and Christian Gruhler, operating as early as 1854. This 1862 advertisement is from the *Miners & Business Men's Directory*.

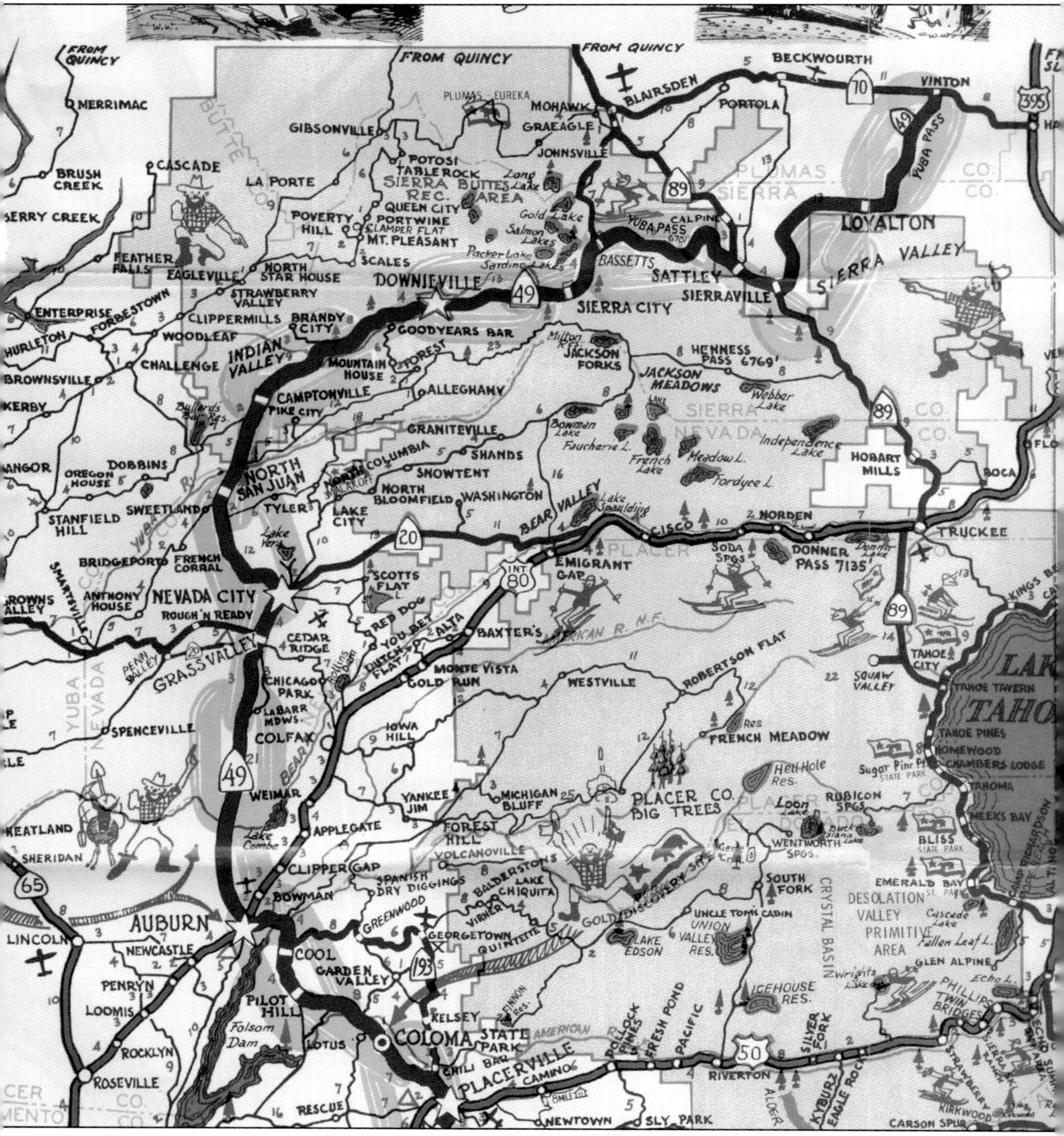

The two most prominent towns in Nevada County today are Grass Valley and Nevada City. Grass Valley was home to the California, City, Grass Valley, and Washington breweries. Nevada City housed the Chicago, City, Milwaukee, Nevada, Nevada City, Sierra Nevada, and the United States breweries, just to name a few. Passing through Yuba County, the next major brewery was the Downieville Brewery in Sierra County. (Courtesy Golden Chain Council.)

Six

Nevada and Sierra Counties
The Northern Mines

"There is a fountain filled with beer, where the Thirsty Thousands drink."

—Drinking song lyric, published in the *Independent*, 1904.

Most miners made their way to Nevada County's northern mines by catching a riverboat from Sacramento to Marysville. From Marysville, they packed their gear on their back or, if they had funds, on the back of a mule, heading into the foothills to try their luck. Mining in the northern mines ran the spectrum from the simple placer mine, to massive hydraulic mines, to deep hardrock mining. Some of these mines gained so much notoriety that, although no longer functioning mines, they warranted preservation as California state parks. Chief among these are the Empire Mine and Malakoff Diggins. And where there were miners, there was beer. By 1858, there were as many as seven breweries in Nevada County, producing 44,000 gallons of beer annually. By 1879, that number had grown to 15, and their annual production had reached 500,000 gallons.

Highway 49 travels through Yuba County for less than 10 miles of its 300-mile route. It is in Sierra County that the last of the Motherlode's rich gold deposits were to be found. Formed in 1852, the county's towns of Downieville, Sierra City, and Goodyear's Bar all had significant gold strikes. The brewery in Downieville struck it rich with liquid gold, making a living that was equal or better—and certainly far more comfortable—than most miners who were out in the open elements scrounging for a days' wages. While the town of Vinton, in Plumas County, is at the literal end of Highway 49, for all intents and purposes, Sierra City is the end of the tour along the Golden Chain Highway.

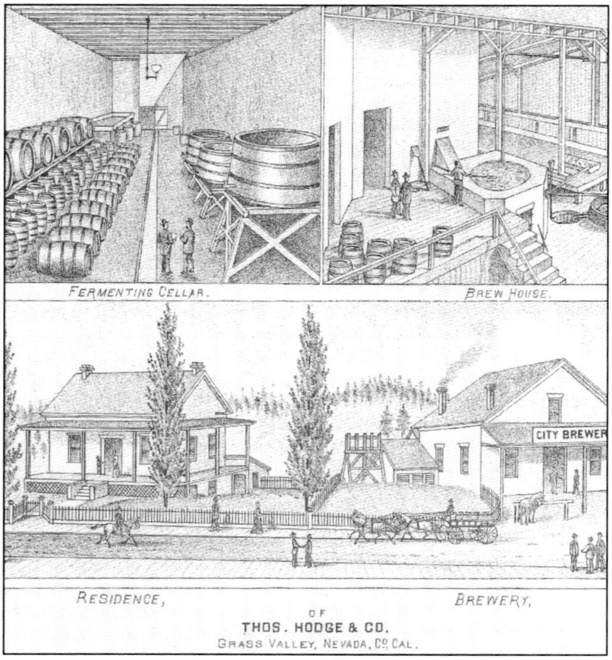

This Thompson and West lithograph shows the Thomas Hodge residence and his adjacent City Brewery as they appeared c. 1880. Note the delivery wagons loaded with kegs of beer in the lower image. The view on the upper right shows the interior of the brew house. One man is tending the large brew kettle with a hearth below it. A drain pipe runs from the brew kettle to the mash tub to the right, which is being tended by a second man. The pipe exiting the mash tub through the hole in the floor likely ran downstairs to the fermentation cellar shown in the image to the upper left. The image of the fermentation room shows the open fermenters, kegged beer, and gas lighting.

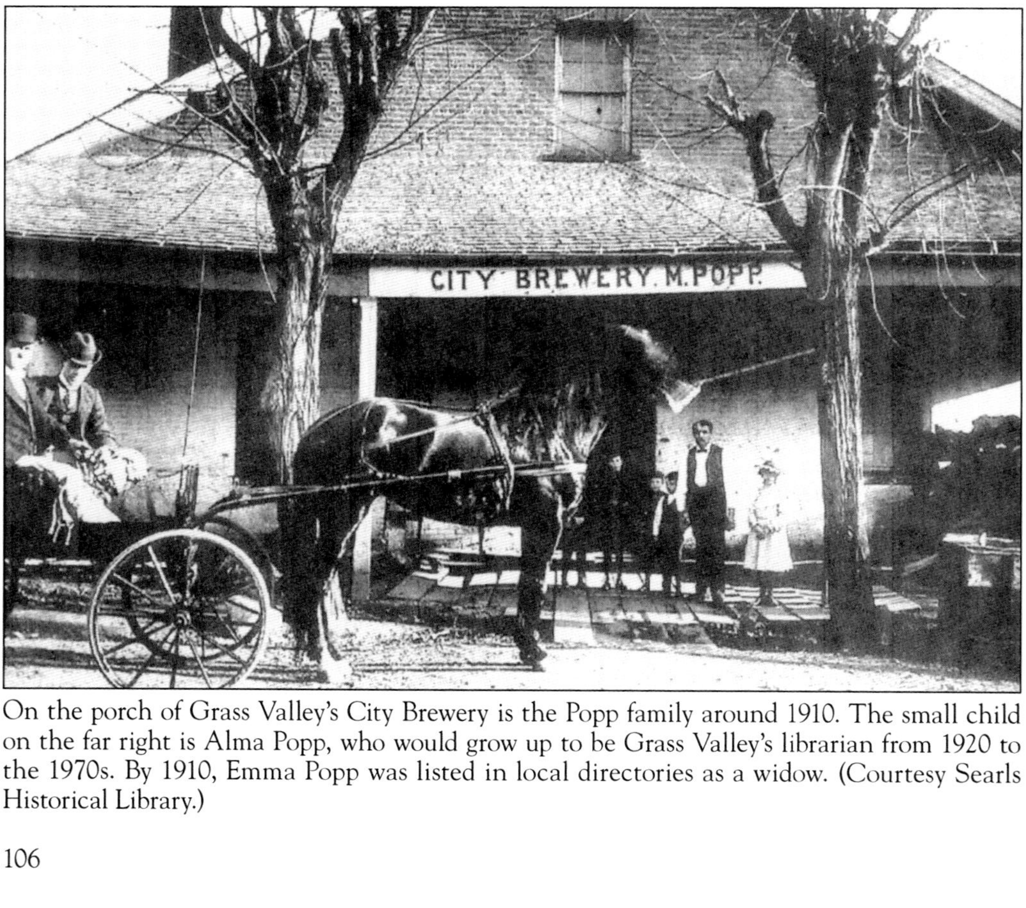

On the porch of Grass Valley's City Brewery is the Popp family around 1910. The small child on the far right is Alma Popp, who would grow up to be Grass Valley's librarian from 1920 to the 1970s. By 1910, Emma Popp was listed in local directories as a widow. (Courtesy Searls Historical Library.)

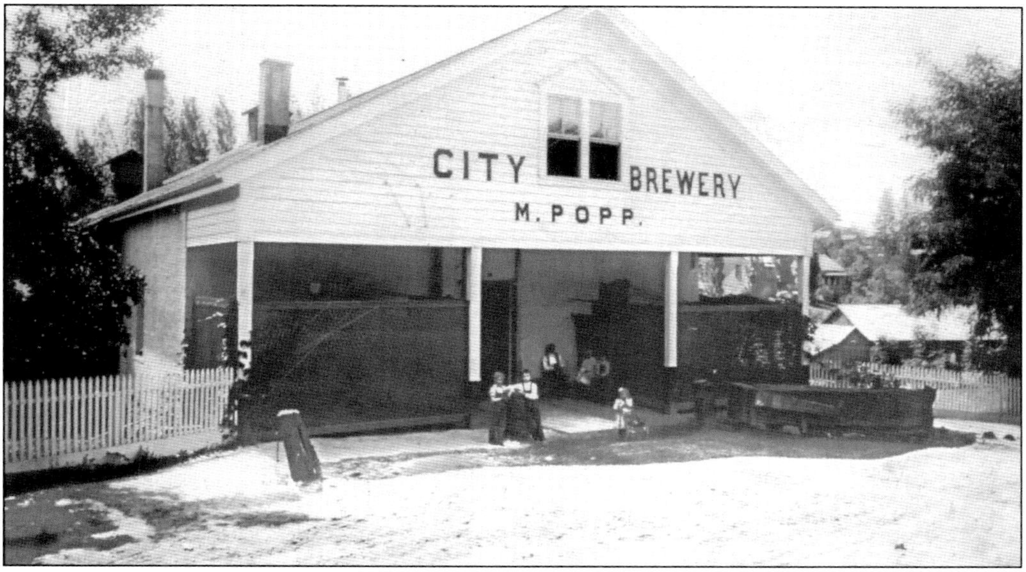

This image shows what must be a later view of the City Brewery after a face-lift. Note the multiple chimneys, indicating the locations of the brew kettle and malt kiln. The 1891 Sanborn map of the City Brewery notes the presence of a saloon in the lower left corner of the brewery on the map. Also present are a malt kiln and malt floor, indicating they were producing their own malt. By 1898, the brewery had been expanded and was operating under W.F. Mitchell. (Courtesy Searls Historical Library.)

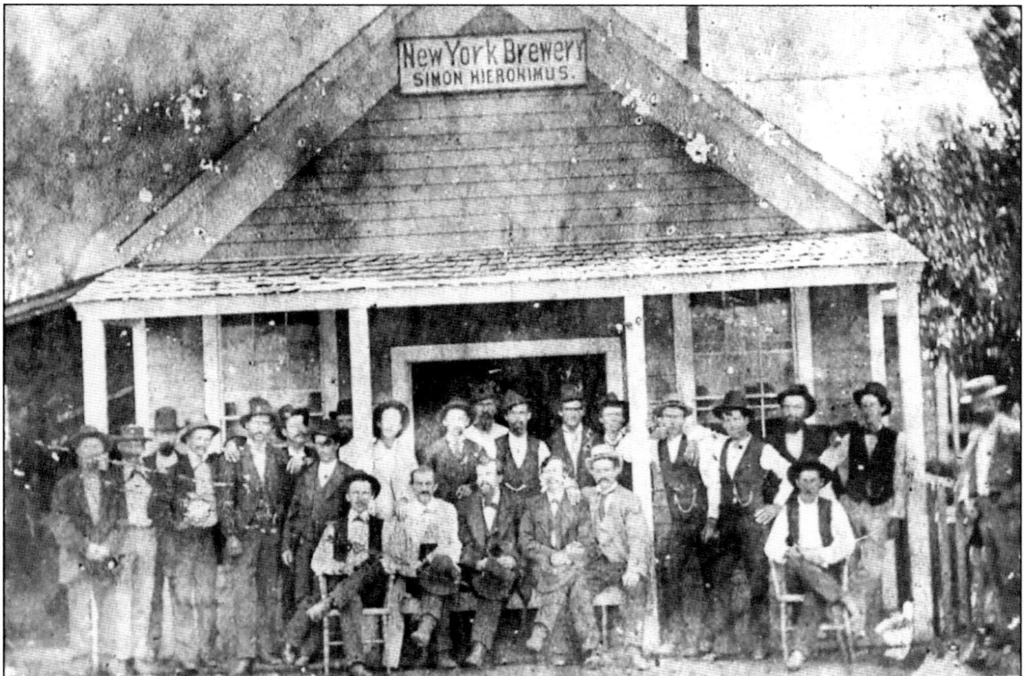

This c. 1878 image is of Simon Hieronimus's New York Brewery in the community of North Bloomfield. Once the site of some of California's most expansive hydraulic mining, North Bloomfield is now located in Malakoff Diggins State Park. By 1905, the brewery was closed. (Courtesy Searls Historical Library.)

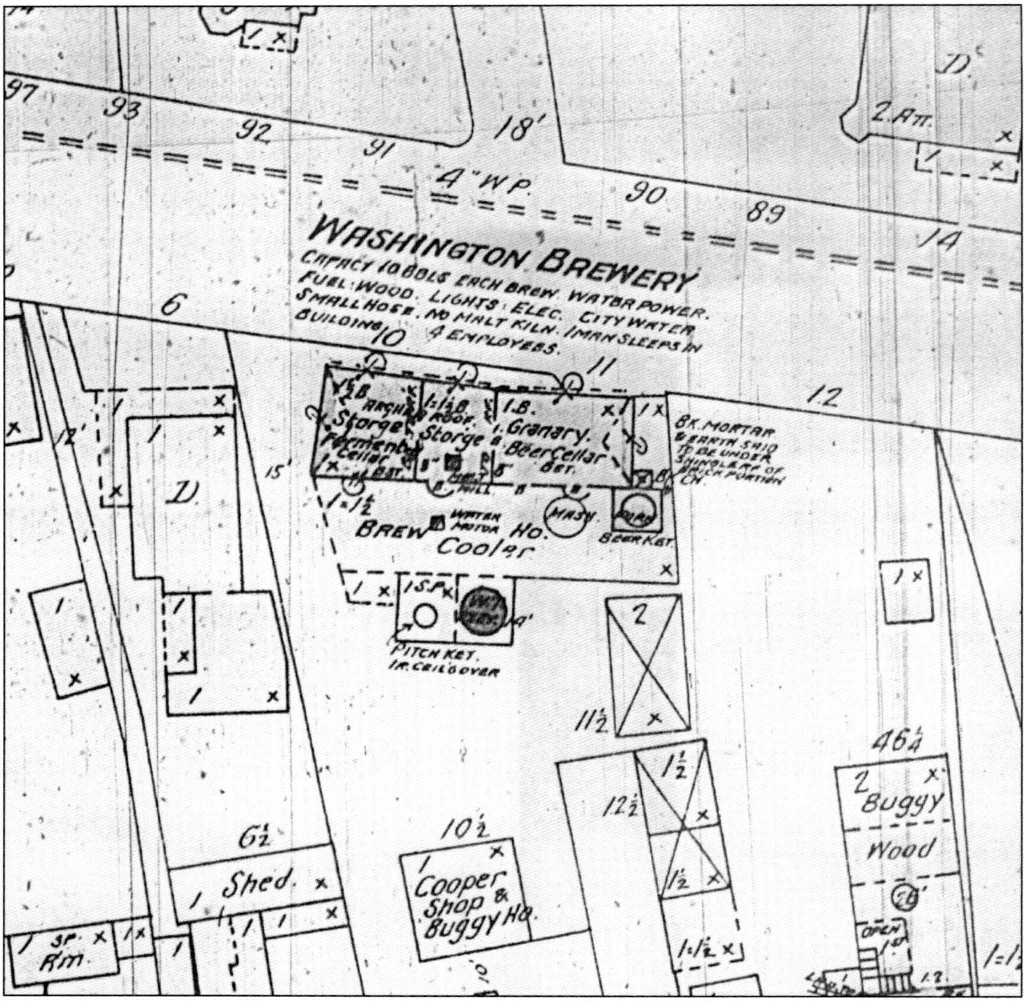

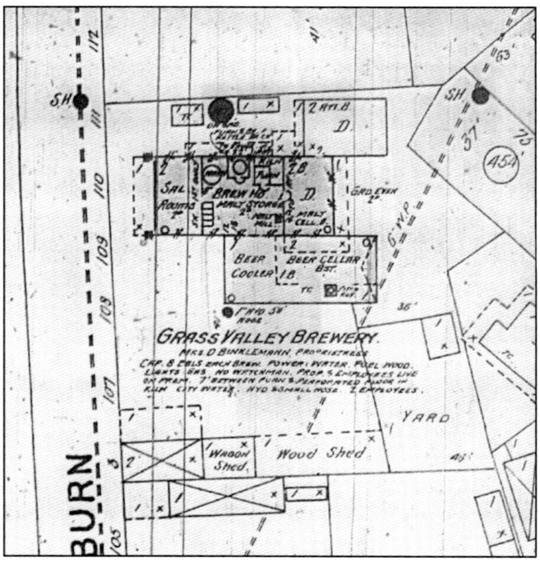

These 1891 Sanborn maps show details of the Washington and Grass Valley breweries, which were within two city blocks of one another, as was the California Brewery. The Washington Brewery spanned from Washington to Main Streets. Depicted is the malt house, indicating they created their own malt, as well as the brew kettle. The proprietress of the California Brewery, which also had a saloon, is Mrs. D. Binklemann. The brewery had a capacity of eight barrels per brew, two less than its rival, the Washington Brewery.

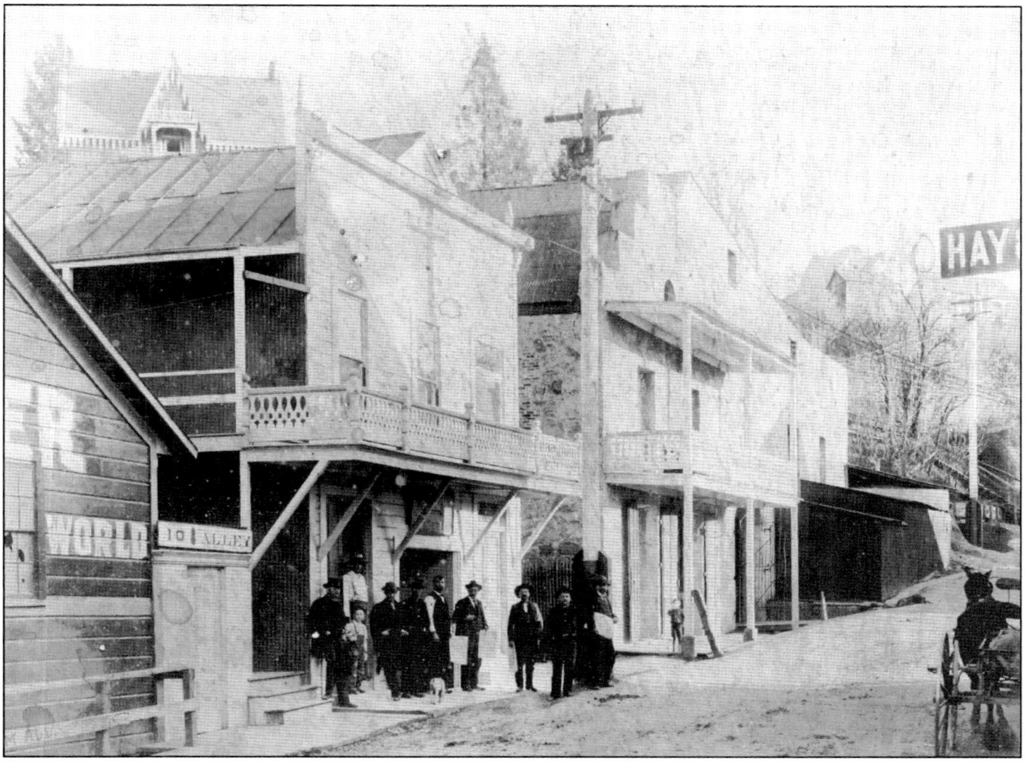

The stone building at the center right of this image was a brewery operated by Holdbelner and Gildrelerne. The image below is a modern view of the Holdbelner Brewery building. It was reopened as a brewery in the 1990s, but closed again a few years later. It currently stands at 107 Sacramento Street in Nevada City. (Above, courtesy Searls Historical Library; below, courtesy authors' collection.)

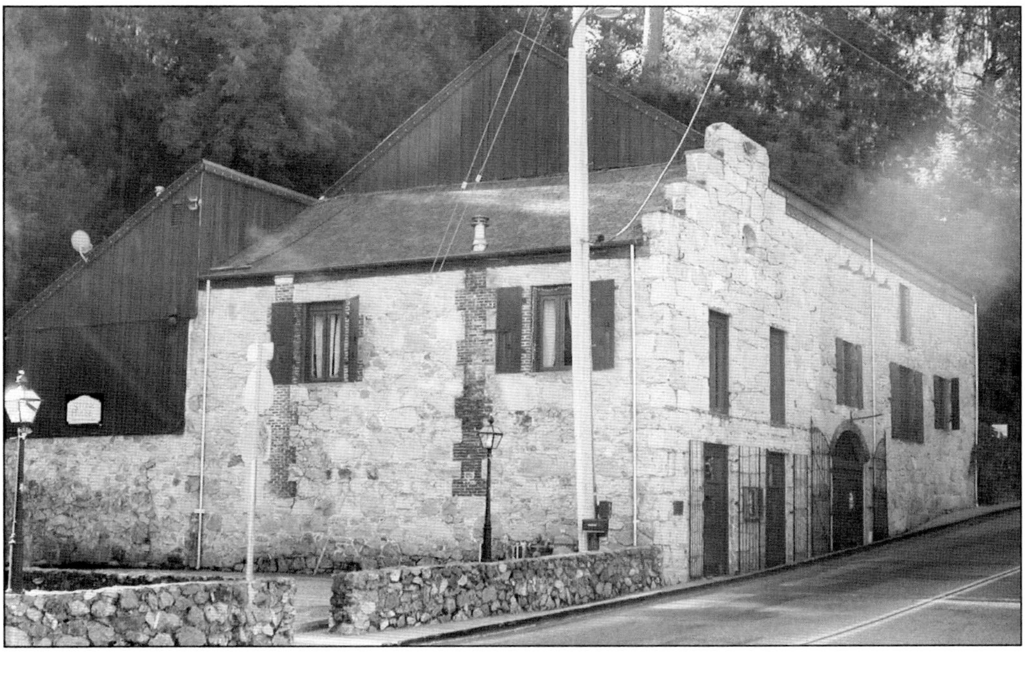

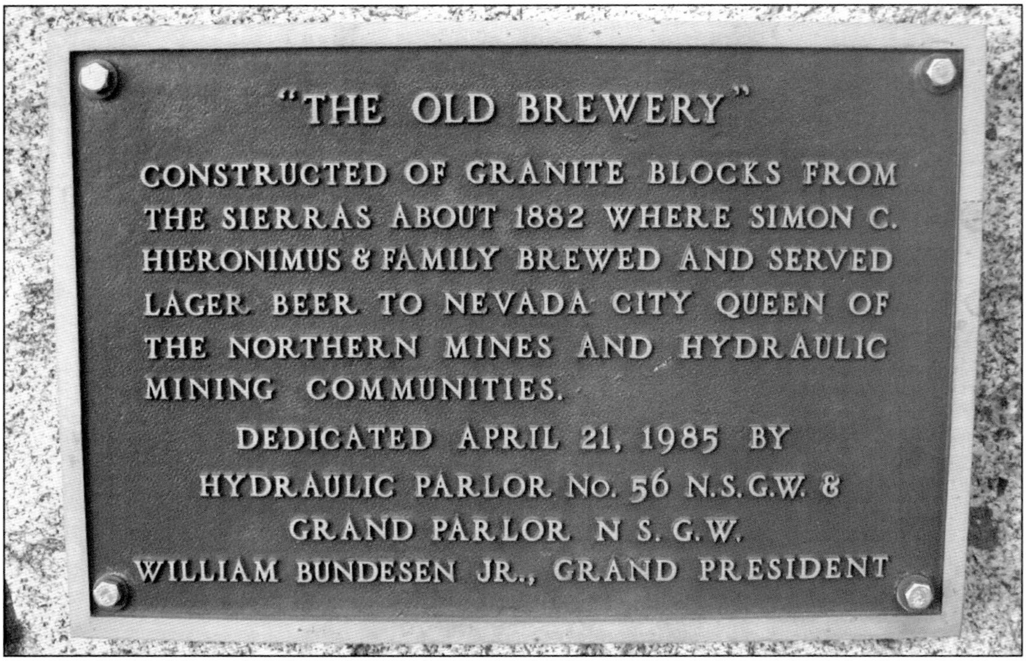

This historical marker is mounted on the brewery building shown on the previous page. While the plaque indicates the brewery was built in 1882, an earlier brewery operated here in the 1850s. Initially run by Holdbelner and Gildrelerne, it was later operated by Simon Hieronimus, who also operated the New York Brewery in North Bloomfield. Below is a detail of the beautiful granite work from the 1882 construction; the 1857 date refers to the earliest brewery operations. (Both, courtesy authors' collection.)

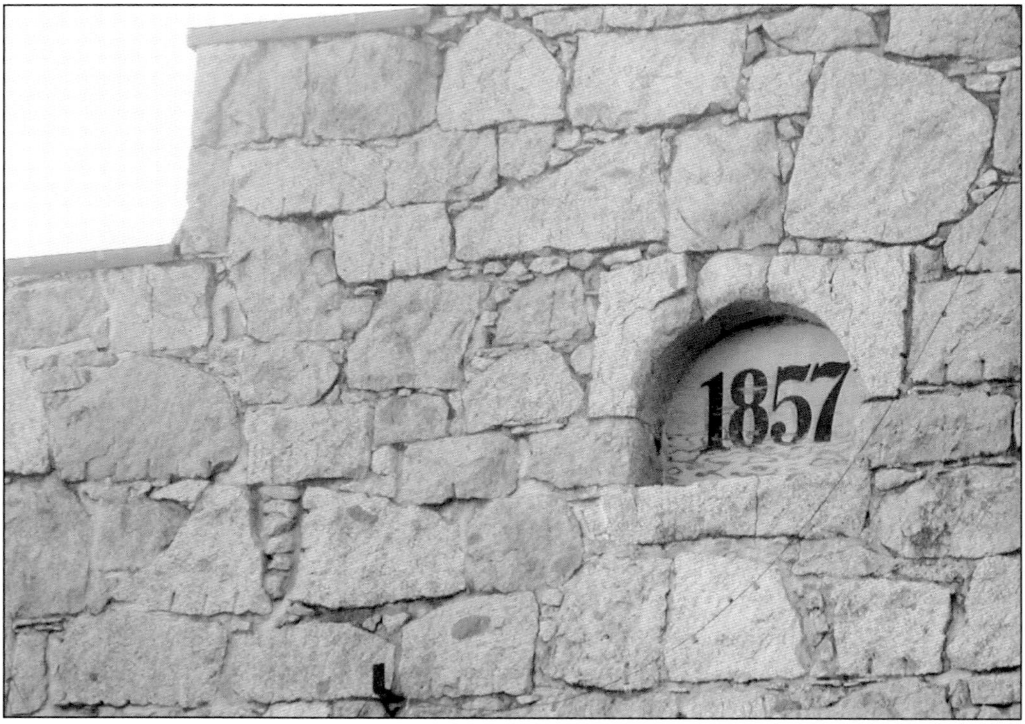

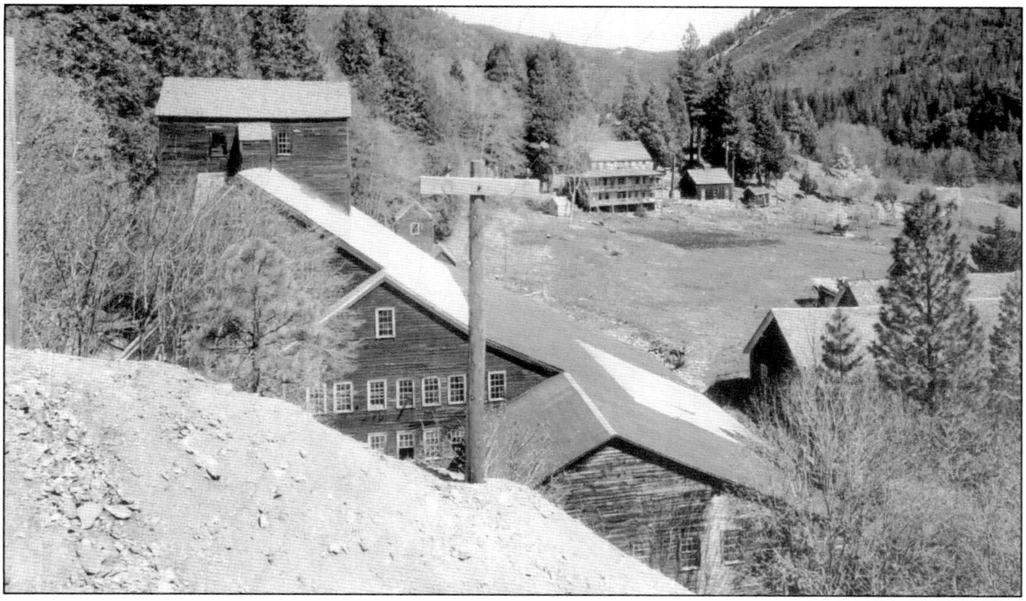

The Golden Chain Highway passes briefly through Yuba County, with no major mining communities along Highway 49 (though Marysville had a large, early brewery that surely many a miner stopped at on the way to the gold fields). Miners travelling to Sierra County faced more extremes of climate and geography than almost any other Motherlode county. Much of the county's gold was found up the steep washes and canyons that surrounded the main towns. Pictured here c. 1934 is a large, unidentified mine near Sierra City, possibly the Kentucky Mine. (Courtesy authors' collection.)

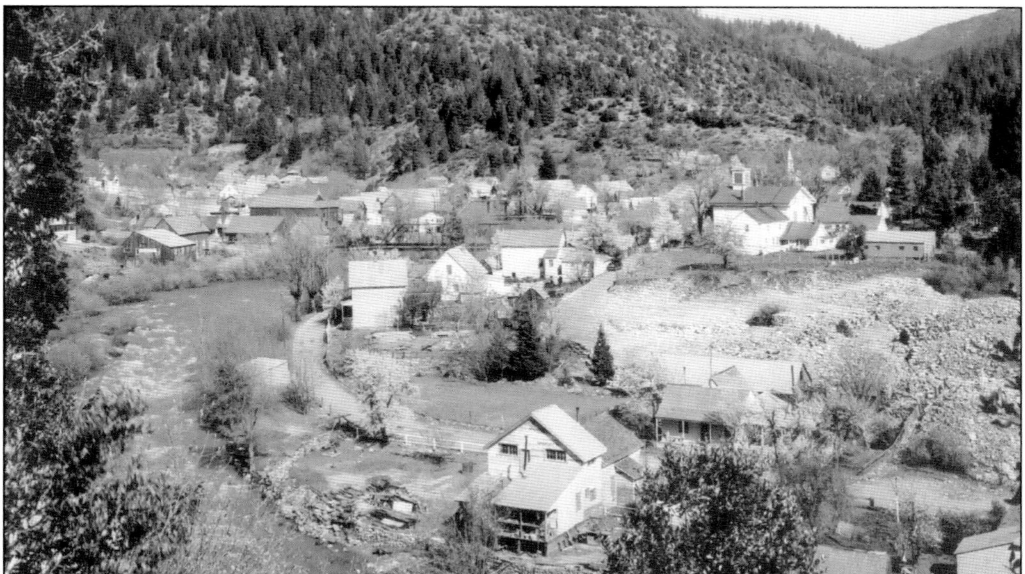

Downieville, seen in this 1934 overview, is considered to be one of the most intact Gold Rush towns in California. Located at the junction of the north and south forks of the Yuba River—from which its earliest name, The Forks, was derived—mining began early in the area. The town was established by 1849, and it became the county seat in 1852. The town is named for Maj. William Downie, an early miner and explorer of the region, and like a good Gold Rush town, housed several breweries. (Courtesy authors' collection.)

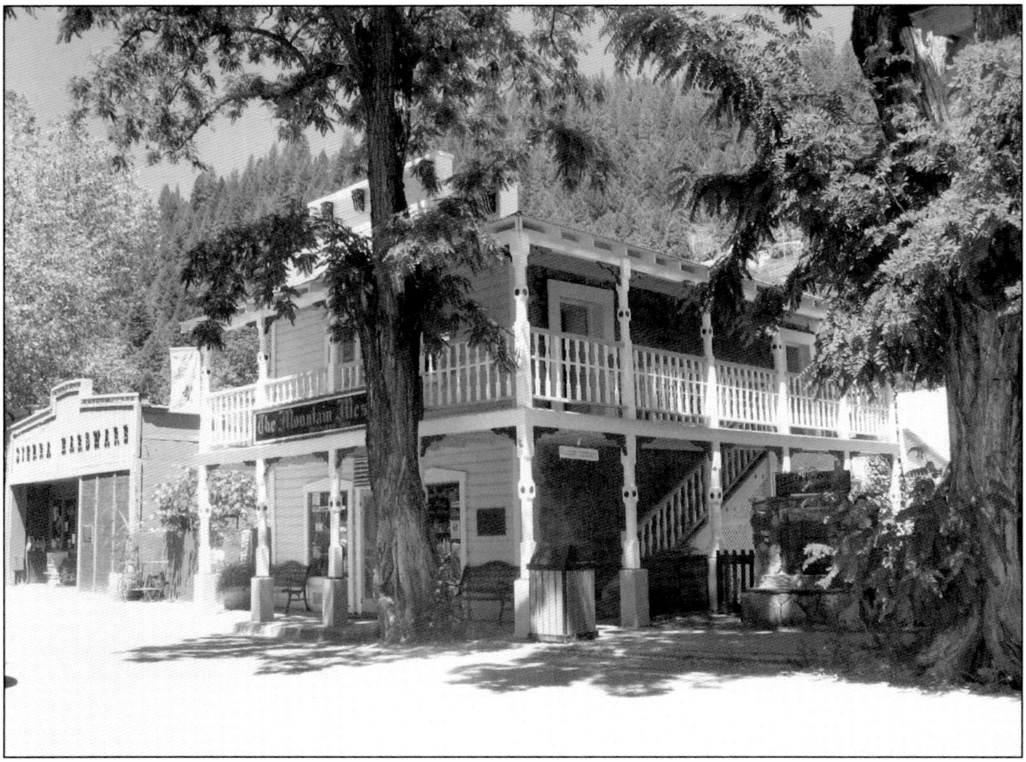

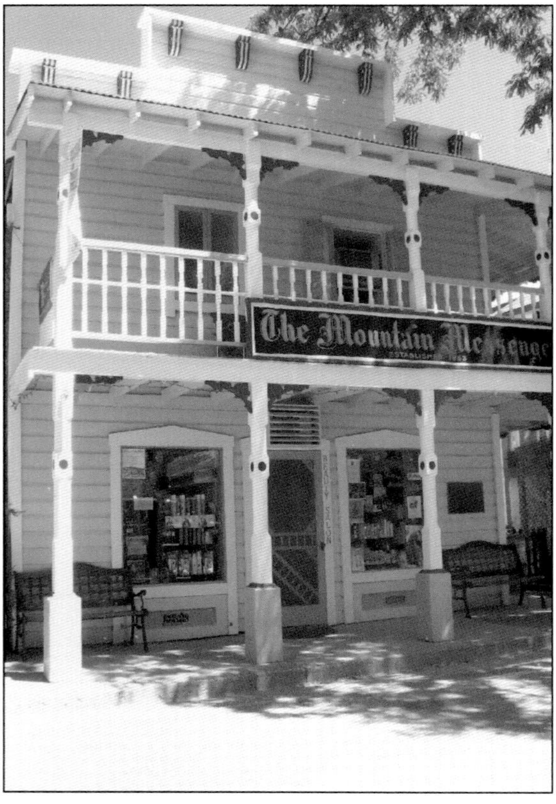

The Mackerman building, built in 1852, initially housed Joseph Mackerman's family and brewery; little is known about the brewery's history. As quoted in the 1882 *Sierra County History*: "The two breweries of Downieville make an excellent quality of beer. The amber fluid was first brewed here in 1854, by Borge, who two years after sold his brewery to Scammon and Schultz, and they to John Rupp and another party. Ferdinand Busch [sic] bought the property in 1858, and still owns it. The Monte Cristo Brewery [5 miles north of Downieville] was built in 1861. L. Nessler and Joseph Wackman became the proprietors the same year. The former purchased the latter's interest in 1866; but in 1868, and for eight years after, J. A. Blohn was a partner, Mr. Nessler being now the only proprietor. The brewery was burned in 1864, involving a loss of $10,000, and a second time was consumed in 1870. John August Blohn was operating the Sierra Brewery in Downieville." (Photographs by S. Whittle, courtesy HMdb.org.)

The town's most famous brewery, the Downieville Brewery, was built in 1854. This 1874 map shows all the communities that Bosch's brewery, and other existing regional breweries served. Note the town of Monte Cristo, home to an early brewery, northwest of Downieville. Bosch delivered to mining communities such as Goodyear's Bar, Forest City, and Alleghany. Forest City, southwest of Downieville, was a hub for Bosch. One advertisement reads: "Bosch's Beer will always be found on tap at Forest City. . . Drink Bosch's Beer if you want to grow fat and happy." What could be a better selling point? The Downieville Brewery Depot at Forest City listed Charles Spanseil as the manager.

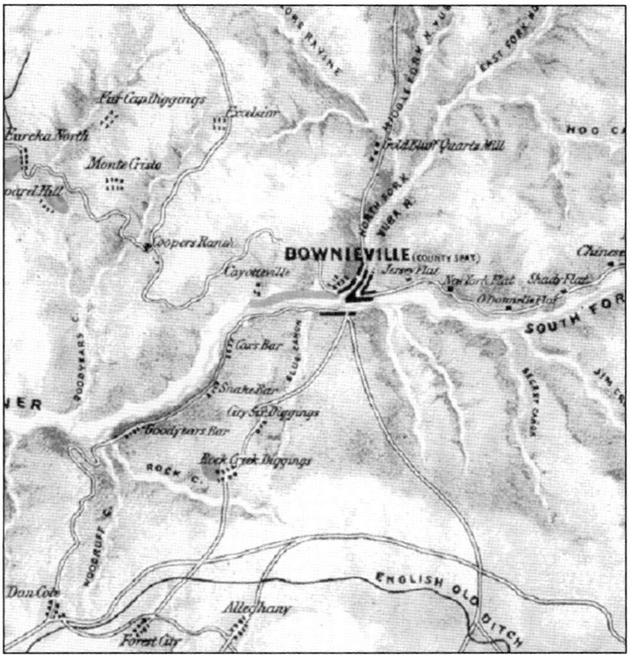

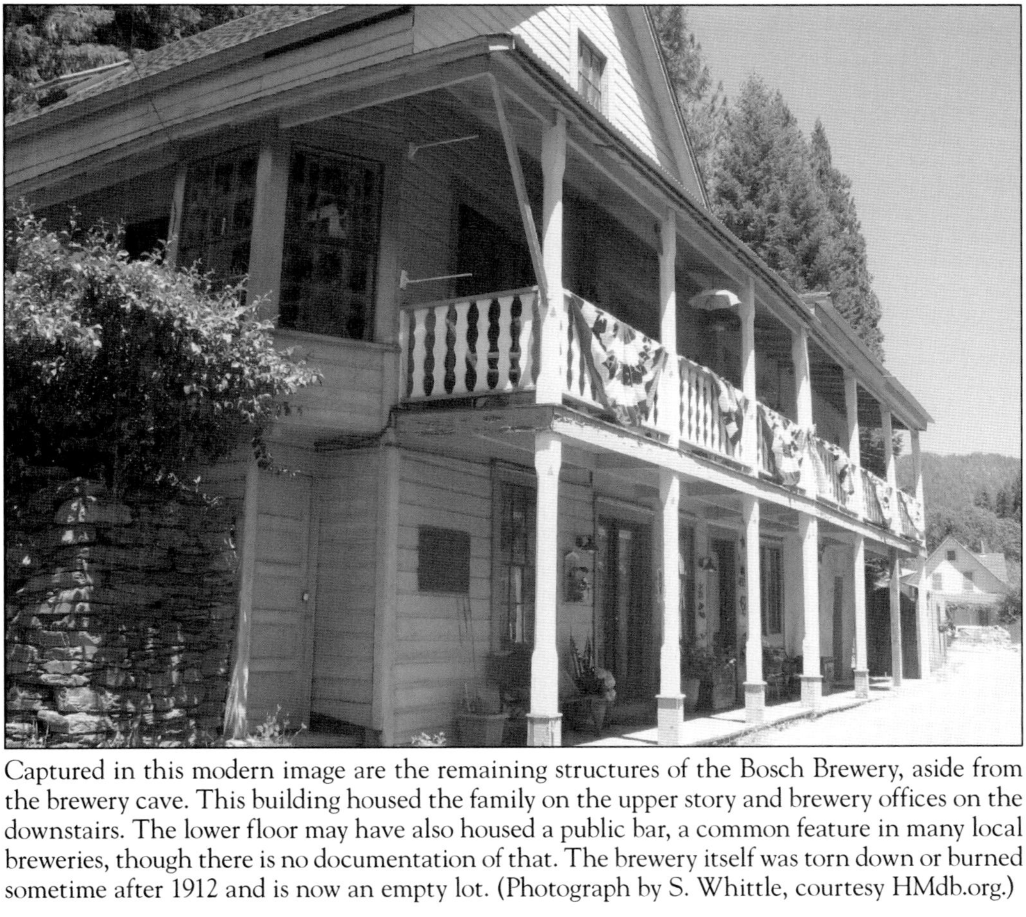

Captured in this modern image are the remaining structures of the Bosch Brewery, aside from the brewery cave. This building housed the family on the upper story and brewery offices on the downstairs. The lower floor may have also housed a public bar, a common feature in many local breweries, though there is no documentation of that. The brewery itself was torn down or burned sometime after 1912 and is now an empty lot. (Photograph by S. Whittle, courtesy HMdb.org.)

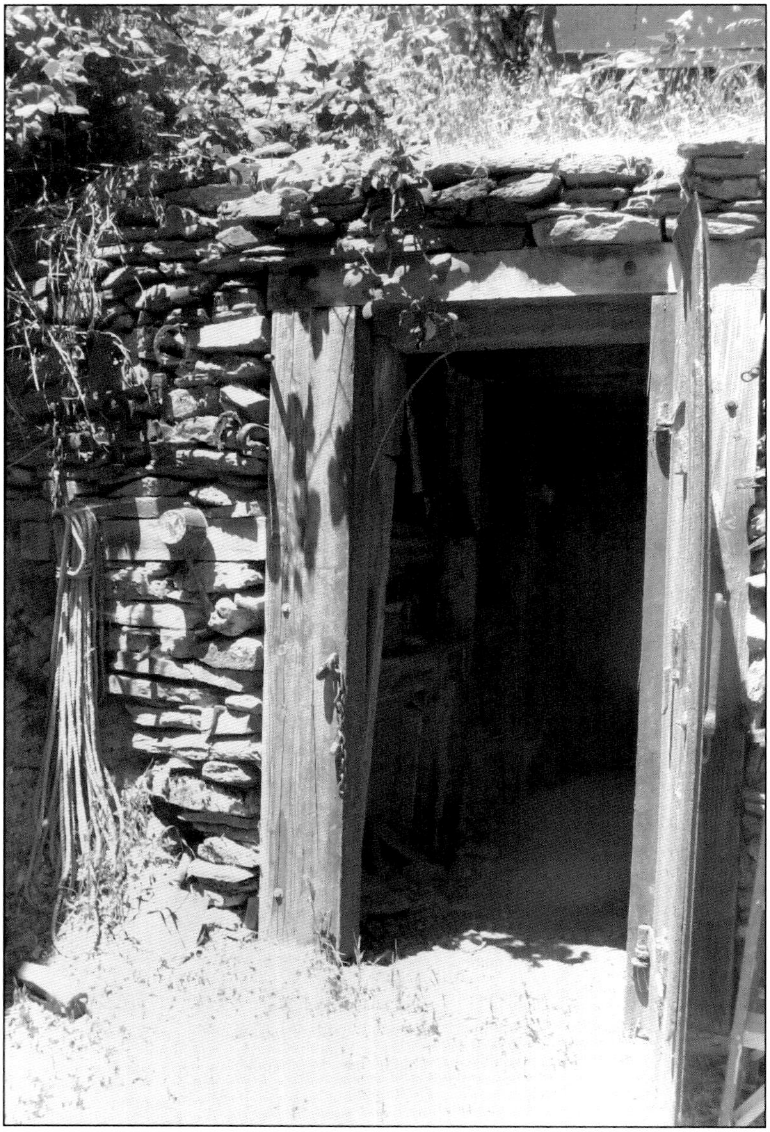

One of the more interesting features of the Downieville Brewery was the use of what is thought to be an abandoned mine adit for cold storage. The authors came across only one other brewery, the Mokelumne Hill Brewery in Calaveras County, that made use of a mine adit for storage (see Chapter 2). There is also the possibility that the cave was excavated specifically for this purpose, a point the proprietor makes in this undated advertisement: "Country orders promptly filled, and satisfaction guaranteed. Beer supplied from the Downieville Brewery Cave." (Above, photograph by S. Whittle, courtesy HMdb.org; below, courtesy Cherry Simi.)

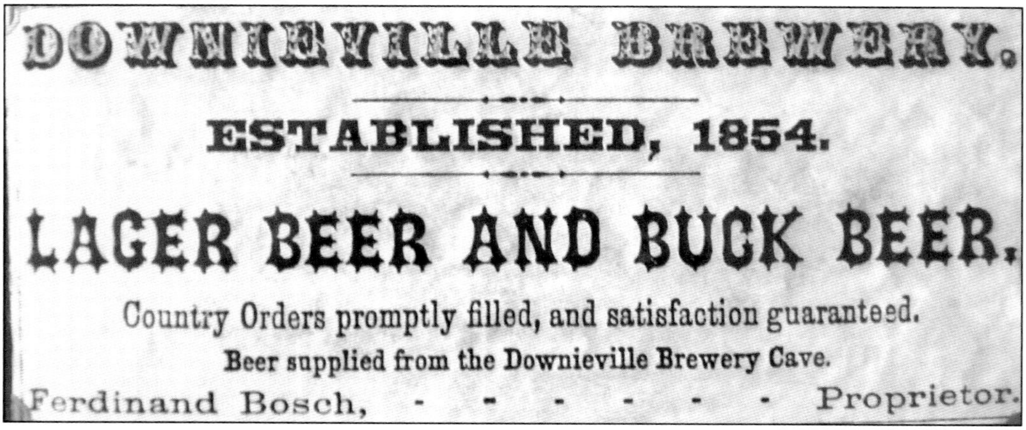

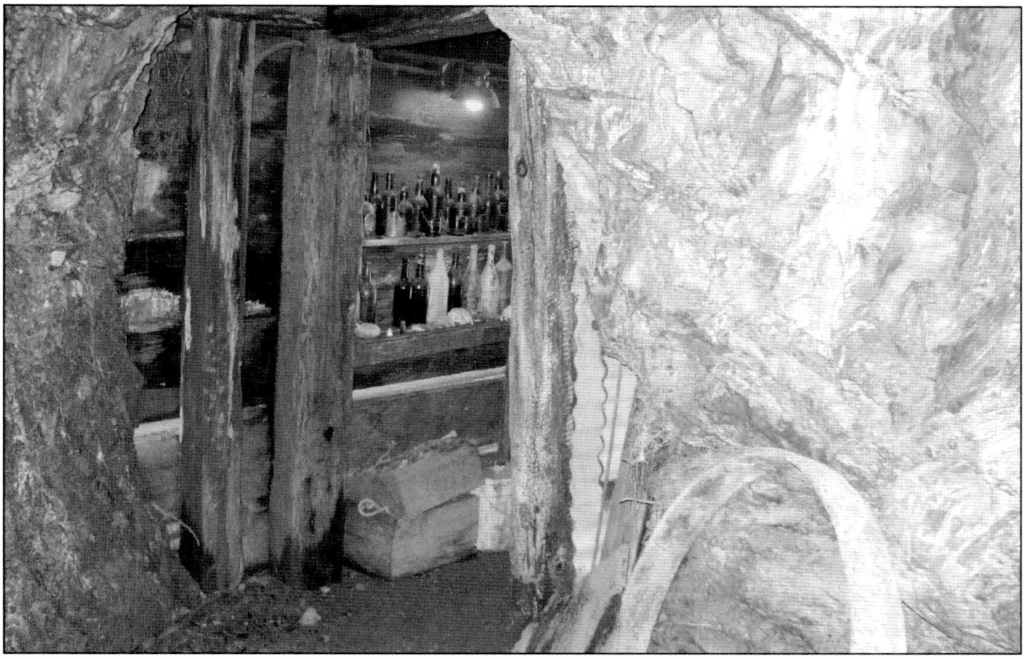

The interior of the Downieville Brewery Cave would have been a naturally cool place to store beer. The tunnel was also used to load and unload the company's freight wagons. According to the building's owner, Cherry Simi, few bottles were found during the remodeling of the brewery. What she did find were lots of ceramic stoppers (see Page 61 for a stopper example). (Photograph by S. Whittle, courtesy HMdb.org.)

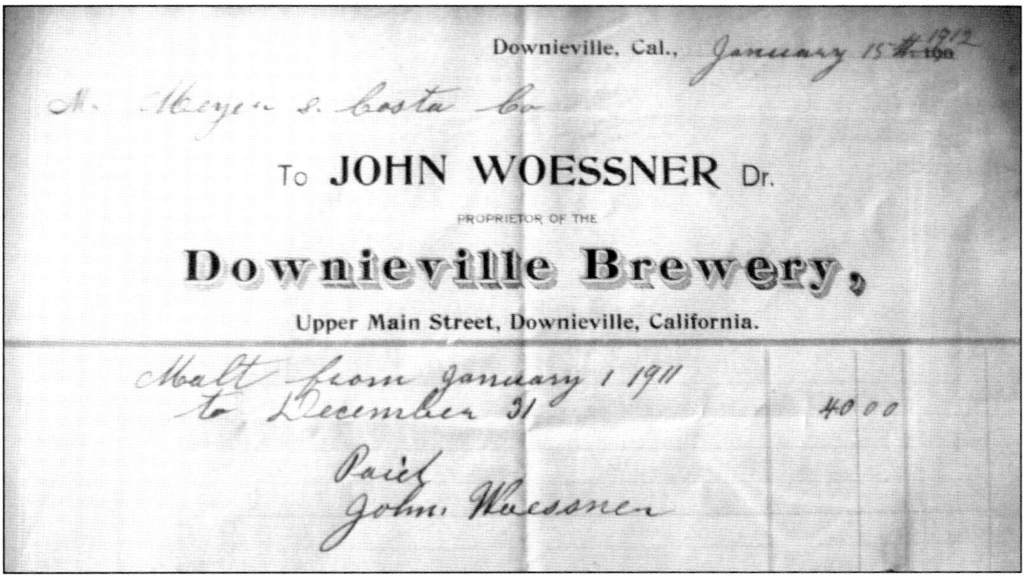

Downieville, Cal., January 15th 1912

N. Meyer & Costa Co

To JOHN WOESSNER Dr.

PROPRIETOR OF THE

Downieville Brewery,

Upper Main Street, Downieville, California.

Malt from January 1 1911 to December 31 — 40 00

Paid
John Woessner

Pictured is a rare billhead for the Downieville Brewery, located on Upper Main Street, when John Woessner (also Weussner) was the proprietor. Prior to buying the brewery, Woessner had worked as a brewer with Ferdinand Bosch. This receipt for malt, signed by Woessner, dates to January 1912, two years after he reportedly died. When he did finally pass away, he left the brewery to a bartender from another local brewery, Henry Zwiefel, who turned it into a laundry. (Courtesy Cherry Simi.)

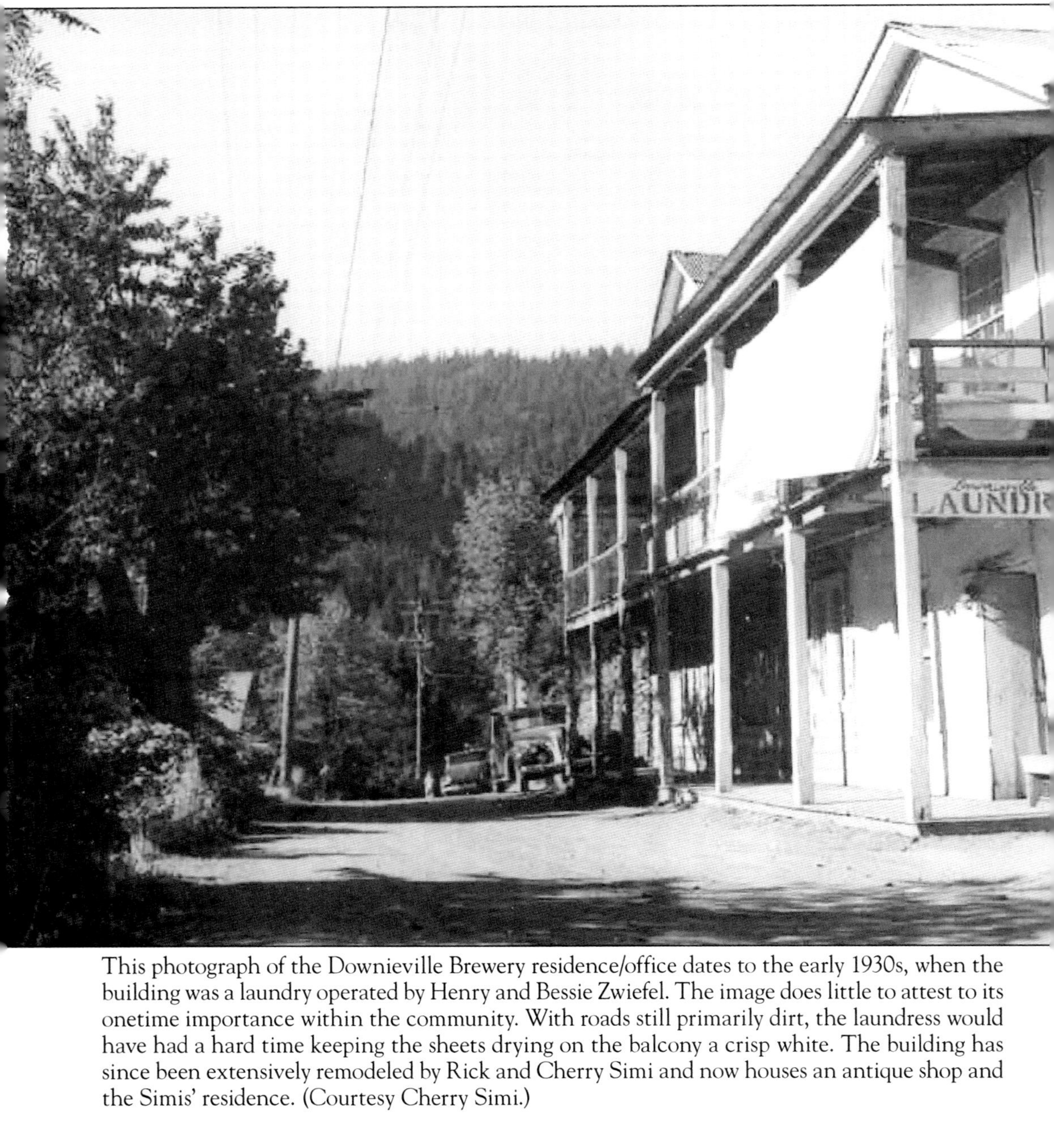

This photograph of the Downieville Brewery residence/office dates to the early 1930s, when the building was a laundry operated by Henry and Bessie Zwiefel. The image does little to attest to its onetime importance within the community. With roads still primarily dirt, the laundress would have had a hard time keeping the sheets drying on the balcony a crisp white. The building has since been extensively remodeled by Rick and Cherry Simi and now houses an antique shop and the Simis' residence. (Courtesy Cherry Simi.)

Seven

The Beginning and the End

Steam Beer to Prohibition

"Once, during Prohibition, I was forced to live for days on nothing but food and water."

—W.C. Fields

The origins of steam beer are vague. According to one story, during the Gold Rush a man by the name of Pete Steam came to California to try his hand in the mining industry. He soon became disheartened with mining, and turned to his trained profession: brewing. When Steam tried to adapt brewing to the local region, he actually rediscovered an old-world method of beer making called *kraüsening.* His "Steam" beer caught on and was soon being copied at small breweries along the Sierras. Other versions of this brew's origins can be found in the following pages. After Prohibition, most US breweries concentrated on lagers; regional varieties, including steam beer, fell by the wayside. By the middle of the 20th century the only producer of steam beer was the famous Anchor Steam Brewery of San Francisco.

The lead up to Prohibition was a long one, with roots in the Temperance movements throughout the country, before California even became a state. The primary forces were the National Prohibition Party, the Women's Christian Temperance Union, and the Anti-Saloon League. These efforts were galvanized by the Progressive ideals of the emerging 20th century and anti-immigrant sentiments in the face of looming war.

These groups finally achieved their goal in 1919 with the passage of the 18th Amendment to the Constitution, which barred the sale of alcohol, ushering in Prohibition. The result was the demise of small breweries and the takeover of beer production and distribution by organized crime. In response, law enforcement spent millions of dollars trying to enforce the laws, and in 1933 the federal government finally ended Prohibition. It was too late, and in most cases the small, regional breweries were not able to holdout during Prohibition. Only the largest, most well-financed firms were able to hang on. The result was a landscape of nationwide corporate beer production in the United States. It would be almost half a century before small-scale brewing came back in the form of microbreweries.

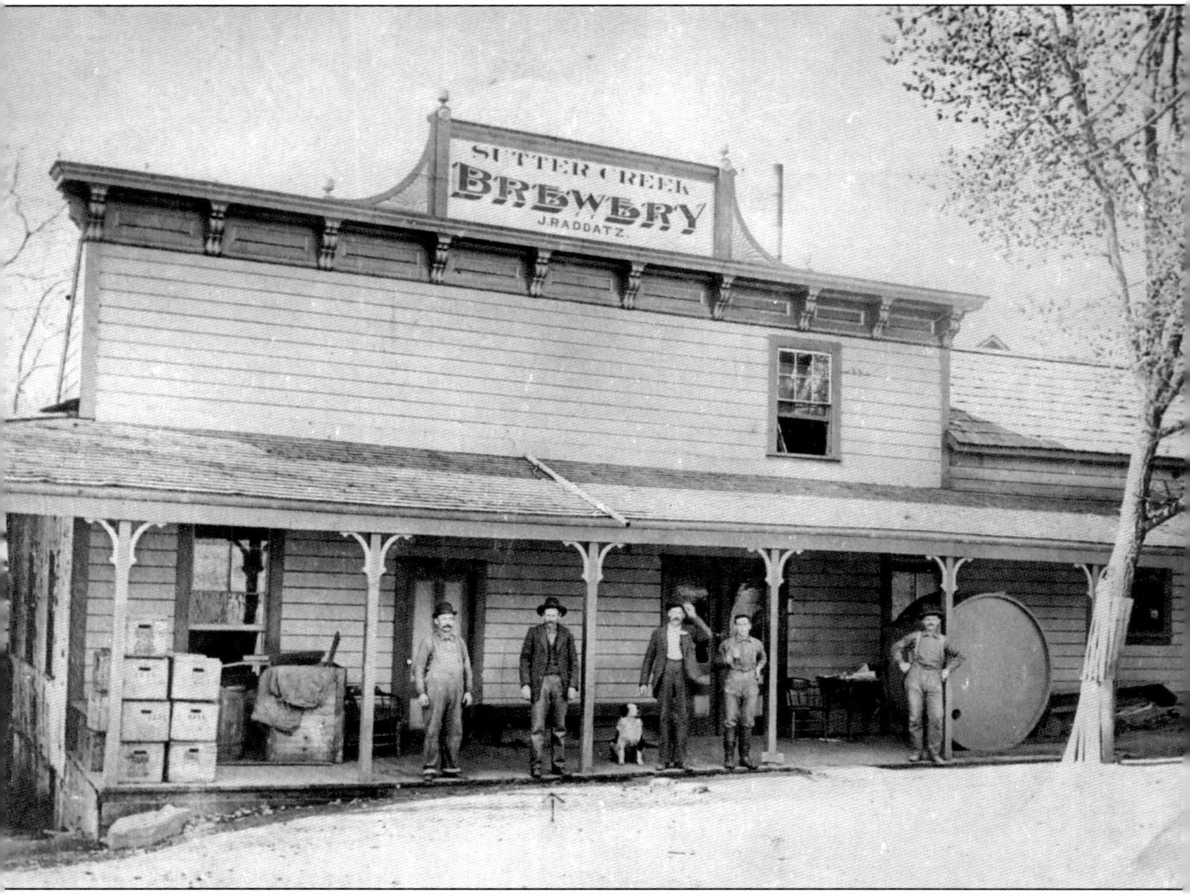

Steam beer was developed in California during the Gold Rush and is the only style of beer indigenous to the United States. One of the key brewing aspects that characterize steam beer is the fermentation of yeasts at higher than traditional temperatures, approximately 60–70 degrees Fahrenheit. This method of brewing is generally attributed to the inability of pioneer California brewers to cool the wort with ice, as eastern brewers did. Seen here is the Rabolt/Raddatz Brewery that operated in Sutter Creek from the 1860s onward. An unknown resident recalled: "A German family by the name of Raddatz owned the brewery. Their steam beer was really wonderful!" For more information about the brewery, please see Chapter 3. (Courtesy Amador County Archives.)

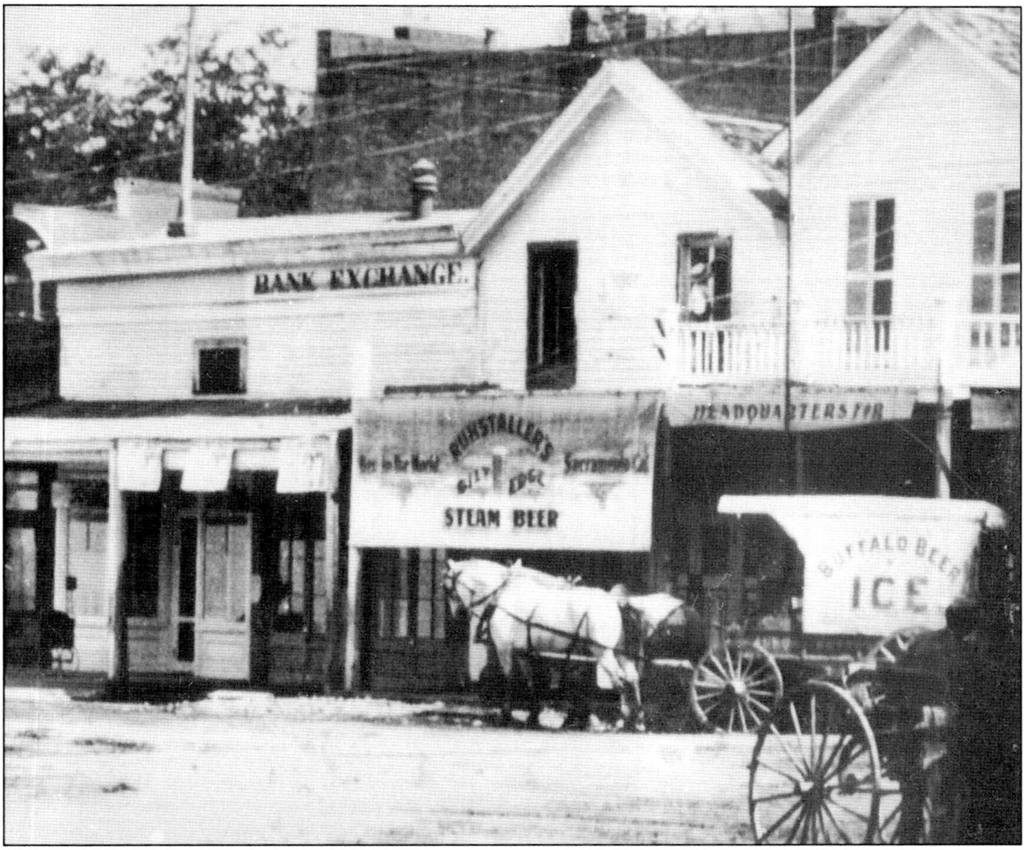

This image from Auburn shows a saloon advertising Ruhstaller's steam beer on a large banner; in front is the competition, a Buffalo Brewing Co. delivery wagon. Ruhstaller's and Buffalo, regional breweries from Sacramento, both produced steam beer. The San Francisco–based company Anchor Steam Brewing says of the invention of steam beer: "It was produced in San Francisco during the 1800s, this was done because in San Francisco, the temperatures were much higher and they could not keep beer as cold. Beer was often made at temperatures in excess of 60 degrees. The beer was then pumped into kegs where beer continued to ferment and build up carbonation. When the process was finished, the cap from the keg was removed and a bolt of steam shot out." (Above, courtesy Placer County Museums; below, courtesy authors' collection.)

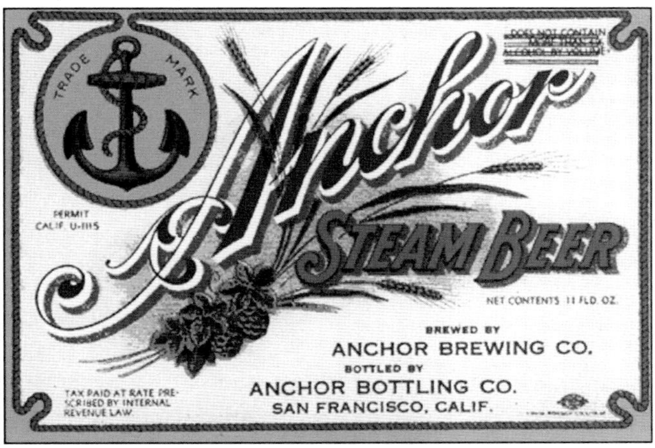

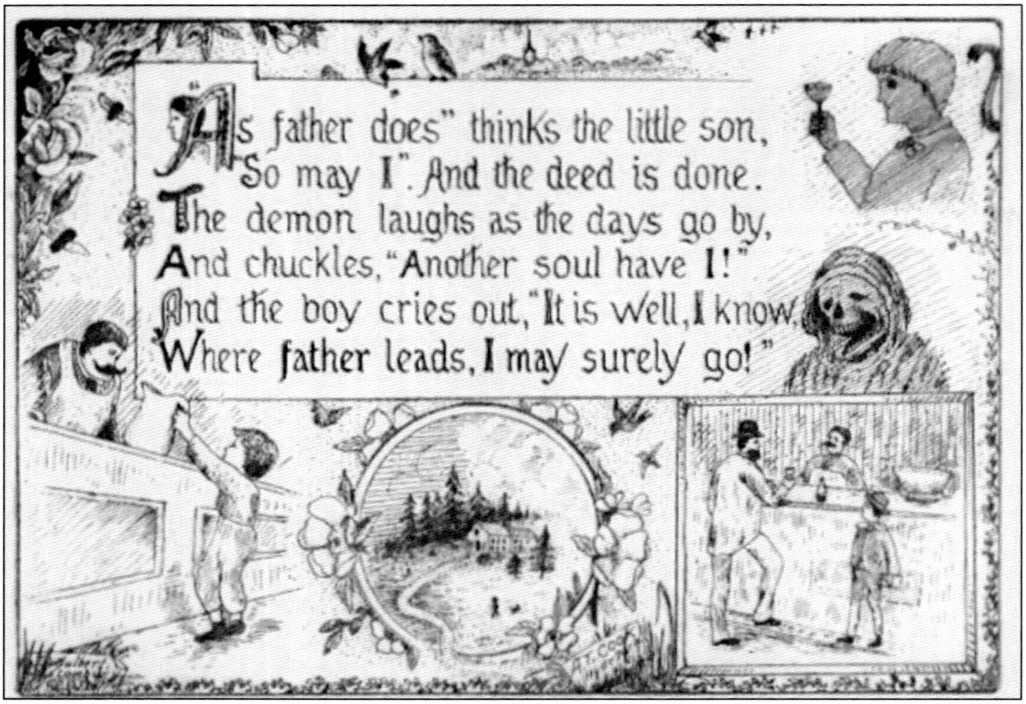

Temperance literature was designed to make one stop and think before lifting a glass. For teetotalers, alcohol was the cause of many societal problems, including domestic violence and poverty. Postcards, such as this one, tried to demonize drink, though for many of the newly arrived ethnic groups to the gold fields, and later in the state's history, beer drinking was part of the everyday cultural traditions. A portion of this postcard reads: "The demon laughs as the days go by, and chuckles, Another soul have I!" Note the image of the little boy bringing a pitcher of beer home from the bar or brewery for his family. (Courtesy authors' collection.)

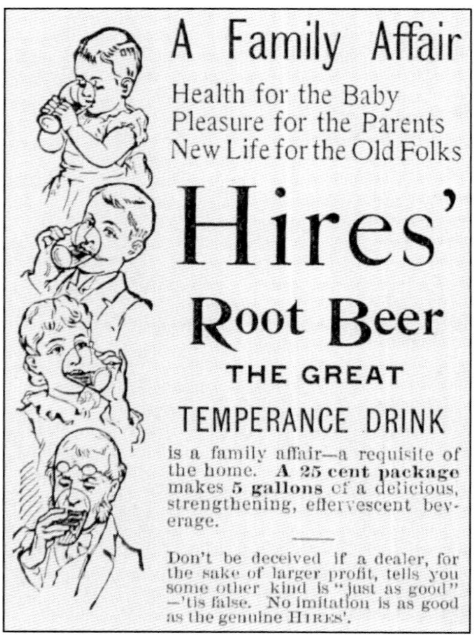

Seen here is a Hires' Root Beer advertisement from the early 1890s, where the entire family—from grandpa to baby—is enjoying a "temperance drink." Root beer, a drink which was often brewed to have an alcohol content before it became popular as a soda, apparently offered "Health for the Baby, Pleasure for the Parents, New Life for the Old Folks." Coca-Cola was also being marketed at this time as a temperate alternative, though the manufacturer did not completely discard cocaine as an ingredient until 1929, which makes one wonder just how temperate a drink it was. (Courtesy authors' collection.)

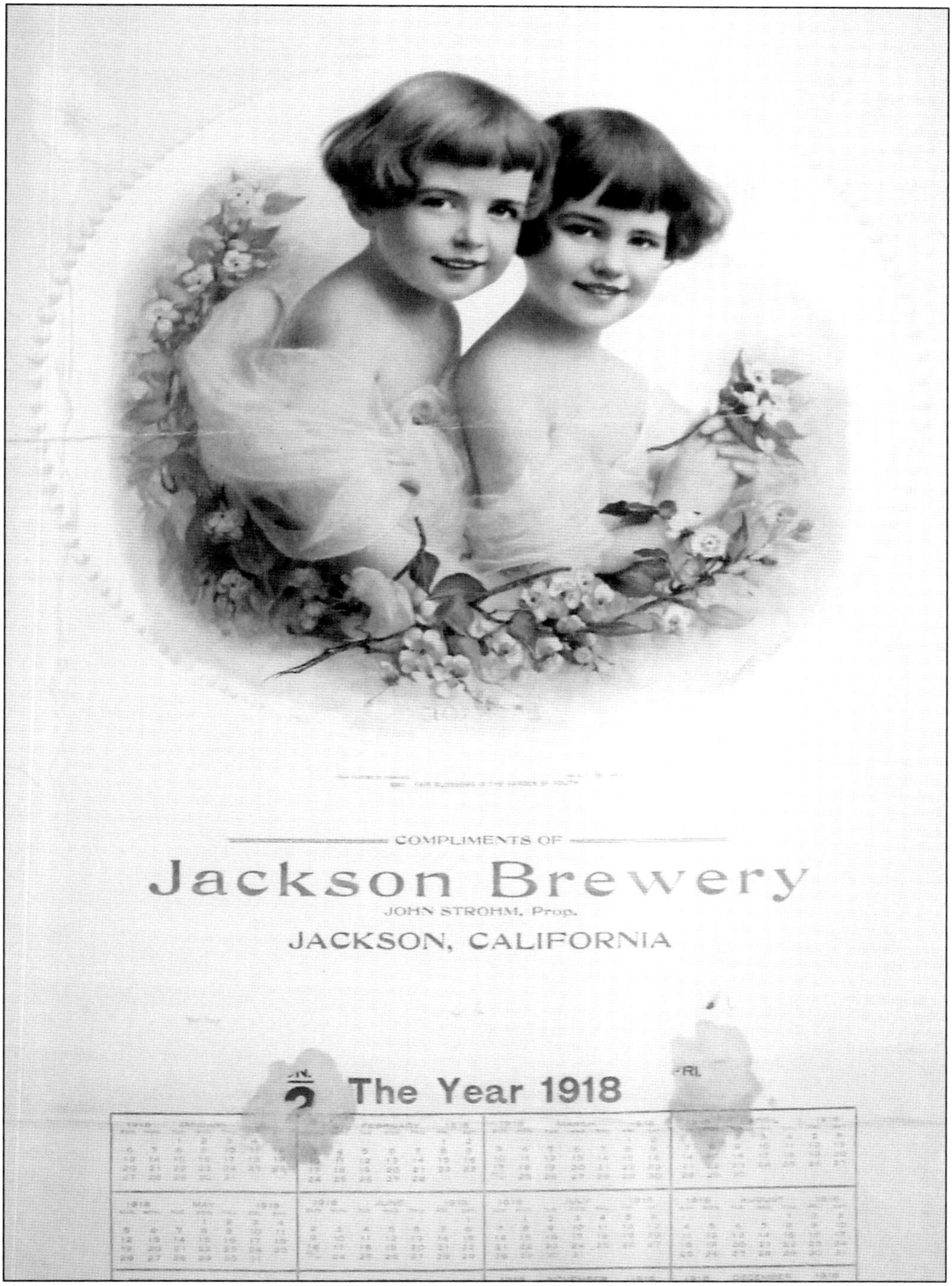

Images of beautiful women could be found on many of the complimentary gifts breweries handed out to customers (see Page 52 for a Buffalo Brewery tray and Page 32 for an advertising coaster). Printed in 1918 by John Strohm of the Jackson Brewery, this charming calendar was produced only one year before Prohibition was legally enacted. It may be that the image of these two angelic children was meant to soften the association between beer and the growing perception of the negative social behaviors associated with alcohol consumption. (Courtesy Amador County Archives.)

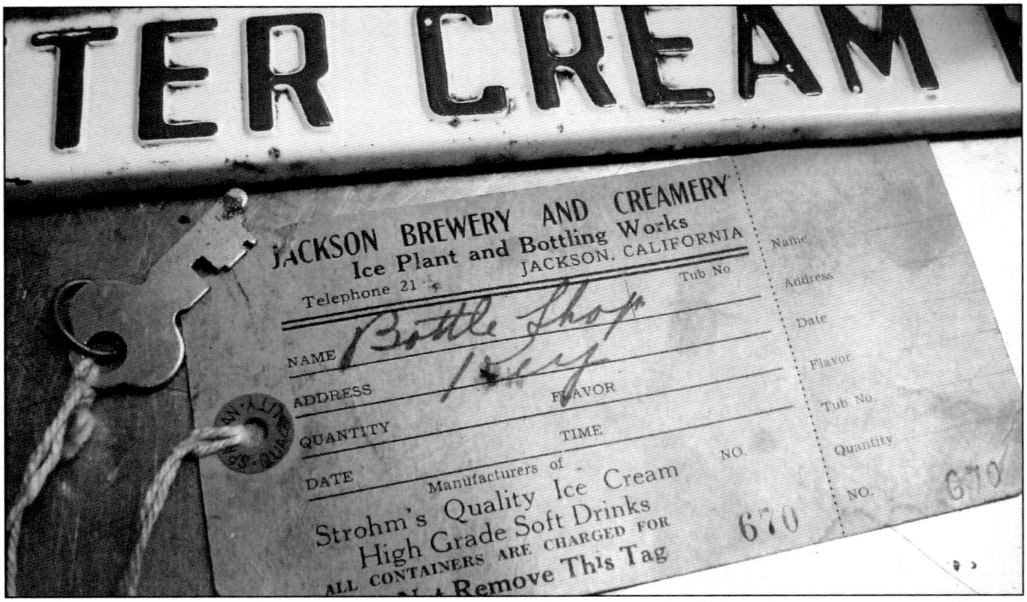

With the advent of Prohibition, many breweries were forced to adapt to survive, as is evidenced from this commercial product tag from the Jackson Brewery and Creamery, which was now also an ice plant and bottling works, selling "Strohm's Quality Ice Cream" and "High Grade Soft Drinks." Strohm proved to be a creative businessman, and his "Golden Nugget butter" received a first place at the 1920 California State Fair. The Ione Brewery, actually operated by Strohm at this juncture, had also transitioned to a creamery and ice house, but neither facility survived Prohibition. (Courtesy Michael Backovich.)

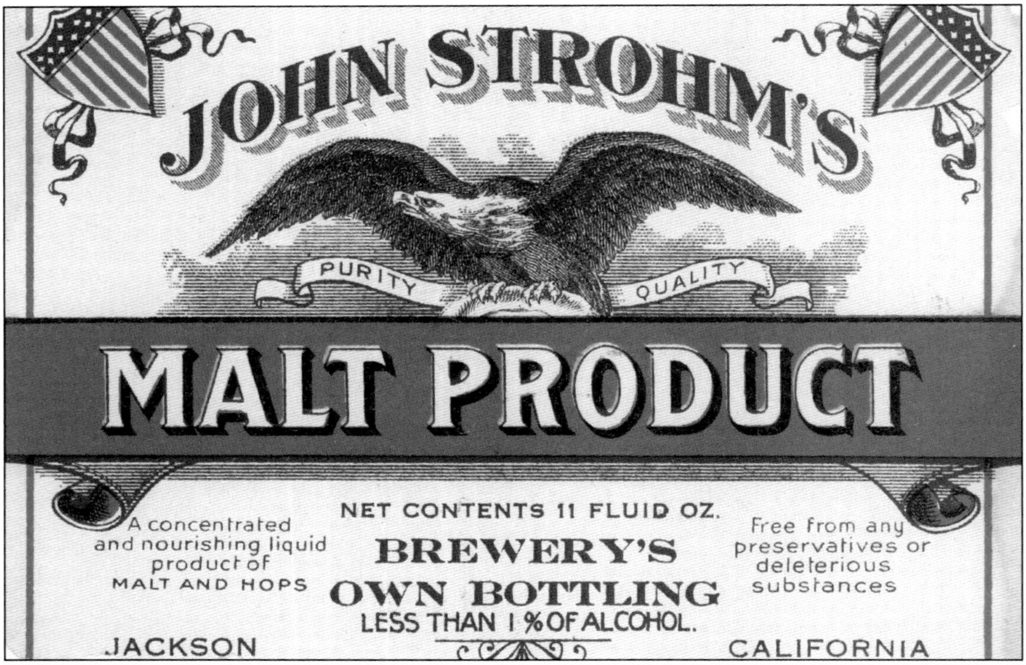

Selling malt products was another way for breweries to get by during Prohibition. The "nourishing liquid of malt and hops" was being sold as a restorative, but it probably tasted much better when brewed into an illegal lager. (Courtesy Amador County Archives.)

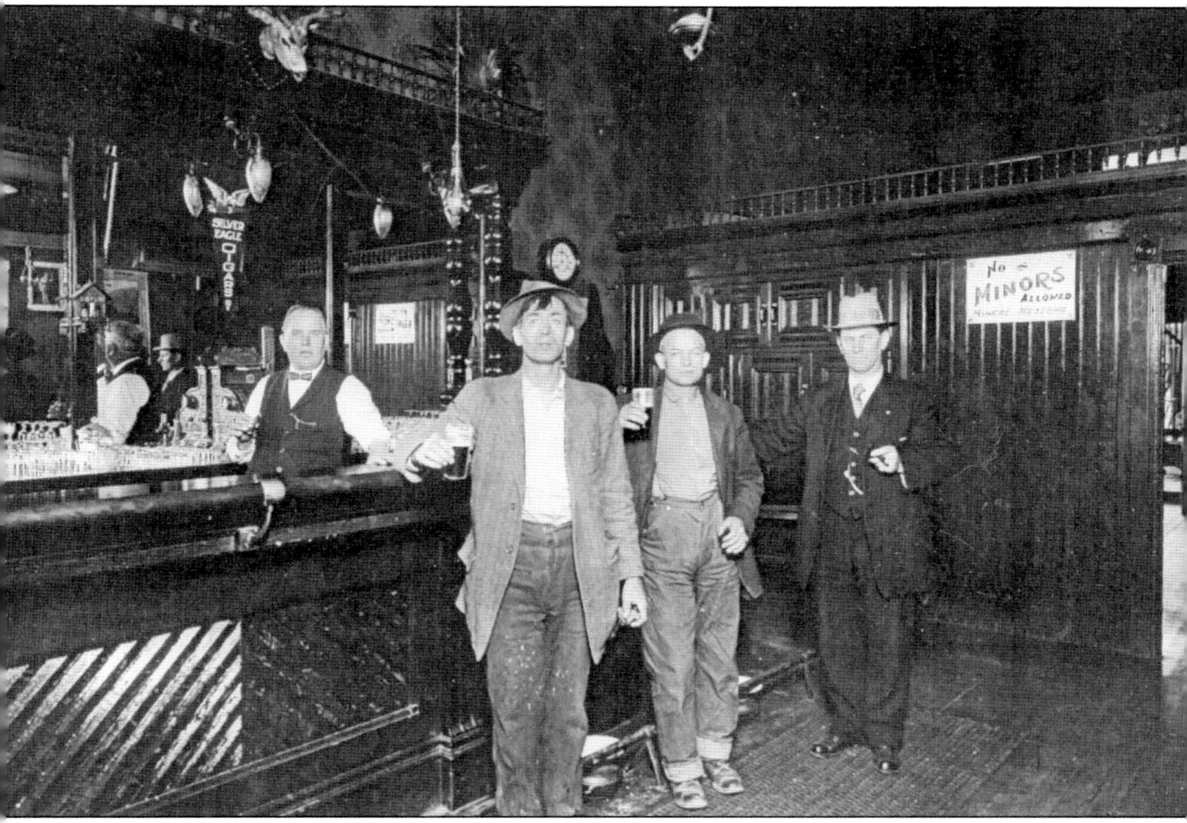

Shown here is a local bar just prior to—or perhaps even during—Prohibition. Note the sign that says: "Miners allowed, No Minors allowed." Some communities, such as Jackson, Amador County, did little to adhere to Prohibition, acquiring a statewide reputation. Alcohol, gambling, and prostitution all thrived here—actually much longer than any of the county's local breweries—until illegal operations were closed down in the 1950s. (Courtesy Amador County Archives.)

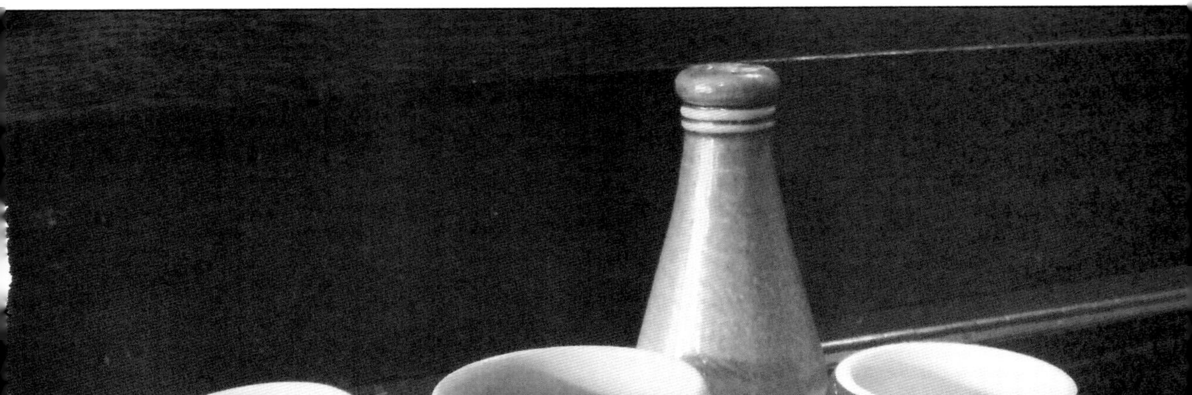

Prohibition did little to stop crime in the United States, instead creating a new outlet for those willing to take advantage of the system. What Prohibition effectively did was eliminate the country's small local and regional breweries, along with the variety that brewers brought to their trade. Communities were left with fewer choices, and larger corporations, such as Budweiser (seen on one of the mugs above), began to dominate in a way it had not had opportunity to do before. Within a few years, local and regional brewers became a thing of the past, to be found only within the pages of history books. (Courtesy authors' collection.)

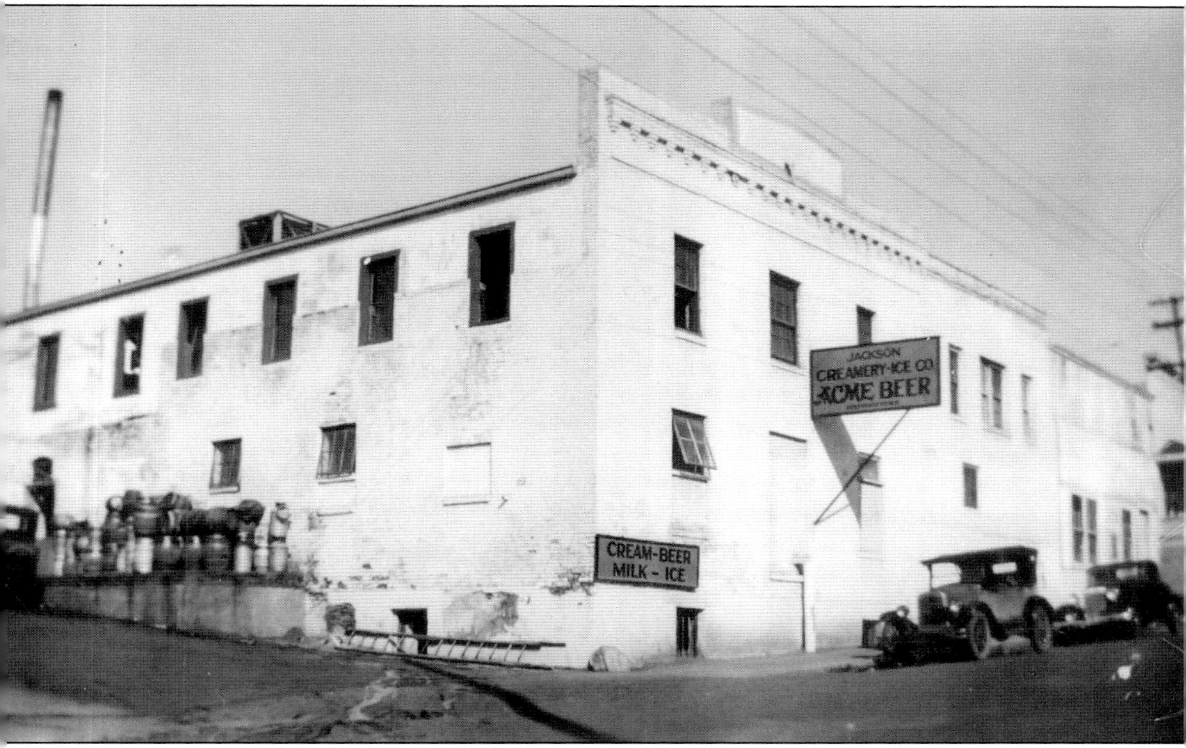

Forced to adapt to Prohibition, John Strohm, who bought Amador County's Jackson Brewery in the 1890s, never removed the title "Brewery" from his building, but simply added "Creamery." Beer brewing was part of the traditions German immigrants brought from their home countries and many saw no reason to give up. This image of the freshly whitewashed brewery dates to 1933; perhaps the owner was celebrating the repeal of Prohibition. The brewery would close within the next decade and would be torn down in 1958, almost 100 years after it was originally built. (Courtesy Amador County Archives.)

Current Breweries

The following is a brief summary of Gold Country breweries open at the time this volume was being written. As the previous chapters have shown, regional breweries—frequently referred to as microbreweries—come and go with some regularity, so the following list may not be entirely accurate at the time the reader reviews this. Should the readers find themselves touring the Motherlode, please take the time to responsibly sample the many fine beers provided by these local breweries.

El Dorado Brewing Company
4384 Harness Tract Road
Camino, CA 95709
eldobrew.com

Chappell Brewery
5024 Highway 140
Mariposa, CA 95338
209-274-4500

Fox Barrel Cider Company
1213 S. Auburn St.
Colfax, CA 95713
foxbarrel.com

Placerville Brewing Company
155 Placerville Drive.
Placerville, CA 95667
530-295-9166
placervillebrewing.com

Gold Hill Brewing Co.
5660 Vineyard Lane
Placerville, CA 95667
530-626-6522
goldhillvineyard.com

Snowshoe Brewing Company
2050 Highway 4
Arnold, CA 95223
209-795-2272
Snowshoebrewing.com

Jack Russell Brewing Company
2380 Larsen Dr.
Camino, CA 95709
530-647-9420
jackrussellbrewing.com

Lockdown Brewing Company
11327 Trade Center Drive, #350
Rancho Cordova, CA 95742
916-835-7416
Lockdownbrewingco.com

Further Reading

The following bibliography provides a short list of other texts that may be of regional or topical interest to the reader of this volume.

Carroll, Ed. *Sacramento's Breweries*. Golden Notes Volume 53(1), 2010.
Marvin, Judith, Julia Costello, and Salvatore Manna. *Northern Calaveras County*, Charleston, SC: Arcadia Publishing, 2007.
Poultney, John. *Amador County*. Charleston, SC: Arcadia Publishing, 2006.
Radanovich, Leroy. *Mariposa County*. Charleston, SC: Arcadia Publishing, 2005.
Wooten, Kimberly and R. Scott Baxter. *Sutter Creek*. Charleston, SC: Arcadia Publishing, 2006.
———*Shenandoah Valley and Amador Wine Country*. Charleston, SC: Arcadia Publishing, 2008.